Reconstruction Era
Biographies

Reconstruction Era Biographies

Roger Matuz

Lawrence W. Baker,
Project Editor

U·X·L

An imprint of Thomson Gale,
a part of The Thomson Corporation

THOMSON

GALE

Detroit • New York • San Francisco • San Diego • New Haven, Conn. • Waterville, Maine • London • Munich

THOMSON

GALE

Reconstruction Era: Biographies

Roger Matuz

Project Editor Lawrence W. Baker	**Imaging and Multimedia** Lezlie Light, Mike Logusz, Denay Wilding	**Composition** Evi Seoud
Permissions Margaret Abendroth, Denise Buckley, Margaret Chamberlain	**Product Design** Pamela A. E. Galbreath, Kate Scheible	**Manufacturing** Rita Wimberley

Cover photographs reproduced courtesy of the Library of Congress (clockwise from top left, Hiram Revels, Andrew Johnson, and Susan B. Anthony).

While every effort has been made to ensure the reliability of the information presented in this publication, Thomson Gale does not guarantee the accuracy of data contained herein. Thomson Gale accepts no payment for listing; and inclusion in the publication of any organization, agency, institution, publication, service, or individual does not imply endorsement by the editors or publisher. Errors brought to the attention of the publisher and verified to the satisfaction of the publisher will be corrected in future editions.

LIBRARY OF CONGRESS CATALOGING-IN-PUBLICATION DATA

Matuz, Roger.
    Reconstruction era : biographies / Roger Matuz ; Lawrence W. Baker, project editor.
        p. cm. — (Reconstruction Era reference library)
    Includes bibliographical references (p.) and index.
    ISBN 0-7876-9218-2 (alk. paper)
    1. Reconstruction (U.S. history, 1865–1877)—Biography—Juvenile literature. I. Baker, Lawrence W. II. Title. III. Series.

    E668.M38 2004
    973.8'1'0922—dc22   2004017300

This title is also available as an e-book.
ISBN 1-4144-0454-9
Contact your Thomson Gale sales representative for ordering information.

Printed in the United States of America
10 9 8 7 6 5 4 3 2 1

Reconstruction Era: Biographies

Reader's Guide

Reconstruction Era: Biographies presents twenty-five entries covering twenty-eight people who lived during the Reconstruction era, the period stretching roughly from the end of the American Civil War in April 1865 to the inauguration of President Rutherford B. Hayes in 1877. Reconstruction was a federal policy intended to restore the relationship between the former Confederate states and the federal Union, to oversee the transition of the newly freed slaves into citizens, and to help convert the Southern economy from one based on slave labor to one based on paid labor. Reconstruction officially ended following the resolution to the controversial presidential election of 1876 in which an electoral commission declared Hayes the victor, just days before he was inaugurated in March 1877. The new president had federal troops removed from the former Confederate region in the South to bring an end to the Reconstruction era.

Coverage and features

Reconstruction Era: Biographies profiles a diverse mix of personalities, from political leaders to famous authors and artists, and from social activists to scientists. The variety of people included reveals the many different concerns and issues Americans faced during a dynamic and difficult period when the wounds of the Civil War were healing and the pursuit of social equality for African Americans and women sparked controversy and debate.

During the Reconstruction era, a president was nearly removed from office; slavery was abolished, but attempts to protect the rights of former slaves were an ongoing and often frustrating challenge; famous works of literature and art were introduced that are still beloved and respected today; and the beginning of professional baseball and the establishment of Yellowstone as a national park were among the sports and recreational developments that balanced the more profoundly serious issues of the day. The biographies reflect the events of the day: those featured include Andrew Johnson, the embattled president who was nearly removed from office by Congress, and Ulysses S. Grant, the Civil War hero whose presidency was riddled by scandal; congressmen who challenged President Johnson for control of Reconstruction policy, including Thaddeus Stevens and Charles Sumner, as well as the first African Americans to serve in the legislative body, including Blanche K. Bruce and Hiram Revels; activists for women's rights (Susan B. Anthony and Julia Ward Howe) and for African American rights (Frederick Douglass); and popular writers, like Louisa May Alcott and Bret Harte.

Reconstruction Era: Biographies also features sidebars containing interesting facts about people and events related to the Reconstruction era. Within each full-length biography, boldfaced cross-references direct readers to other individuals profiled in the volume, helping readers compare and contrast the viewpoints and approaches taken by different people faced with similar challenges during the time period. Finally, each volume includes nearly eighty photographs and illustrations, a "Reconstruction Era Timeline" that lists significant dates and events of the Reconstruction era, and an index.

U•X•L Reconstruction Era Reference Library

Reconstruction Era: Biographies is only one component of the three-part U•X•L Reconstruction Era Reference Library. The other two titles in this set are:

- *Reconstruction Era: Almanac:* This volume presents a comprehensive overview of the Reconstruction era. Its nine chapters are arranged chronologically and explore such topics as the effects of freedom on black family life, Radical Republicans, carpetbaggers and scalawags, amnesty for white Southerners, Black Codes, the impeachment of President Andrew Johnson, the rise of the Ku Klux Klan, attempts to restore the old order in the South, the disputed presidential election of 1876, and the Compromise of 1877. The *Almanac* also contains nearly sixty black-and-white photographs and maps, "Words to Know" boxes, a timeline, research and activity ideas, and an index.

- *Reconstruction Era: Primary Sources:* This title tells the story of the Reconstruction era in the words of the people who lived and shaped it and the laws that contributed to it. Nineteen complete or excerpted documents provide a wide range of perspectives on this period of history. Included are excerpts from abolitionist Frederick Douglass's famous article about Reconstruction, Frances Butler Leigh's account of life after slavery as the daughter of a plantation owner, former slave John Paterson Green's experiences with the Ku Klux Klan, and U.S. senator Charles Sumner's argument in favor of the impeachment of President Andrew Johnson, *Primary Sources* also contains nearly sixty black-and-white photographs and illustrations, a timeline, and an index.

- A cumulative index of all three titles in the U•X•L Reconstruction Era Reference Library is also available.

Acknowledgments

Thanks to copyeditor Rebecca Valentine; proofreader Amy Marcaccio Keyzer; the indexers from Synapse, the Knowledge Link Corporation; and typesetter Jake Di Vita of the Graphix Group for their fine work.

Comments and suggestions

We welcome your comments on *Reconstruction Era: Biographies* and suggestions for other topics to consider. Please write: Editors, *Reconstruction Era: Biographies*, U•X•L, 27500 Drake Rd., Farmington Hills, Michigan 48331-3535; call toll free: (800) 877-4253; fax to (248) 699-8097; or send e-mail via http://www.gale.com.

Reconstruction Era Timeline

1622 The first African slaves are brought to the British colonies in North America, which will eventually become the United States of America.

1803 The Louisiana Purchase adds about 800,000 square miles of new territory to the United States.

1820 The Missouri Compromise allows Missouri to be admitted to the Union as a slave state, while Maine is admitted as a free state, thus maintaining the balance between states where slavery is allowed and where it is illegal. Slavery is prohibited in any of the lands of the Louisiana Purchase that are north of the Missouri border.

1848 The U.S. victory in the Mexican-American War brings a large area of new territory into the United States, including what will become the states of Texas, New Mexico, Arizona, and California.

February 28, 1854 The Republican Party is formed by politicians—most of them from the Northern states—who favor protections for business interests, public support for internal improvements (like roads and services), and social reforms, especially an end to slavery.

May 30, 1854 The Kansas-Nebraska Bill, which reverses the Missouri Compromise by allowing the status of slavery in Kansas and Nebraska to be decided by settlers, is signed into law.

May 19–20, 1856 U.S. senator **Charles Sumner** of Massachusetts gives his "Crime against Kansas" speech in which he insults proslavery supporters of the Kansas-Missouri bill of 1854.

August 21, 1858 Future president Abraham Lincoln and U.S. senator Stephen A. Douglas of Illinois hold the first in a series of seven debates on the issue of slavery; they take place over a period of two months.

November 6, 1860 Illinois Republican Abraham Lincoln is elected president, sending shockwaves of panic through the South, where many believe that Lincoln will immediately take steps to outlaw slavery.

February 4, 1861 Seven Southern states that have seceded (broken away) from the Federal Union form a government of their own called the Confederate States of America, or the Confederacy. They establish their capitol in Richmond, Virginia, with former U.S. senator **Jefferson Davis** of Mississippi as president. In April and May, four more Southern states will join the Confederacy.

April 12–13, 1861 A successful Confederate attack on the Union outpost at Fort Sumter, South Carolina, marks the beginning of the American Civil War.

May 24, 1861 Three Virginia slaves who have escaped from their plantation and fled to a Union army camp are labeled "contraband" (property confiscated during a war) by Union general Benjamin Butler.

July 21, 1861 The Confederate army defeats Union forces at the first Battle of Bull Run in Virginia, not far from Washington, D.C.

November 7, 1861 The U.S. Navy occupies the city of Port Royal in the Sea Islands off the shore of South Carolina. The white plantation owners in the area have already fled, leaving behind a large population of slaves.

February 24, 1862 The Union army takes control of Nashville, Tennessee. In early April, they will also win a victory at Shiloh, Tennessee.

March 13, 1862 Congress passes an Article of War that prohibits the Army from returning runaway slaves to their masters.

April 25, 1862 Union naval forces under Commander David Farragut capture the important southern city of New Orleans, Louisiana.

May 13, 1862 South Carolina slave Robert Smalls steals a Confederate navy ship from Charleston Harbor and turns it over to the Union forces.

July 17, 1862 President Abraham Lincoln signs the Second Confiscation Act, which declares free all slaves who escape to the Union lines.

September 17, 1862 The Union army wins a decisive victory at the Battle of Antietam near Sharpsburg, Maryland.

September 27, 1862 The First Louisiana Native Guard, made up of African Americans from New Orleans's free black community, becomes the first official black regiment to join the Union Army.

1863 The Militia Act, passed on July 17, 1862, allows former slaves to enroll in the U.S. army.

January 1, 1863 President Abraham Lincoln signs the Emancipation Proclamation, which declares forever free most of the four million slaves living in the Confederate states. Excluded are approximately 450,000 slaves in the loyal border states, the 275,000 in Union-held Tennessee, and those in the parts of Virginia and Louisiana that are under Union control.

January 25, 1863 The Fifty-fourth Massachusetts Infantry becomes the first African American regiment in the North to join the Union army.

March 1863 The group of idealistic northern missionaries and teachers known as Gideon's Band arrives in Port

Royal, South Carolina, intending to assist the large population of former slaves living there.

May 1863 The all-black Fifty-fourth Massachusetts Regiment departs from Boston for South Carolina, where the soldiers will win acclaim for their bravery during a battle at Fort Wagner.

July 1–3, 1863 At Gettysburg, Pennsylvania, the Union army wins an important victory, forcing the Confederate army to retreat into Virginia.

July 4, 1863 After an eight-week siege, Union forces under General **Ulysses S. Grant** defeat Confederate troops in Vicksburg, Mississippi.

July 13–16, 1863 Nearly a thousand people are killed or wounded in a bloody race riot in New York City that highlights northern opposition to the war and white hostility toward African Americans.

November 1863 At Beaufort, South Carolina, the First South Carolina Volunteers become the first Union regiments of black soldiers to be formed in the Confederate states.

December 8, 1863 President Abraham Lincoln issues his Proclamation of Amnesty and Reconstruction, also known as the Ten Per Cent Plan. The plan allows almost any Southerner who will take an oath of loyalty to the United States to receive a full pardon and all rights of a U.S. citizen. Once 10 percent of a Southern state's population have signed the oath, the state may form a new government. Lincoln's plan is criticized by several members of Congress as too lenient toward the Confederacy.

March 1864 Davis Bend, Mississippi, is the site of an experiment in which about 5,000 blacks are given control over their own land and labor. The freed people not only establish their own government but, by 1865, raise almost 2,000 bales of cotton, earning a profit of $160,000.

July 4, 1864 President Abraham Lincoln pocket-vetoes the Wade-Davis Bill, which would have allowed a Southern state to be readmitted to the Union only after 50 percent of those who voted in 1860 signed a loyalty oath.

September 2, 1864 The Southern city of Atlanta, Georgia, falls to Union forces under General William T. Sherman.

November 8, 1864 Abraham Lincoln is reelected president.

November 16, 1864 Union general William T. Sherman leaves Atlanta, Georgia, and begins his "March to the Sea," which ends on December 21 when he takes control of the coastal city of Savannah without a fight.

January 16, 1865 Union general William T. Sherman issues his Special Field Order #15, which sets aside land along the Georgia coast for settlement by African Americans.

January 31, 1865 Congress passes the Thirteenth Amendment, officially abolishing slavery in the United States.

March 3, 1865 The U.S. Department of War establishes the Freedmen's Bureau, a federal agency authorized to assist the former slaves in their transition to freedom by distributing clothing, food, fuel, and medical care and to help coordinate the establishment of black schools. Later, the agency's powers will be expanded to set up black schools and handle legal cases brought by blacks.

April 3, 1865 Union forces capture Richmond, Virginia, the Confederate capitol. The next day, President Abraham Lincoln travels down from Washington, D.C., to stroll through the city.

April 9, 1865 Confederate general **Robert E. Lee** formally surrenders to the Union army at Appomattox Courthouse, Virginia.

April 14, 1865 Southern actor John Wilkes Booth shoots Abraham Lincoln while the president is attending a play at Ford's Theatre in Washington, D.C. Lincoln dies the next day, and Vice President **Andrew Johnson** is sworn in as president.

May 29, 1865 Choosing not to wait until Congress is in session, President Andrew Johnson announces his plan for the Reconstruction of the South. His program is so lenient toward the Confederacy that it will allow most of those who dominated Southern politics before the war to return to power.

Summer 1865 The Southern states hold conventions to form state governments under President Andrew Johnson's plan. They put in place new laws called Black Codes that are meant to restrict the employment options and personal freedom of African Americans. At the same time, Southern blacks hold Freedmen's Conventions throughout the South, at which they discuss and record their views.

Fall 1865 Noted orator and writer **Frederick Douglass** undertakes a speaking tour in support of voting and civil rights for freedmen. The following year, Douglass speaks and writes against the policies of President Andrew Johnson, who refused to use his federal powers to pursue voting rights for freedmen or to interfere with states on civil rights issues.

September 1865 Former Confederate general Robert E. Lee becomes president of Washington College, in Lexington, Virginia.

December 1865 Politician and former Union general Carl Schurz reports on conditions in the South, warning that blacks need the federal government's protection from hostile white Southerners. Although President Andrew Johnson ignores the report, many Northerners are horrified by its contents.

December 6, 1865 In an address to the Thirty-ninth Congress, President Andrew Johnson announces that the Reconstruction of the South has been completed. Congress disagrees, and refuses to seat the new Southern representatives and senators.

December 18, 1865 After being named House chairman of a joint congressional committee on Reconstruction, U.S. representative **Thaddeus Stevens** of Pennsylvania declares that it is the duty of Congress to supervise Reconstruction and demand tough terms of the former Confederate states, rejecting President Andrew Johnson's authority to define the terms of Reconstruction.

1866 Ogala Sioux Chief **Red Cloud** organizes resistance to encroachment on Sioux lands in Wyoming and Montana. What becomes known as Red Cloud's War (also referred to as the Bozeman War) lasts until 1868.

January 1866 **Alexander Stephens**, former vice president of the Confederate States of America, is elected to the U.S. Senate in Georgia under the Reconstruction Plan initiated by President Andrew Johnson. Congress, however, rejects the plan and does not allow Stephens to serve.

April 9, 1866 A Congress dominated by a group called the Radical Republicans passes the Civil Rights Bill over President Andrew Johnson's veto. This legislation guarantees that all persons born in the United States (except for Native Americans) are to be considered U.S. citizens with full protection of "person and property" under the law.

May 1, 1866 A three-day race riot begins in Memphis, Tennessee. When it is over, forty-six blacks will have died.

June 13, 1866 Congress approves the Fourteenth Amendment to the U.S. Constitution, which makes it illegal for any state to deny equality before the law to any male citizen.

July 16, 1866 Over President Andrew Johnson's veto, Congress passes a bill extending the life and expanding the powers of the Freedmen's Bureau.

July 30, 1866 Thirty-four blacks and three whites die in a race riot in New Orleans, Louisiana.

August 28, 1866 President Andrew Johnson embarks on what will prove to be a disastrous "swing around the circle" speaking tour.

November 1866 The Republicans win a landslide victory in the midterm elections. They are now in control of every Northern state legislature and government, and the Radicals Republicans in the U.S. Congress are at their peak of power.

March 2, 1867 Over President Andrew Johnson's veto, Congress passes the first in a series of Reconstruction Acts. This one divides the South into five military districts, to be run by military commanders until the states meet the federal requirements for forming new governments. Seeking to prevent Johnson from overriding the Republicans' Reconstruction efforts, Congress also passes the Tenure of Office Act, which limits the president from dismissing government officials who have been approved by Congress.

May 1867 Former Confederate general Nathan Bedford Forrest becomes the first Grand Wizard of the Ku Klux Klan, a white terrorist group formed a year earlier.

Fall 1867 In accordance with the Reconstruction Act, the former states of the Confederacy hold constitutional conventions. Nearly a million and a half voters are registered, including about seven hundred thousand African Americans.

1868 **Francis L. Cardozo** is elected secretary of state of South Carolina, becoming the first African American to hold an elected position in the state. That year he also helped found the Avery Institute, a school for African American youth and for the training of teachers, in Charleston, South Carolina.

February 1868 After President Andrew Johnson dismisses Secretary of War **Edwin Stanton**, whose political views differ from his own, Congress impeaches him on the grounds that he has violated the Tenure of Office Act and other charges.

May 1868 U.S. senator Charles Sumner of Massachusetts offers a fierce argument in favor of removing President Andrew Johnson from office.

May 16, 1868 President Andrew Johnson is acquitted of violating the Tenure of Office Act. He escapes being dismissed from office by one vote.

June 1868 The states of Alabama, Arkansas, Florida, Georgia, Louisiana, North Carolina, and South Carolina are readmitted to the Union under the Reconstruction plan developed by the Republicans in Congress.

Summer 1868 **Louisa May Alcott**'s *Little Women,* the first of eight novels in the "Little Women" series, is published.

August 11, 1868 The death of U.S. representative Thaddeus Stevens of Pennsylvania a longtime advocate for black equality, represents waning congressional advocacy concern for African American civil rights.

November 3, 1868 Civil War hero Ulysses S. Grant is elected president. The votes cast by newly enfranchised African Americans play a key role in his win.

1869 The newly formed Reconstruction governments are established.

1869 The first all-professional baseball team, the Cincinnati Red Stockings, is established by manager and center-fielder **Harry Wright.** Two years later, the first professional baseball league, the National Association of Baseball Clubs, is founded. The National League of Professional Baseball Clubs, which began in 1876, continues today as Major League Baseball's National League.

February 26, 1869 Jefferson Davis, former president of the Confederate States of America, is released from prison following delays in his trial and a general amnesty proclamation for ex-Confederates by President Andrew Johnson.

May 1869 The National Woman Suffrage Association (NWSA) is founded by **Susan B. Anthony** and Elizabeth Cady Stanton.

1870 The Tweed Ring, a corrupt group of New York City politicians, is exposed by a coalition of reformers, including lawyer and politician **Samuel J. Tilden.** Tilden's reputation as a reformer would lead to his becoming New York's Democratic Party chairman, the state's governor, and the Democratic Party's nominee for president in 1876.

February 25, 1870 Hiram Revels of Mississippi, the first African American to serve in the U.S. Senate, takes over the seat once occupied by former Confederate president Jefferson Davis.

Spring 1870 Bret Harte's collection of stories set in California mining settlements, *The Luck of Roaring Camp and Other Sketches,* is published. The collection proves so popular that Harte signs in 1871 the highest paying publishing contract in American history to that time.

March 30, 1870 The Fifteenth Amendment, which bars state governments from denying or abridging voting rights "on account of race, color, or previous condition of servitude," becomes part of the U.S. Constitution.

May 31, 1870 In response to the widespread violence that had terrorized Southern blacks, Congress passes the first of three Enforcement Acts designed to protect the civil and political rights of African Americans.

September 1870 Social activist and suffragette **Julia Ward Howe** issues an essay, "Appeal to Womanhood throughout the World," calling for a general congress of women to promote the alliance of different nationalities.

November 1870 **Zebulon Vance**, a former congressman and Confederate leader of North Carolina is elected to the U.S. Senate, but is not allowed to serve. The Fourteenth Amendment, passed in 1867, included a provision against former members of the Confederacy that made it illegal for them to serve in the federal legislature or executive branch unless the "disability" was removed by a vote of two-thirds majority in both houses of Congress. Later, in 1879, Vance would be elected to the U.S. Senate and would serve until his death in 1894.

1871 Congress declares that the Indian nations are no longer sovereign, an act that will lead to the gradual relocation of all Native Americans onto reservations.

April 20, 1871 The second Enforcement Act, known as the Ku Klux Klan Act, is passed by Congress.

1872 *Picturesque America,* featuring drawings of spectacular natural scenes of the United States by such illustrators as **Harry Fenn**, is a popular and acclaimed publication.

March 1, 1872 After explorer and geologist **Ferdinand V. Hayden** impresses Congress with descriptions, specimens, photographs and paintings of northwest Wyoming, President Ulysses S. Grant signs a bill into law declaring that over 2 million acres in Wyoming around the Yellowstone River would forever be "dedicated and set apart as a public park or pleasuring ground for the benefit and enjoyment of the people."

May 1, 1872 The Liberal Republican Party nominates New York newspaper editor **Horace Greeley** for president. Two months later, the Democratic Party also nominates Greeley.

November 5, 1872 President Ulysses S. Grant wins reelection.

December 11, 1872 African American P. B. S. Pinchback becomes acting governor of Louisiana, serving for a little less than one month.

1873 **Ellen H. Richards** becomes the first woman to earn a bachelor of chemistry degree in America. She would later found the discipline called home economics.

September 18, 1873 The period of serious economic decline known as the Panic of 1873 begins, set off by the bankruptcy of **Jay Cooke,** one of the most powerful bankers in the country. More than a million people lose their jobs, thousands of businesses close, and agricultural prices and land values fall. Miners and factory workers react to wage cuts with violent strikes.

March 11, 1874 With the death of U.S. senator Charles Sumner of Massachusetts, the waning influence of the Radical Republicans of Congress effectively ends. The Radical Republicans had controlled Reconstruction policy.

Fall 1874 To keep blacks away from the polls in the November elections in Mississippi, a program of terrorism called the "Mississippi Plan" is put into effect. Widespread violence and intimidation are successfully employed as weapons to prevent blacks from exercising their voting rights. Similar effects will be achieved by the same means in other states during the 1876 elections, leading to victories by white supremacists across the South.

November 1874 Blanche K. Bruce of Mississippi becomes the first African American to be elected to a full term to the U.S. Senate.

March 1, 1875 Congress passes the Civil Rights Act, which is meant to reinforce the government's commitment to protecting black rights. Key provisions of the act will be found unconstitutional in the Slaughterhouse Cases, which will come before the Supreme Court in the 1880s.

December 9, 1875 The Whiskey Ring corruption scandal erupts when President Ulysses S. Grant's private secretary, Orville E. Babcock, is charged with participating in fraud involving tax revenues.

Summer 1876 National exhibitions are held in Philadelphia, Pennsylvania, and Washington, D.C., in honor of the one hundredth anniversary of the signing of the Declaration of Independence. **Thomas Eakins's** painting, *The Gross Clinic,* which would become famous in the twentieth century, is displayed in a portion of the Philadelphia exhibit dedicated to the medical sciences.

June 25, 1876 Warriors of the Cheyenne, Sans Arcs, Miniconjoux Sioux, Oglala Sioux, Blackfeet and Hunkpapa Sioux defeat the forces of General George Armstrong Custer on the banks of the Little Big Horn River in southern Montana. The Battle of the Little Big Horn also becomes known as Custer's Last Stand.

November 7, 1876 The results of the presidential election in which Republican **Rutherford B. Hayes** narrowly beats Democrat Samuel J. Tilden are disputed. Four months later, in a compromise that will allow the Redemption movement to overthrow the southern Reconstruction governments, Democrats agree to accept Hayes's election if the government will leave the South to manage its own affairs.

April 1877 Federal troops are withdrawn from the state capitols of South Carolina and Louisiana, allowing white supremacists known as "Redeemers" to take control of these states' governments. Soon the Redemption movement will have overthrown all of the Reconstruction governments.

Summer 1877 President Rutherford B. Hayes tours the South and makes speeches announcing the end of Reconstruction.

Fall 1877 A state constitutional convention is held in Georgia and dominated by **Robert Toombs**, former secretary of state of the Confederate States of America. Under Toombs's leadership, no action is taken to protect the voting rights of freedmen.

Spring 1879 Discouraged by the overthrow of the multiracial Reconstruction governments by white supremacists, some Southern blacks migrate to the new western state of Kansas. Members of the Exoduster movement, as it is called, seek wider employment opportunities, protection of civil rights, and an escape from the anti-black violence that plagues the South.

1880 Poverty is widespread in the South, where the per capita income is only 40 percent of that of the North.

1881 Influential black leader Booker T. Washington is named principal of the Tuskegee Institute, which will soon become the leading black educational institution in the nation.

1887 The first Jim Crow law is enacted in Florida. This system of legalized segregation mandates separate schools and public facilities (such as hospitals, prisons, hotels, restaurants, parks, waiting rooms, elevators, cemeteries, and drinking fountains) for blacks and whites.

1894 W. E. B. Du Bois, who will become the leading black intellectual and founder of the Niagara Movement, earns a Ph.D. from Harvard University.

September 18, 1895 African American activist Booker T. Washington delivers his famous Atlanta Compromise Speech, in which he tells a white audience that blacks are more interested in economic advancement than political and social equality.

1896 In the *Plessy v. Ferguson* case, the Supreme Court validates the concept of "separate but equal," asserting that the Fourteenth Amendment was never intended to prevent social segregation.

January 1, 1913 African American communities across the nation hold Jubilee celebrations to commemorate the fiftieth anniversary of the signing of the Emancipation Proclamation.

1929 The stock market crash marks the onset of the Great Depression, a period of economic hardship that will last until the entrance of the United States into World War II.

1955–56 Civil rights advocates take part in the Montgomery Bus Boycott, refusing to ride on the city buses of Montgomery, Alabama, until they are integrated. Many believe that this event inaugurates the Civil Rights Movement.

1965 The passage of the Voting Rights Act marks a new era in public and government commitment to the guarantee of black civil and political rights.

Reconstruction Era
Biographies

Louisa May Alcott

Born November 29, 1832
Germantown, Pennsylvania

Died March 6, 1888
Roxbury, Massachusetts

Writer and editor

Louisa May Alcott is most famous as the author of *Little Women* (1868) and the seven novels that followed in the "Little Women" series. The novels are realistic and entertaining accounts of the March family, and show children developing as independent and thoughtful individuals, facing and learning from conflicts, and sharing a warm and loving family life. Alcott enjoyed widespread popularity in her lifetime as a children's author. Meanwhile, she was secretly successful as a magazine writer of sensational fiction about crime, revenge, and romance. Alcott was not revealed as the writer of those stories until more than fifty years after her death.

"Far away there in the sunshine are my highest aspirations. I may not reach them, but I can look up and see their beauty, believe in them, and try to follow where they lead."

Keeping a journal

Louisa May Alcott was born on November 29, 1832, in Germantown, Pennsylvania. She was the second of four daughters of Amos Bronson Alcott, a noted philosopher and educator, and Abigail May, a descendant of one of Boston's more prominent families. The family moved to Boston, Massachusetts, in 1834 when Alcott's father founded a school

Louisa May Alcott. *The Granger Collection, New York. Reproduced by permission.*

based on some of his principles of education. Bronson Alcott believed that education should emphasize play and the imagination as activities through which children learn and develop physically, intellectually, emotionally, and spiritually. His educational system was too different from conventional educational practices of the time to become firmly established. The family was often in need of money, and they moved several times between Boston and Concord, Massachusetts.

Alcott and her sisters were taught at home by their father, who brought them into contact with some of America's greatest writers, including Ralph Waldo Emerson (1803–1882), Nathaniel Hawthorne (1804–1864), Henry David Thoreau (1817–1862), and Margaret Fuller (1810–1850). The Alcott girls were required to keep journals, and together they wrote a family newspaper and plays in which they performed. Their education also included domestic skills, from housekeeping to sewing and clothes-making.

About the time Alcott turned eleven in 1843, the family joined a communal living experiment at Fruitlands, a farm in Harvard, Massachusetts. (Communal living involves several people or families who live together as a group—sharing work, expenses, and the fruits of their labor). Alcott wrote about the experiences in her journal, which were later published, in 1889, in *Louisa May Alcott: Her Life, Letters, and Journals*. She described life at Fruitlands as a kind of vacation, but later she would note the experiment failed because the adults were not prepared for the demands of farming.

The family moved back to Concord and lived there from 1845 to 1850. Beginning in her mid-teens, Alcott worked at such jobs as seamstress, governess, teacher, and servant. In 1848, at age sixteen, she taught neighborhood children in a school in Concord. Many of her lessons were conveyed as fairy tales. One of the students, Ellen Emerson, daughter of Ralph Waldo Emerson, loved the tales, so Alcott wrote them down for her in a notebook. Ellen's mother, Lidian Emerson, read them and recommended that Alcott try to publish the stories.

Writing career begins

In 1848, the family moved back to Boston, where Alcott's mother founded an employment service. While Alcott worked as a teacher and seamstress, she continued writing and was published before she turned twenty. Her poem "Sunlight" appeared in *Peterson's Magazine* in September 1851 under the pseudonym Flora Fairfield. (A pseudonym is a fictitious name a writer sometimes uses to conceal his or her identity, especially if the writer is involved in different styles of writing.) Alcott published her first story, "The Rival Painters," in the May 1852 issue of the

Famous Rejection Letter

After submitting her story "How I Went Out to Service" to publisher James T. Fields in 1874, Louisa May Alcott received a reply from him: "Stick to your teaching, Miss Alcott. You can't write."

Olive Branch, another leading magazine of the time. While these pieces were tame and sentimental, Alcott realized she could make money regularly to help support the family by submitting stories for magazines. Magazines wanted sensational (curious, unusual, emotional) stories, and Alcott began writing and submitting them under the pseudonym A. M. Barnard.

Alcott's first book, *Flower Fables,* was published when she was twenty-three. The book collected stories she used when teaching and had written down for Ellen Emerson. Among other activities during this time, Alcott performed as an actress in free theater productions. She also wrote two plays during the mid-1850s. *Nat Batchelor's Pleasure Trip* was accepted in 1855 and performed later at Harvard University in 1860. *The Rival Prima Donnas,* which she adapted from one of her short stories, was accepted by the Boston Theater in 1856 but never performed.

The late 1850s proved a harrowing time for Alcott. Violence had erupted in the United States over slavery and Alcott's strongly abolitionist (antislavery) family helped provide refuge for runaway slaves. Meanwhile, Alcott provided care for her sister, Elizabeth, who died in 1858 after a long illness.

When the American Civil War (1861–65) began in 1861, Alcott became determined to help the Union cause. The Civil War was a conflict that took place between the Northern states (Union) and the Southern seceded states (Confederacy). Alcott began working as a nurse in December 1862 at the Union Hotel Hospital in the Georgetown section of Washington, D.C. However, six weeks later, she contracted typhoid fever (a bacterial disease that causes fever, headaches, and intestinal problems) and had to stay at home. She suffered there for three months before she could leave her room. Treatment for her illness left her with bouts of headaches for the rest of her life.

Upon regaining her health, Alcott quickly returned to writing. Letters she wrote to her family while serving as a nurse were published in 1863 as *Hospital Sketches*. Rich with detail and related by a witty narrator named Tribulation Periwinkle, *Hospital Sketches* relates the experiences of an idealistic young woman working as a nurse in a war hospital. She becomes more mature after viewing the horrors of war, but gains an important sense of balance between her imagination and the reality around her.

Hospital Sketches was well-received, providing Alcott with some clout with publishers and confidence as a writer. The following year, she published *Moods,* a novel she had completed in 1860. She trimmed back the original manuscript, and while some critics found the story uneven, the book was immediately popular and provided enough money for Alcott to travel to Europe. (*Moods* was later republished with both the original, complete text and the cut version.)

When Alcott returned from Europe in the summer of 1866, her family was in need of money. Alcott returned to writing anonymous stories for magazines. These stories, which often featured crimes and romantic entanglements, were never attributed to Alcott during her lifetime. Not until a 1943 article by Leona Rostenberg, "Some Anonymous and Pseudonymous Thrillers of Louisa M. Alcott," was published in *Papers of the Bibliographical Society of America,* was Alcott revealed to have made money and written in the popular sentimental and sensational style. Most of the stories Alcott published anonymously or under the pseudonym of A. M. Barnard were documented and collected in publications after 1970.

Big success with *Little Women*

In 1867, Alcott became editor of *Merry's Museum,* a leading children's monthly magazine. During that year, she was approached by Thomas Niles, an editor at Roberts Brothers, the firm that published Alcott's books. He suggested that Alcott write a novel for girls. Drawing on her own family and their experiences, including those of her sisters Anna, Eliza-

An illustration of *Little Women* character Marmee (in bonnet) surrounded by her daughters—the four March sisters. *Illustration by Rene Cloke. Reproduced by permission of P. R. Gawthorn Ltd.*

beth, and May, Alcott produced the manuscript for *Little Women* within two months. Niles and Alcott were unsure about whether the book would sell, but their doubts were eased when Niles's young niece read the book with delight, then immediately began rereading it. *Little Women* was published in October 1868 and became an immediate sensation.

Book reviewers praised the novel's refreshing approach. Children's literature of the time typically presented youngsters as merely cute and precious, with simple conflicts; the approach of *Little Women,* however, was more realistic, showing children as unique individuals with ranges of emotion, who learn from their experiences. Subsequent critics have shown how the novels demonstrate Alcott's values: the characters learn the limits of equating happiness with money and possessions; the importance of coeducation (where boys and girls are educated equally and together) and other theories of education held by her father are shown; and the girls grow into independent young women who pursue their own paths in life, not merely what society expects of them. *Little Women* relates the adventures of the four March sisters as they strive to improve themselves and become "good girls" on their own terms. The

An Excerpt from *Little Women*

Margaret, the eldest of the four, was sixteen, and very pretty, being plump and fair, with large eyes, plenty of soft brown hair, a sweet mouth, and white hands, of which she was rather vain. Fifteen-year-old Jo was very tall, thin, and brown, and reminded one of a colt, for she never seemed to know what to do with her long limbs, which were very much in her way. She had a decided mouth, a comical nose, and sharp, gray eyes, which appeared to see everything, and were by turns fierce, funny, or thoughtful. Her long, thick hair was her one beauty, but it was usually bundled into a net, to be out of her way. Round shoulders had Jo, big hands and feet, a fly-away look to her clothes, and the uncomfortable appearance of a girl who was rapidly shoot-ing up into a woman and didn't like it. Elizabeth, or Beth, as everyone called her, was a rosy, smooth-haired, bright-eyed girl of thirteen, with a shy manner, a timid voice, and a peaceful expression which was seldom disturbed. Her father called her "Little Miss Tranquillity," and the name suited her excellently, for she seemed to live in a happy world of her own, only venturing out to meet the few whom she trusted and loved. Amy, though the youngest, was a most important person, in her own opinion at least. A regular snow maiden, with blue eyes, and yellow hair curling on her shoulders, pale and slender, and always carrying herself like a young lady mindful of her manners. What the characters of the four sisters were we will leave to be found out.

children in *Little Women* are imperfect, and many readers found traits in one of the sisters that they could see in themselves.

When hundreds of letters poured into the publisher from fans asking for more stories about the March sisters, Alcott quickly wrote a sequel in 1869 published as *Little Women or, Meg, Jo, Beth and Amy, Part Second,* which was another big seller. In all, Alcott would produce eight novels grouped as the "Little Women" series. After the first two volumes, Alcott wrote *An Old-Fashioned Girl* (1870), *Little Men* (1871), *Eight Cousins* (1875), *Rose in Bloom* (1876), *Under the Lilacs* (1878), *Jack and Jill* (1880), and *Jo's Boys and How They Turned Out* (1886). These novels follow the lives of the March sisters and their families as they grow older while evoking the local color of the New England towns where they lived. All of the books remained immensely popular. During the twentieth century, the books were adapted to major motion pictures in 1933, 1949, and 1994 and as a television movie in 1978.

Prolific writer

With the financial success of *Little Women*, Alcott took another trip to Europe. She returned to Boston during the summer of 1871 after receiving news of the death of her brother-in-law. While she was in Europe, the editor of *Merry's Museum* published *Will's Wonder-Book,* a collection of eight stories by Alcott that were published when she worked for the magazine. The stories are based on animals and show the value of kindness and friendliness. Alcott was also active in the women's suffrage (women's right to vote) movement, writing for the *Woman's Journal,* a women's activist magazine. In 1879, she became the first woman in Concord to register to vote in the village's school committee election.

Alcott turned forty in 1871 and spent what would be the last fifteen years of her life writing books and caring for her mother and father in their old age, as well as for other members of her family. She served as legal guardian of her sister May's daughter and later adopted her sister Anna's son. Alcott had a novel, *A Modern Mephistopheles,* published anonymously in 1877. The tale tells of a man who sells his soul to the devil. In 1887, a year before her death, Alcott gave permission for her publisher to reprint *A Modern Mephistopheles* under her name, along with "A Whisper in the Dark," one of her early sensation stories.

Between 1870 and 1880, Alcott published many books, including five of the "Little Women" novels as well as six volumes of short stories under the title *Aunt Jo's Scrap-Bag.* During this period, her mother died, and in 1879, following the death of her sister, May, Alcott took in May's infant daughter. In 1882, Alcott's father suffered a stroke, and Alcott cared for him as well.

In 1885, the family moved to Boston. The following year, Alcott published *Jo's Boys, and How They Turned Out* (1886), a sequel to *Little Men* and the final book in the "Little Women" series. Alcott died on March 6, 1888, two days after her father died.

An avid readership of Alcott, particularly for *Little Women,* has continued through the generations. A year after she died, *Louisa May Alcott: Her Life, Letters, and Journals* provided more material for her adoring fans. The publication of Alcott's sensation stories beginning in 1975 inspired interest nearly a century later in several adult novels she had published. Meanwhile, the sustained popularity of Alcott's *Little*

Women attests to the significance of the writer Alcott's biographer Ednah Dow Cheney called "the Children's friend."

For More Information

Books

Alcott, Louisa May. *Girlhood Diary of Louisa May Alcott, 1843–1846: Writings of a Young Author.* Edited by Kerry A. Graves. Mankato, MN: Blue Earth Books, 2001.

Alcott, Louisa May. *Louisa May Alcott: Her Life, Letters, and Journals.* Boston: Roberts Brothers, 1889. Multiple reprints.

Cheney, Ednah Dow. *Louisa May Alcott: The Children's Friend.* Boston: Prang, 1888. Reprint, New York: Chelsea House Publishing, 1980.

Eiselein, Gregory, Anne K. Phillips, and Madeleine B. Stern. *The Louisa May Alcott Encyclopedia.* Westport, CT: Greenwood, 2001.

Gormley, Beatrice. *Louisa May Alcott: Young Novelist.* New York: Simon & Schuster, 1999.

Keyser, Elizabeth Lennox. *Little Women: A Family Romance.* New York: Twayne, 1999.

Stern, Madeleine B. *Louisa May Alcott: From Blood and Thunder to Hearth and Home.* Boston: Northeastern University Press, 1998.

Web Sites

"Little Women." *American Studies at the University of Virginia.* http://xroads.virginia.edu/~hyper/alcott/lwhp.html (accessed on June 16, 2004).

Louisa May Alcott Memorial Association. *Orchard House—Home of the Alcotts.* http://www.louisamayalcott.org/ (accessed on June 16, 2004).

Susan B. Anthony

Born February 15, 1820
Adams, Massachusetts

Died March 13, 1906
Rochester, New York

Activist for women's rights,
abolition of slavery, and temperance

S usan B. Anthony was an early and longtime activist for women's rights and a leader of the American woman's suffrage (right to vote) movement. She spoke throughout the country, was arrested once for voting, helped start a magazine, contributed to the compilation of a multivolume history of the women's suffrage movement, and supported temperance (abstaining from alcohol) and the abolition of slavery through speeches and petitions. In honor of her tireless work and achievements, Anthony's image was chosen for a new dollar coin in 1979, making her the first woman to be depicted on U.S. currency.

"The true republic—men, their rights and nothing more; women, their rights and nothing less."

Outspoken teen

Susan Brownell Anthony was born on February 15, 1820, in Adams, Massachusetts, one of seven children to Daniel and Lucy Read Anthony. Her father built the town's first cotton mill. When Anthony was six, the family moved to Battenville, New York, north of Albany. Anthony's parents encouraged self-reliance and principled convictions. As mem-

Susan B. Anthony.
Photograph by L. Condon. The Library of Congress.

bers of the Quaker religion, the family lived modestly and practiced nonviolence and respect for all people, regardless of race or background.

When Anthony was four years old, she was sent to the home of her paternal grandparents with her two sisters while their mother prepared to give birth to another baby. The girls were tutored in reading by Anthony's grandfather, who insisted on long hours of practice. Anthony suffered eyestrain from the intense reading experience and her left eye remained crossed for the rest of her life.

At home, the daughters were expected to help their mother with domestic chores, keeping house for the family as well as helping to feed workers at the mill, whose numbers typically ranged from ten to two dozen at any given time. After their daily chores and homework were done, the children were free to roam the hills surrounding the family home.

When Anthony's father was able to earn good wages by managing a mill, he sent Anthony and a sister to be educated at a boarding school in Philadelphia, Pennsylvania, run by the Friends of the Quakers. Anthony completed her schooling at the age of fifteen and began teaching at the school for a modest salary as well as a free room. When she learned that she was making only 20 percent as much as equally qualified male teachers, Anthony protested to the school's administrators. Her protests, combined with her habit of visiting with nearby African American families, led to her dismissal from the school, and Anthony returned home.

The family moved to Rochester, New York, in 1845. Anthony's father became a leading abolitionist and regularly hosted important guests at the family farm, including journalists **Frederick Douglass** (c. 1817–1895; see entry) and William Lloyd Garrison (1805–1879). Anthony had continued teaching and became principal of the Girls' Department at Canajoharie Academy in Rochester. At the time, teaching was the best way young women could have a career and be economically independent. She retired from teaching around 1848 and managed her parents' farm just outside of Rochester. She became acquainted with an extensive community of social reformers who lived in the area.

Activism begins

Anthony shared her family's dedication to abolition, temperance, and women's rights. Her parents attended the Women's Rights Convention in Seneca Falls, New York, in 1848 and signed the first Declaration of Women's Rights, which was drafted at the convention. In 1851, Anthony became president of the local chapter of the Daughters of Temperance. In the spring of 1851, she traveled to Seneca Falls to attend an antislavery meeting. She stayed at the home of Amelia Bloomer (1818–1894), editor of *The Lily,* a temperance magazine.

Anthony and Bloomer met Elizabeth Cady Stanton (1815–1902; see box), who had also come to Seneca Falls for the convention. The meeting initiated a friendship and collaboration between Anthony and Stanton that lasted the rest of their lives. They made a good team: Anthony was a great organizer, speaker, and tireless traveler, while Stanton was better with ideas and writing.

A significant event that contributed to Anthony becoming a leader for women's suffrage occurred in 1852, when she attended a meeting of the Sons of Temperance in Albany. At one point, Anthony rose to speak but was ignored by the men of the meeting. Angered and insulted, she stormed out and soon founded the Women's State Temperance Society. The incident convinced Anthony that the right to vote was the cornerstone of women's fight for respect and equality. Anthony attended her first women's-rights convention in 1852. From then until the end of the American Civil War (1861–65), she campaigned from door to door, in legislatures, and in meetings for the abolition of slavery and promotion of women's rights. Her efforts helped lead to the passage in New York of legislation that for the first time allowed married women to own property, keep their own wages, and have custody of their children in the event of separation or divorce.

During the Civil War, Anthony focused on abolition. She organized the Women's National Loyal League, which sponsored petition drives to support the Thirteenth Amendment to the Constitution to abolish slavery. The league gathered petitions with four hundred thousand signatures, which were presented to Congress by U.S. senator **Charles Sumner** (1811–1874; see entry) of Massachusetts. As the Fourteenth

Elizabeth Cady Stanton: "I Forged the Thunderbolts and She Fired Them"

Elizabeth Cady Stanton was born in Johnstown, New York, in 1815. She had little formal education, but taught herself by using her brother's books on Greek and Latin. She developed an interest in the temperance and abolition movements. At the age of twenty-four, she married Henry Stanton, an abolitionist. The couple's belief in equality in their marriage was reflected in their marriage vows, in which Henry Stanton agreed to leave out the word "obey."

Stanton had seven children. Her responsibilities as a mother limited her participation in the reform movements, but she proved to be an excellent and impassioned writer. She helped to organize the first American women's rights convention at Seneca Falls, New York, in 1848. Stanton drafted the Declaration of Sentiments and Resolutions (similar in tone to the Declaration of Independence) that the convention adopted. She insisted, despite resistance of some delegates at the convention, that voting rights would be part of the resolution. With her victory on that issue, the women's suffrage movement was launched.

Stanton met Susan B. Anthony at an antislavery meeting in Seneca Falls in 1851. Stanton helped convince Anthony that advancement of women's rights would fuel many other reforms. Stanton and Anthony became the leaders of the women's movement. Stanton wrote speeches while Anthony, who was not married, traveled around the country drumming up support. As Stanton described their collaboration, "I forged the thunderbolts and she fired them."

Stanton and Anthony would work together for over fifty years. They agreed to and Fifteenth Amendments were being drafted (providing citizenship and protecting voting rights for African Americans, respectively) during the next few years, Anthony lobbied for inclusion of women's suffrage in the amendments. The male political establishment of the time, however, wanted to focus solely on ensuring rights of freed men. Publisher and journalist **Horace Greeley** (1811–1872; see entry), a leading abolitionist, told the suffragettes, "This is the Negro's hour."

Anthony and Stanton responded by severing their ties with the American Woman Suffrage Association. The Association was made up of men and women seeking suffrage and rights for African Americans and for women. Anthony and Stanton then formed the women-only National Woman's Suffrage Association in 1869.

Elizabeth Cady Stanton. *AP/Wide World Photos. Reproduced by permission.*

voting rights for African Americans. Anthony joined Stanton in creating a new organization in 1869, the National Woman Suffrage Association. Stanton and Matilda Joslyn Gage (1826–1898) wrote the Declaration of Rights of the Women of the United States, which Anthony presented, uninvited, during the Centennial celebration in Washington, D.C., in 1876 (the one-hundredth anniversary of the signing of the Declaration of Independence).

In 1889, Stanton and Anthony merged their National Woman Suffrage Association with their old group, the American Woman Suffrage Association, to form the National American Woman Suffrage Association. Stanton agreed to serve as president of the organization for two years. Elizabeth Cady Stanton died in 1902.

leave the American Woman Suffrage Association when the group decided to delay pursuit of women's suffrage to focus on

Long fight for the vote

During the late 1860s, Anthony had spent some time in Kansas with the family of her brother, Daniel, a newspaper publisher. She learned enough about publishing to help the National Woman Suffrage Association produce a weekly periodical, *The Revolution*, beginning in 1868. The periodical promoted women's causes and provided information and insight on such issues as divorce, prostitution, and unequal pay for women who performed jobs requiring the same responsibilities as men. When the journal went bankrupt in 1870, Anthony began a lecture tour to pay off the debts. She was popular enough to extend her speaking tour for six years, through the end of 1876.

Meanwhile, in 1872, Anthony and over a dozen others from Rochester became the first women ever to vote in a

national election. When stopped at the polls, Anthony read aloud the Fifteenth Amendment, which has no wording that indicates the right to vote is restricted to men. When the women were arrested, Anthony used the case as a test of women's legal right to vote under the Fifteenth Amendment. With the trial set for 1873 in Rochester, Anthony went on a speaking tour to address the question, "Is It a Crime for a U.S. Citizen to Vote?" She lost her court case, however, after the judge refused to let Anthony testify and he directed the jury to find her guilty. Anthony was fined $100 and her attorney's motion for a new trial was denied.

Anthony continued to tour the country in support of the federal suffrage amendment. She spoke before Congress, political conventions, labor meetings, and town meetings in every part of the country. She wrote articles on women's history and lobbied for social change. Along with colleagues like Stanton, Anthony contributed to the five-volume *History of Woman Suffrage* during the mid-1870s. After this project, Anthony worked with biographer Ida Husted Harper (1851–1931) on two volumes of *The Life and Work of Susan B. Anthony,* with incidents and comments drawn largely from scrapbooks, diaries, and letters Anthony maintained.

The Fifteenth Amendment

Susan B. Anthony argued that the Fifteenth Amendment, which follows, did not contain wording that specifically restricted voting to men.

1. The right of citizens of the United States to vote shall not be denied or abridged by the United States or by any State on account of race, color, or previous condition of servitude.

2. The Congress shall have power to enforce this article by appropriate legislation.

In 1889, Anthony and Stanton's National Woman's Suffrage Association merged with the American Woman Suffrage Association to form the National American Woman Suffrage Association. In 1890, Wyoming became the first state to allow women to vote.

By the end of the nineteenth century, Anthony could feel some sense of triumph as women had entered professional and vocational fields and were more economically independent, and as colleges became more open to women students. In 1900, Anthony persuaded the University of Rochester to admit women.

By then, in her seventies, Anthony had settled in Rochester. For the first time in her life, she had time to entertain guests in her own home. Still, she traveled often. She was on the road until a month before her death in Rochester. She had traveled to Baltimore, Maryland, to attend the National American Woman Suffrage Association's annual convention, and then went to Washington, D.C. Anthony closed her last public speech on women's suffrage with the words, "Failure is impossible."

Four states (Wyoming, Colorado, Idaho, and Utah) had granted women the right to vote at the time of Anthony's death on March 13, 1906. Finally, in 1920, the Nineteenth Amendment gave women the right to vote in national elections.

For More Information

Books

Anthony, Susan B., Elizabeth Cady Stanton, and Matilda Joslyn Gage, eds. *History of Woman Suffrage*. New York: Fowler & Wells, 1881–1922. Reprint, Salem, NH: Ayer Co., 1985.

Harper, Ida Husted. *Life and Work of Susan B. Anthony*. Indianapolis and Kansas City: Bowen-Merrill Co., 1898–1908. Reprint, New York: Arno, 1969.

Harper, Judith. *Susan B. Anthony: A Biographical Companion*. Santa Barbara: ABC-CLIO, 1998.

Kendall, Martha E. *Susan B. Anthony: Voice for Women's Voting Rights*. Berkeley Heights, NJ: Enslow, 1997.

Sherr, Lynn. *Failure Is Impossible: Susan B. Anthony in Her Own Words*. New York: Three Rivers Press, 1996.

Web Sites

The Susan B. Anthony Center for Women's Leadership. http://www.rochester.edu/SBA/sbaecs.html (accessed on June 16, 2004).

The Susan B. Anthony House. http://www.susanbanthonyhouse.org/ (accessed on June 16, 2004).

Blanche K. Bruce

Born March 1, 1841
Farmville, Virginia

Died March 17, 1898
Washington, D.C.

U.S. senator, educator, and farmer

Blanche K. Bruce was the first African American to serve a full term in the U.S. Senate. Prior to his political career, he founded a school in Hannibal, Missouri, and later helped establish a strong, countywide system of twenty-one schools in Mississippi. Bruce was also a successful farmer. Following his term in the Senate, Bruce was a chairperson of the Republican National Convention in Chicago in 1880 and served in the administrations of presidents Benjamin Harrison (1833–1901; served 1889–93) and William McKinley (1843–1901; served 1897–1901).

Up from slavery

Born Blanche Bruce in 1841 on a plantation in Farmville, Virginia, he was one of eleven children of Polly Bruce, a slave. Bruce's father was probably Pettus Perkinson, the slaveowner of the plantation. Polly encouraged her children to take advantage of learning opportunities. Bruce learned to read and write while taking care of his half-brother, Willie Perkinson. Pettus Perkinson moved his extended family

"I have confidence, not only in my country and her institutions, but in the endurance, capacity and destiny of my people. We will, as opportunity offers and ability serves, seek our places.... Whatever our ultimate position in the composite civilization of the Republic and whatever varying fortunes attend our career, we will not forget our instincts for freedom nor our love for country."

Blanche K. Bruce. *The Library of Congress.*

several times within six years, and at a young age Bruce moved with his family to Missouri. He fled Missouri during his teens and worked various odd jobs, most of the time in Kansas, as a fugitive slave.

When Bruce returned to Missouri in 1864, he was a free man. The Emancipation Proclamation of 1863 freed slaves, but was binding only in slave states that had remained in the Union. Missouri was one of them. (Eleven slave states had left the Union and formed the Confederate States of America). At the age of twenty-three, Bruce founded a school for African American children in Hannibal. During this period, Bruce may have attended Oberlin College in Ohio, but that cannot be firmly verified. It was during this time he added a middle name, Kelso.

In 1868, Bruce purchased land in Floreyville, Mississippi, and began preparing it for farming. Over the next few years, he accumulated additional parcels of land and transformed a swampy area into a fertile and profitable 640-acre cotton plantation. During this period, Bruce also worked as a teacher. He became superintendent of county schools and brought strong administrative skills to a weak school system. In the process, Bruce ensured that African American children of the area would have educational opportunities equal to those of their white peers.

Becomes local leader

As a successful landowner and administrator, the charming and persuasive Bruce quickly became recognized as a local leader. Mississippi's military governor, Adelbert Ames (1835–1933), appointed him conductor of elections for a nearby Mississippi county. (A military governor is appointed by the government of an occupying military force. During the Reconstruction era—from the end of the Civil War [1861–65] in 1865 to the end of Reconstruction in 1877—Southern states that had seceded from the Union were run by military governors to ensure that peace and civil rights were protected.) In 1870, Bruce became sergeant at arms in the state senate.

Bruce's political rise in Mississippi was swift: he became an assessor (one who appraises the value of property for local tax purposes) for Bolivar County in 1871, was named county sheriff in 1872, and won a place on a state board that supervised tax assessors that year. Respected by the local community, Bruce was able to maintain calm when violence by a group of white men threatened to become a race riot in his home county.

In 1873, Bruce was offered the opportunity to run for lieutenant governor of Mississippi. He declined, believing he had an opportunity instead to win election to the U.S. Senate. In the Senate election of 1874, Bruce faced two challengers who had migrated from the North to take advantage of opportunities into the war-ravaged South. (Such opportunists were called "carpetbaggers" because many arrived in the South with their possessions in a cheap suitcase). When one of his opponents attempted to make Bruce's background a political issue, Bruce replied, "It is true that I was a house slave. But I freed myself, educated myself, and raised myself up in the world. If my opponent had started out where I did, he would still be there." Bruce won the election.

Civil rights advocate

On the first official day of work for a first-time senator, the new senator takes the oath of office and is introduced to the Senate. It is customary for the new senator to be escorted to the Senate floor by the other senator from the same state. However, when Bruce was walking from his seat to the Senate floor on his first day to take his oath, fellow Mississippi senator James Lusk Alcorn refused to escort Bruce. Alcorn was angry that Bruce did not assist him in a political struggle against Mississippi's military governor. Bruce was halfway down the aisle when another senator rose and accompanied him to the floor. That senator was Roscoe Conkling, a powerful fellow Republican from New York.

During his tenure in the Senate, Bruce supported civil rights. He opposed bills that would place limits on the immigration of Chinese people (many Chinese came to the United States following the Civil War for jobs related to railroad construction or to work in growing cities in the West). Bruce was a leading proponent on such issues as desegregation of the U.S. Army. He also fought for pensions for African American

Union army veterans (over 10 percent of the Union army was African American at the end of the Civil War in 1865). Bruce also supported more aggressive government action in issuing western land grants to African Americans. Land grants were made available by the government to encourage settlement on the western frontier.

Representing the interests of his home state and region, Bruce supported development of a channel and levee system (pertaining to water irrigation) and construction of the Mississippi Valley and Ship Island Railroad. He participated in a Senate inquiry into fraud and violence in Mississippi elections of 1875.

Among his most significant roles as senator, Bruce chaired an investigation into the Freedmen's Savings and Trust scandal. In 1865, following the end of the Civil War and passage of the Thirteenth Amendment, which outlawed slavery, the federal government authorized the creation of a bank that would help former slaves become economically stable. Mismanagement and corruption, however, had plagued Freedmen's Savings and Trust. By 1874, the bank had collapsed. Bruce's six-member committee issued a report naming bank officials who were guilty of fraud and incompetence. Eventually, over sixty thousand customers victimized by the bank's 1874 failure received a portion of their money.

U.S. senator Roscoe Conkling of New York, who treated the African American senator Blanche K. Bruce with honor and respect on his first day in the Senate. *Photograph by Mathew Brady. The Library of Congress.*

Distinguished career after Congress

In 1878, near the end of his Senate term, Bruce married Josephine Beall Wilson, a teacher. They would have one child, Roscoe Conkling Bruce, named in honor of the senator who had shown respect for Bruce on his first day in the Senate. Bruce and his wife were active in Washington society. On February 14, 1879, Bruce presided over the Senate as part of a customary practice of rotating presiding officers during routine floor proceedings. This instance proved far from routine by setting an historical precedent. Bruce had a personal background that no other senator before could claim: He had been born into slavery.

Following the end of his term in the Senate, Bruce became, in 1880, the first African American to chair the Republican National Convention. From 1881 to 1885, he served in the Treasury Department in the administrations of President James A. Garfield (1831–1881; served 1881) and, following Garfield's assassination in 1881, Chester A. Arthur (1830–1886; served 1881–85). Bruce and his family settled in Washington, D.C., where Bruce operated a successful business handling investments, claims, insurance, and real estate.

At the 1888 Republican National Convention, Bruce received eleven votes for vice president at the convention that nominated Benjamin Harrison for president. He was appointed Recorder of Deeds of the District of Columbia by President Harrison, administering property documents from 1889 to 1893. Bruce served in the Department of Treasury in the administration of President William McKinley in 1897. However, he served only three months before an illness forced him to leave the position.

Bruce received an honorary degree from Howard University in 1893 and served on the university's Board of Trustees from 1894 to 1898. On March 17, 1898, the fifty-seven-year-old Bruce died from diabetic complications in Washington, D.C. He was buried in Suitland, Maryland, the final resting place of many other prominent African Americans.

 Senator Bruce Recalls His First Day on the Job

Mr. Alcorn [Bruce's fellow senator from Mississippi] made no motion to escort me, but was buried behind a newspaper, and I concluded I would go it alone. I had got about half-way up the aisle when a tall gentleman stepped up and said, "Excuse me, Mr. Bruce, I did not until this moment see that you were without escort, permit me. My name is Conkling," and he linked his arm in mine and we marched up to the desk together. I took the oath and then he escorted me back to my seat.

For More Information

Books

Buckmaster, Henrietta. *The Fighting Congressmen: Thaddeus Stephens, Hiram Revels, James Rapier, Blanche K. Bruce.* New York: Scholastic Book Services, 1971.

Sterling, Philip. *Four Took Freedom: The Lives of Harriet Tubman, Frederick Douglass, Robert Smalls and Blanche K. Bruce.* Garden City, NY: Doubleday, 1967.

Swain, Charles. *Blanche K. Bruce, Politician.* New York: Chelsea House, 1996.

Web Sites

"Former Slave Presides over Senate." *The U.S. Senate.* http://www.senate.gov/artandhistory/history/minute/Former_Slave_Presides_Over_Senate.htm (accessed on June 17, 2004).

Francis L. Cardozo

Born February 1, 1837
Charleston, South Carolina

Died July 22, 1903
Washington, D.C.

Minister, educator, and politician

Francis L. Cardozo served as an educator and politician in his native South Carolina and in Washington, D.C. His efforts in education resulted in two highly respected high schools: the Avery Institute in Charleston, South Carolina, and the Paul Laurence Dunbar High School in Washington, D.C. Cardozo was an effective elected official during the Reconstruction era in South Carolina, helping smooth the transition from an economy based on slavery to one that aimed to provide equal opportunity.

From carpenter to minister

Francis Louis Cardozo was born in Charleston, South Carolina, in 1837. His father, a journalist, was white, and Cardozo's mother was of mixed African and Native American ancestry. Cardozo had at least two siblings, a brother and a sister. He attended a school for African Americans in Charleston until he was twelve. Cardozo was then apprenticed (bound by contract) to a carpenter. As an apprentice, Cardozo had on-the-job training to learn the skills of carpentry. He remained an appren-

"One of the greatest of slavery bulwarks was the infernal plantation system.... I maintain that our freedom will be of no effect if we allow it to continue. What is the main cause of the prosperity of the North? It is because every man has his own farm and is free and independent. Let the lands of the South be similarly divided."

Francis L. Cardozo. *The Library of Congress.*

Edward Bouchet, Educator and Scientist

Like Francis Cardozo, there were many educators who improved schools for African American children following the Civil War. Edward Bouchet was one of them. He spent twenty-six years in Philadelphia, Pennsylvania, teaching at the Institute for Colored Youth and speaking often before church, trade, and community groups. Bouchet was the first African American to receive a doctorate degree, graduating from Yale University with his Ph.D. in physics in 1876.

Bouchet was born on September 15, 1852, in New Haven, Connecticut. He attended the Artisan Street Colored School, the oldest of four primary schools for African American children in New Haven. An excellent student, Bouchet moved to a private school, where he graduated first in his class and gave the valedictory address (the speech given by the most outstanding member of a graduating class) at graduation. He entered Yale College in 1870 and was one of the top students of his class. In his senior year, Bouchet was approached by Alfred Cope about remaining at Yale and obtaining his doctorate in physics. Cope was on the Board of Managers of the Institute for Colored Youth (ICY), a Quaker school for African American children located in Philadelphia. Cope wanted to develop a science program for ICY and wanted Bouchet to direct the department.

After receiving his Ph.D., Bouchet started the science department and taught at ICY for twenty-six years. During this period, he became a member of the Franklin Institute, one of the country's oldest scientific societies, founded in 1824. He was also a member of the American Academy of Po-

tice for five years and then became a journeyman (one who possesses the skills to be licensed as a professional carpenter).

During this time, Cardozo had joined the Second Presbyterian Church in Charleston. He saved enough money from his carpentry work to travel to Scotland, where he attended the University of Glasgow while continuing to support himself through odd jobs. Cardozo moved from Glasgow to Edinburgh, Scotland, and then to London, England, to study for the ministry. He returned to the United States in 1864 at age twenty-seven and was appointed minister to the Temple Street Congregational Church in New Haven, Connecticut.

Cardozo married Catherine Romena Howell of New Haven. The couple would have four sons, two daughters, and a few famous grandchildren. Among them were Eslanda litical and Social Science and sat on the board of directors of the Century Building and Loan Association in Philadelphia, which was organized in 1886.

In 1902, the curriculum of ICY changed, de-emphasizing the humanities and science to focus on the mechanical trades to prepare young people to enter the workforce. Bouchet left the Institute in protest and spent the rest of his life in a variety of positions. He taught in a college preparatory program at Sumner High School in St. Louis, Missouri, in 1902; worked as a business manager at a St. Louis hospital the following year; moved to New Orleans in 1905 and worked for two years as U.S. Inspector of Customs for the Louisiana Purchase Exposition; returned to education in 1905 as the director of academics at St. Paul's Normal and Industrial School in Lawrenceville, Virginia; and then became principal of Lincoln High School in Galipolis, Ohio, in 1908.

Bouchet's five years at Lincoln High School were typical of his career. He arrived at a school in neglect and helped students overcome obstacles to learning, improving the facilities and curriculum and pursuing his philosophy of training young African Americans so they were prepared to enter college.

In 1913, Bouchet joined the faculty of Bishop College in Marshall, Texas. However, he soon began suffering heart problems and was forced to retire. By this time, he was seventy-six years old. Bouchet returned to his hometown of New Haven and lived there until his death in 1918.

Goode Robeson (1896–1965), an anthropologist and wife of noted actor Paul Robeson (1898–1976), and W. Warrick Cardozo (1905–1962), a physician who was a pioneer researcher in the disease sickle cell anemia.

Teacher and politician

Cardozo discovered he wanted to be an educator rather than a minister. His brother and sister were both teaching in Flushing, New York. Following the end of the Civil War (1861–65) in the spring of 1865, Cardozo asked the American Missionary Association (AMA) to send him to the South to establish a school to train black teachers. Cardozo was appointed head of an AMA school back in his hometown of Charleston. Cardozo and his family were joined by his brother and sister and their families in Charleston, and the Cardozo siblings all taught at the school. Cardozo ran the school until April 1868, helping to establish what would become the Avery Institute, an acclaimed teacher training facility.

At the school, Cardozo directed an integrated staff of white teachers from the North and African American teachers from both the North and South. Cardozo led his school under difficult conditions. The ownership of the school building was under dispute: It had been taken over by the AMA during the Civil War, but some townspeople claimed they were the real owners. Meanwhile, Cardozo had heard of a plan by the estate of Charles Avery to contribute $10,000 to build a school in Atlanta, Georgia. Avery had created a fortune earlier in the century as a medicine supplier based in Pittsburgh, Pennsylvania. A staunch abolitionist (antislavery activist), Avery had helped slaves escape the South through the Underground Railroad, a series of safe havens where runaway slaves stayed as they moved north toward freedom in Canada. Upon his death, Avery left an estate that provided a large sum of money to help in "the education and elevation of the colored people of the United States and Canada."

Cardozo was able to gain support from local politicians, who provided letters of recommendation that helped him secure money from the Avery estate. He also received financial assistance from the Freedmen's Bureau, a banking institution established by the federal government after the Civil War to assist African Americans to become economically stable. In April 1867, Cardozo and his teachers moved to a temporary location for their school while a new school was being built. The Avery Institute opened the following April as a school and as an institute for teacher training.

Enters politics

Meanwhile, Cardozo had become well known in the Charleston community. He served on a board advising South Carolina's military commander about voter registration regulations in 1866. (A military governor is appointed by the government of an occupying military force. During the Reconstruction era—from the end of the Civil War in 1865 to the end of Reconstruction in 1877—Southern states that had seceded from the Union were run by military governors to ensure that peace and civil rights were protected.) In 1868, he was elected to the South Carolina state constitutional convention. States like South Carolina that had seceded from and fought against the Union in the Civil War were required to amend or rewrite their state constitutions to include approval of the Thirteenth and Fourteenth Amendments (outlawing slavery and protecting voting rights, respectively), as part of the requirements for rejoining the Union.

At the convention, Cardozo emphasized the need to make land grants available to freedmen. Land grants provide parcels of land by loan or for free with the condition that the land is used and maintained. Cardozo claimed that the plantation system of the South, where huge tracts of land were owned by one family, had fostered slavery and would stifle economic growth opportunities. Cardozo argued that plantations should be divided into smaller tracts that could be developed independently so many more people would enjoy economic freedom and earn a living.

Cardozo and Plantations

The following is an excerpt from Francis Cardozo's speech at the South Carolina Constitutional Convention of 1868 on the subject of plantations.

One of the greatest of slavery bulwarks was the infernal plantation system, one man owning his thousand, another his twenty, another fifty thousand acres of land. [Providing land grants for freedmen] is the only way by which we will break up that system, and I maintain that our freedom will be of no effect if we allow it to continue. What is the main cause of the prosperity of the North? It is because every man has his own farm and is free and independent. Let the lands of the South be similarly divided. I would not say for one moment they should be confiscated, but if sold to maintain the war, now that slavery is destroyed, let the plantation system go with it. We will never have true freedom until we abolish the system of agriculture which existed in the Southern States. It is useless to have any schools while we maintain the stronghold of slavery as the agricultural system of the country.

Cardozo attended the convention while he was still heading the school, but he no longer had the time to teach. His participation in the convention led Republicans to recommend that Cardozo should run for state government office. Cardozo ran for and was elected secretary of state, becoming the first African American to hold an elected position in the history of South Carolina. Still, his election victory was bittersweet. The new responsibilities led Cardozo to resign from his school position just days before the formal dedication of the

Avery Institute, for which he had worked so hard. Cardozo was reelected in 1870 and served in the office until 1872, when he became state treasurer.

Political career

As secretary of state, Cardozo reorganized the state's Land Commission, which administered the use and sale of land. He made the agency honest and effective. In his role as state treasurer from 1872 to 1877, he supported the efforts of state Republicans to reform taxes and ensure that the state spent its money wisely. After Southern Democrats won control of the state in the elections of 1876, Cardozo and his family left South Carolina in 1877 for Washington, D.C.

Cardozo accepted a position in the Treasury Department during the administration of **Rutherford B. Hayes** (1822–1893; served 1877–81; see entry). In 1881, Cardozo became principal of the Colored Preparatory High School in Washington, D.C., and molded it into the leading black college preparatory school in the United States. In addition to classes that prepared students for college, Cardozo introduced business courses intended solely to teach business skills to students, regardless of their career choices. The institution was later renamed Paul Laurence Dunbar High School, after the famous poet.

Cardozo began easing his workload as the nineteenth century ended and he reached his sixties. Cardozo died on July 22, 1903. In 1928, a new business and vocational high school in Washington, D.C., was named in his honor.

For More Information

Books

Appiah, Kwame Anthony, and Henry Louis Gates Jr., eds. *Africana: The Encyclopedia of the African and African American Experience.* New York: Basic Civitas Books, 1999.

Drago, Edmund L. *Initiative, Paternalism, and Race Relations: Charleston's Avery Normal Institute.* Athens: University of Georgia Press, 1990.

Smith, Jessie Carney. *Black Firsts.* 2nd ed. Detroit: Visible Ink Press, 2003.

Web Sites

"Politician, Minister, and Educator, Francis Cardozo." *The African American Registry.* http://www.aaregistry.com/african_american_history/

1643/Politician_minister_and_educator_Francis_Cardozo (accessed on June 17, 2004).

"South Carolina Encyclopedia Project: Avery Normal Institute." *College of Charleston School of Humanities & Social Sciences.* http://www.cofc.edu/~history/avery_sc_encyclopedia.htm (accessed on June 17, 2004).

Confederate Leaders

Jefferson Davis	Alexander H. Stephens
Born June 3, 1808	Born February 11, 1812
Southwestern Kentucky	Crawfordsville, Georgia
Died December 6, 1889	Died March 4, 1883
New Orleans, Louisiana	Atlanta, Georgia
President	Vice president
Robert E. Lee	**Robert A. Toombs**
Born January 19, 1807	Born July 2, 1810
Westmoreland County, Virginia	Wilkes County, Georgia
Died October 13, 1870	Died December 15, 1885
Lexington, Virginia	Washington, Georgia
General	Secretary of state

"[I favor] the maintenance of the honor, the rights, the equality, the security, and the glory of my native state ... but if these cannot be maintained in the Union, then I am for their maintenance, at all hazards, out of it."

—Alexander Stephens

Confederate leaders (seated, from left): Jefferson Davis, John Reagan, and Alexander Stephens; (standing, from left) Robert E. Lee, Christopher Memminger, and Robert A. Toombs.
Photo by MPI/Getty Images.

The Confederate States of America (CSA) was founded in 1861 after years of often angry debate over slavery and whether the federal government or states had the power to abolish, maintain, or expand the institution. On February 4, 1861, representatives from the states of Alabama, Florida, Georgia, Louisiana, Mississippi, South Carolina, and Texas met in Montgomery, Alabama, to form a new republic. Those states seceded (separated) from the United States. On February 8, representatives at the convention announced that the Confederate States of America had been created and that members of the convention were serving as the CSA Congress until one could be elected.

Key leaders

Former U.S. senator Jefferson Davis (1808–1889) of Mississippi and former U.S. representative Alexander Stephens (1812–1883) of Georgia were chosen as president and vice president, respectively, and they served in those capacities from the founding of the CSA until it dissolved at the end of the Civil War (1861–65). Robert A. Toombs (1810–1885), also a former U.S. representative from Georgia who had worked with Stephens to defend the expansion of slavery to new territories and states, was named secretary of state. When the Civil War broke out in April 1861, the CSA government was responsible for overseeing the Confederate war effort. Virginia, North Carolina, Tennessee, and Arkansas joined the Confederacy shortly after the war began.

During the war, Robert E. Lee (1807–1870) emerged as the most successful military leader of the Confederacy. Confederate forces won or battled to a draw on most of the early battles of the war, but momentum moved to the Union side during the summer of 1863. Following the Union victory in April 1865, the era of Reconstruction (1865–77) was underway to address key issues: how seceded states would return to the Union; what punishment, if any, should be ordered on members of the former Confederacy; and what federal government support, if any, should be afforded to former slaves (slavery was abolished with the passage of the Thirteenth Amendment in 1865).

Jefferson Davis: soldier and politician

Jefferson Davis served in both houses of U.S. Congress, fought with distinction in the Mexican War (1846–48), and was secretary of war in the administration of President Franklin Pierce (1804–1869; served 1853–57). Davis was elected president of the Confederate States of America in 1861 and served in that position throughout the Civil War.

Davis was born on June 3, 1808, in Christian (now Todd) County, Kentucky. He was the tenth child of Samuel and Jane (Cook) Davis, who had moved westward from Georgia. Davis's father had been a commander during the Revolutionary War (1775–83). The family moved to Mississippi when Davis was a young boy and settled on a small plantation near Woodville. Joseph Emory Davis, the eldest son in the family, became one of the wealthiest men in the South.

An especially bright youngster, Davis was enrolled at age seven in a school at St. Thomas College in Washington County, Kentucky, a thousand miles north of the family home. At nine, he was back in Mississippi and attended local schools before entering Transylvania University in 1821. A Mississippi

Jefferson Davis, president of the Confederate States of America. *The Library of Congress.*

congressman nominated him to the West Point military school, and Davis began studying there in 1824. He graduated in 1828 and became a second lieutenant in the United States Army.

Davis spent seven years stationed on the frontier in Wisconsin and Illinois and fought in the Black Hawk War (1832), which put down a Native American uprising in that area. Stationed at Fort Crawford, Wisconsin, after the war, Davis met and fell in love with Sarah Taylor, the daughter of the fort's commandant and future U.S. president, Zachary Taylor (1784–1850; served 1849–50). The couple eloped and settled in Mississippi.

Davis's wife died three months after marriage from malaria, a disease transmitted by mosquitoes. Davis spent the next ten years working primarily as a farmer. The Davis family was prominent in Mississippi, and Davis was elected to the U.S. House of Representatives in 1844. He married Varina Howell in 1845. At the time Davis entered Congress, the nation was growing more divided over slavery. Davis supported the power of states to determine whether or not to permit slavery.

With the outbreak of the Mexican-American War (1846–48) in 1846, Davis resigned from Congress and accepted command of a volunteer regiment known as the Mississippi Rifles. He served under Taylor, his ex-father-in-law. Along with his Mississippi Rifles regiment, Davis fought with distinction in the war and was selected to fill a vacancy in the U.S. Senate in August 1847 created by the death of Jesse Speight (1795–1847). Davis was elected on his own in 1848 and served until 1851. He served as secretary of war from 1853 to 1857 in the administration of Franklin Pierce, and then was elected again to the U.S. Senate in 1856.

After Abraham Lincoln (1809–1865; served 1861–65) was elected president in 1860, South Carolina seceded from the Union and other Southern states considered secession as well. Davis was against secession until Lincoln declared that there should be no further expansion of slavery. Mississippi then seceded from the union, and Davis withdrew from the Senate in January 1861. On February 18, 1861, at Montgomery, Alabama, he was inaugurated (sworn in) as president of the Confederate States of America.

As the Confederate army was facing defeat in the Civil War in early April 1865, Davis left Richmond, Virginia, the political base of the Confederacy, on April 3. He approved the surrender of the Confederacy in Greensboro, North Carolina, in late April. Davis continued southward, hoping to leave the country. On May 2, 1865, President **Andrew Johnson** (1808–1875; served 1865–69; see entry) offered $100,000 for his arrest under charges that Davis helped plan the assassination of Abraham Lincoln. Davis was captured in Irwinville, Georgia, by the Federal cavalry on May 10. He was held as prisoner in Fortress Monroe in Virginia and charged with treason (disloyalty) and complicity (taking part) in Lincoln's assassination. At first, Davis was kept in irons, but later, when his health began failing, he was provided with comfortable living quarters and his family was permitted to stay with him.

Government lawyers were not sure they would win a case against Davis, and after nearly two years, Davis was released on bond. One of the people putting up bond money (funds paid to free a prisoner as assurance the prisoner will abide by obligations set by a court) was journalist **Horace Greeley** (1811–1872; see entry), a longtime abolitionist. Greeley wanted to bring reconciliation to the nation and put the war behind.

New charges were filed and preparations were made to try Davis in May 1868. However, the case was delayed by the impeachment (formal accusation of wrongdoing) trial of President Johnson. Davis's trial did not begin until November 1868 and, because of constitutional issues, was soon referred to the Supreme Court. In the meantime, on Christmas Day, 1868, President Johnson issued a general amnesty proclamation for ex-Confederates. Davis was finally freed on February 26, 1869.

Davis lived for twenty more years, but he had lost his fortune as well as his home. Despite suffering from a number of health conditions, he managed to travel throughout Europe. As he entered his seventies and the Reconstruction era ended, his health improved. However, Davis failed in business ventures and moved to a home provided to him by a friend of his wife. He spent the years 1878 to 1881 writing *The Rise and Fall of the Confederate Government.* He could have easily won a U.S. Senate seat from Mississippi, but Davis had refused to request a Federal pardon, which was necessary for any ex-Confederate if he wanted to hold federal office. Davis died in New Orleans, Louisiana, on December 6, 1889.

Robert E. Lee: officer and gentleman

Robert E. Lee was the most respected and successful military leader of the Confederacy during the Civil War. He led Confederate forces to impressive victories early in the war, attempted two invasions of the North that were repelled after fierce fighting, and remained in command to the end of the war in 1865. Lee did not fight the war for political reasons. Ultimately, the decision he faced was whether to fight for his country or his state. He chose his state.

Robert Edward Lee was born on January 19, 1807, in Westmoreland County, Virginia. His father, Henry "Light-Horse Harry" Lee, was a member of a famous Virginia family and fought in the Revolutionary War as a cavalry officer. The Lee family moved to Alexandria, Virginia, in 1811, when Lee was four. The family had lost much of its fortune because of bad investments. After attending schools in Alexandria, Lee followed in his father's footsteps and pursued a career in the military that began at West Point Military Academy in 1825. He graduated second in his class in 1829. While serving as an engineer at Fort Monroe, Virginia, from 1831 to 1834, Lee met and married Mary Ann Randolph Custis, granddaughter of the nation's initial first lady, Martha Washington (1732–1802). The Lees would have seven children.

Lee had a variety of other assignments before fighting with distinction in the Mexican-American War. After the war, he was placed in charge of the construction of Fort Carroll, in the harbor of Baltimore, Maryland. In August 1852, at the age of forty-five, Lee was named superintendent at West Point. He returned to military service as lieutenant-colonel of the 2nd

Cavalry in March 1855. He was in Washington, D.C., when abolitionist John Brown (1800–1859) led a small group in a raid of a nearby federal arsenal (weapons supply). Brown wanted to use the weapons to arm slaves to begin a revolt. Lee was sent to the arsenal at Harpers Ferry, Virginia, where he quickly stopped the insurrection (rebellion).

As the nation grew more divided over slavery during the 1850s, Lee was not sympathetic to the movement toward secession by Southern states. Still, he debated whether his state or his country had earned his primary allegiance. He decided that if Virginia seceded, he would support his home state. Lee was summoned to Washington, D.C., in February 1861 and placed on waiting orders, likely to be promoted to a commander if war began. On March 16, 1861, he was made colonel of the 1st Cavalry of the federal army.

Robert E. Lee, general of the Confederate Army. *The Library of Congress.*

Meanwhile, officials in Virginia considered seceding from the union, and Lee realized he could not fight against his own state. When he was offered the field command of the U.S. Army in April 1861, Lee declined the offer. After learning that the Virginia convention voted in favor of secession, Lee resigned his military commission. He was selected, instead, to command the forces of Virginia late in April. He was a general by July and the favorite commander of Confederate president Jefferson Davis.

Lee led Confederate forces to victories in early battles or helped fight off Union forces during the first two years of the Civil War. In 1863, Confederate leaders believed they could invade the North and possibly capture Washington, D.C. Lee's forces reached Gettysburg, in southern Pennsylvania, but the offensive stalled there and Confederates were forced to retreat. For the remainder of the war, Lee led a crafty defense of Virginia and forced the Union into a prolonged offensive, testing its determination.

By 1864, Union forces were making headway in Virginia and the lower Southern states. On February 6, 1865, orders were issued making Lee the general-in-chief of all the Confederate armies. By this time, however, he was consumed with a final defense of Virginia. Forced into a final retreat in early April 1865 and then blocked from retreat, Lee surrendered on April 9, 1865, and the Civil War was effectively over. Lee and his Union counterpart, General **Ulysses S. Grant** (1822–1885; see entry), negotiated an honorable surrender.

Lee was most concerned following the war with national reunification and rebuilding the war-ravaged South. He remained in Richmond and was treated with respect by federal officials. In September 1865, he became president of Washington College in Lexington, Virginia. He wanted to help bring stability and new opportunities for development for younger people, and, as always, led by example. He obeyed the law and counseled all Southerners to do the same. Lee was indicted for treason for his wartime activities. Though he was never brought to trial, neither was he offered a pardon. He died on October 12, 1870, in Lexington. Just over a century later, President Gerald Ford (1913–; served 1974–77) restored Lee's citizenship.

Alexander Stephens: powerful speaker

An engaging speaker, Alexander Stephens attempted to maintain the Union during years leading up to the Civil War, then became an eloquent spokesman for states that seceded and joined the Confederacy. Following the war, he worked actively for reunification of the nation and supported the Reconstruction policies of President Andrew Johnson.

Alexander Hamilton Stephens was born on February 11, 1812, on a farm in Wilkes County (later Taliaferro County), Georgia. Always small, Stephens barely weighed 100 pounds as an adult and was nicknamed "Little Aleck." Stephens grew up working on the farm and going to school. An uncle paid for his education at an academy in Washington, Georgia, where Stephens's admiration for his teacher, Reverend Alexander Hamilton Webster, led him to adopt Hamilton as his middle name. He went on to the University of Georgia and graduated in 1832 at the head of his class. He worked as a teacher before beginning a law practice in 1834 in Crawfordville, near the place of his birth.

Stephens was a good public speaker and was elected to the Georgia legislature and then to Congress in 1843. A staunch supporter of states' rights, Stephens helped launch the Constitutional Union party in Georgia with Robert A. Toombs to aggressively defend Southern interests. Like Toombs, Stephens shifted to the Democratic Party in the mid-1850s. Stephens left Congress in 1859.

Despite suffering from ill health, Stephens resumed his law practice in Crawfordville. He campaigned for Democratic solidarity in 1860, but the party split into three factions and lost the presidential election to Republican Abraham Lincoln. The Georgia legislature was in session when Lincoln was elected. Georgia's governor, Joseph E. Brown (1821–1894), immediately recommended a state convention to address secession. Stephens spoke at the convention and advocated a conference of all the Southern states. "My position," he stated in the conclusion of his speech, "is for the maintenance of the honor, the rights, the equality, the security, and the glory of my native state in the Union, if possible, but if these cannot be maintained in the Union, then I am for their maintenance, at all hazards, out of it." The speech was published and widely distributed, bringing a flood of letters, including one from President Lincoln. Lincoln wrote, "You think slavery is *right* and ought to be extended; while we think it is *wrong* and ought to be restricted." By then, South Carolina had seceded and other Southern states soon followed.

Stephens was elected to be a delegate to the convention in Montgomery, Alabama, in 1861, where the Confederate States of America was formed. At the convention, he was elected vice president of the Confederacy. Stephens attempted several times during the Civil War to forge a peace agreement

Alexander Stephens, vice president of the Confederacy. *The Library of Congress.*

with the federal government. In 1863, he negotiated from a position of some strength, but his last attempt in February 1865 came when Union forces were closing in for victory.

After the end of the Civil War in April 1865, Stephens was taken into custody and held at Fort Warren in Boston Harbor. Upon being released on parole on October 12, 1865, Stephens was greeted by crowds in New York, Washington, D.C., and Atlanta as he traveled home. In January 1866, he was elected to the U.S. Senate under President Andrew Johnson's Reconstruction plan, but Congress rejected the plan and excluded Stephens from serving. Meanwhile, Stephens urged his fellow Georgians to be patient with the Reconstruction program, although he supported the policies of Johnson, not those of Congress.

In April 1866, Stephens testified before the congressional joint committee on Reconstruction. He described his state as willing to participate in the Reconstruction effort. But he was against plans for extending voting rights to African Americans. He did not believe that the federal government had constitutional power to impose conditions on states through Reconstruction programs.

Stephens wrote the two-volume *A Constitutional View of the Late War Between the States,* published in 1868 and 1870. The book caused a sensation in its defense of the Confederacy, and Stephens earned some $35,000 in royalties (a percentage of sales paid to an author). Stephens reacted to critics of the book by collecting reviews and replying to them in *The Reviewers Reviewed* (1872). He later wrote a history book for use in schools, *A Compendium of the History of the United States* (1872) and an illustrated version, *A Comprehensive and Popular History of the United States* (1882).

Stephens had been offered a professorship of political science and history at the University of Georgia, but declined. In 1871, he became part owner of the *Southern Sun,* an Atlanta newspaper. During the election year of 1872, he wrote many editorials in support of presidential candidate Horace Greeley.

Stephens was a candidate for the U.S. Senate in 1872, but was defeated. Later that year, he was elected to the U.S. House of Representatives. Although he entered Congress in failing health and had to use a cane to walk, Stephens remained in Congress for a decade. He supported the decision of the electoral commission that was formed to decide the controversial presidential election of 1876. When the commission decided in favor of Republican **Rutherford B. Hayes** (1822–1893; served 1877–81; see entry) instead of the Democratic candidate, **Samuel J. Tilden** (1814–1886; see entry), Stephens defended the decision and was pleased when Hayes ended Reconstruction in 1877.

Stephens resigned from Congress in 1882. After being bored by retirement, he ran for and was elected governor of Georgia. However, Stephens died on March 4, 1883, in Savannah, Georgia, shortly after he was inaugurated.

Robert A. Toombs: proslavery advocate

Robert Toombs served in both houses of U.S. Congress. As political division between North and South and Democrat and Republican moved Southern states toward secession and the nation toward war during the 1850s, Toombs attempted to find the means for avoiding drastic actions. After the failure of attempts to avoid separation and war, Toombs resigned from the U.S. Senate in January 1861 and served as a delegate the next month to the convention where the Confederate States of America (CSA) was established. He then briefly served as secretary of state for the CSA. "I am not loyal to the existing government of the United States," he said, "and do not wish to be suspected of loyalty."

Robert Augustus Toombs was born on July 2, 1810, in Wilkes County in eastern Georgia. He was the fifth child of Robert Toombs, a wealthy cotton planter who had been a major in the Revolutionary War, and Catherine Toombs. He entered college at the University of Georgia, but completed his education in the North by graduating from Union College in Schenectady, New York, in 1828. Returning to his home state, Toombs began a profitable law practice in Washington, Georgia, in 1830 and accumulated wealth through investments in a plantation and its slaves. In 1830, he married Julia DuBose. The couple would have three children.

Toombs was elected to the Georgia legislature in 1837 as a member of the Whig Party. In 1844, he was elected to Congress. He was especially effective working on financial

Robert Toombs, first secretary of state of the Confederacy and supporter of the Southern states.
Photo by Hulton Archive/Getty Images.

matters. As Congress became divided over slavery in the mid-1840s, Toombs was a leader in defense of the South and the right of states to determine whether or not to permit slavery. During the 1850s, he helped launch the Constitutional Union Party in Georgia to wage an aggressive defense of proslavery measures passed by Congress. He was elected to the U.S. Senate as a member of that party. The Constitutional Union Party did not catch on in other states, so Toombs let it dissolve in Georgia and he became a member of the Democratic Party.

Toombs tried to unite Democrats in opposing Abraham Lincoln's bid for the presidency in 1860, but three different candidates emerged and split the party votes in the presidential election. Toombs hoped to avoid secession if Republicans would support slavery as an issue for states to decide. Republicans refused, and Toombs made a farewell speech to the Senate on January 7, 1861. He was chosen as one of the delegates from Georgia to meet with those of the other states that had seceded in Montgomery, Alabama, in February 1861 to launch the Confederate States of America.

Toombs was named secretary of state for the CSA. Unable to work effectively with Confederate president Jefferson Davis, Toombs applied for and received a military commission in July 1861 as commander of a Georgia brigade on the Virginia front. Toombs was an aggressive military leader. In the Battle of Antietam, his brigade held its position in fierce fighting, while Toombs took a bullet that shattered his left hand. He expected a promotion for his bravery and leadership. When it was refused, Toombs resigned his commission. He was critical of the Confederate leadership, but failed in a bid for election to the Confederate Senate. He reentered the war near the end in the battle for Georgia, leading a division and serving as inspector-general.

When the Confederacy collapsed, Toombs remained at home until Federal troops arrived to arrest him about a month after the war ended. Toombs escaped and made his way to New Orleans, where he boarded a boat. He traveled to Havana, Cuba, and then went on to London, England, before returning to his home in 1867. He did not apply for pardon, a step necessary to regain his citizenship under Reconstruction laws. Toombs started a law practice and soon became influential in state politics.

Toombs focused on protecting Southerners from being victimized by carpetbaggers, Northerners who arrived in Southern states with cloth suitcases and were prepared to take advantage of the war-ravished region and victimized people. He also spoke up against dominance of the South by the federal Reconstruction policy spearheaded by congressional Republicans.

Toombs welcomed the end of Reconstruction as announced by President Rutherford B. Hayes in 1877. A state constitutional convention was held that year in Georgia and Toombs dominated the proceedings: Under his leadership, no action was taken to protect the voting rights of freedmen, the state judiciary system was reorganized, and new regulations were placed on corporations. In 1879, he supported legislation to create a commission to regulate railroad rates.

After turning seventy in 1880, Toombs became less active. He suffered from debilitating eye problems, and mourned the death of his wife in 1883. Toombs was in failing health by then and died on December 15, 1885, in Washington, Georgia. Toombs County, Georgia, was named in his honor.

For More Information

Books

Archer, Jules. *A House Divided: The Lives of Ulysses S. Grant and Robert E. Lee.* New York: Scholastic, 1995.

Burch, Joann Johansen. *Jefferson Davis: President of the Confederacy.* Springfield, NJ: Enslow, 1998.

Cannon, Marian G. *Robert E. Lee.* New York: Franklin Watts, 1993.

Cooper, William J. *Jefferson Davis, American: A Biography.* New York: Alfred A. Knopf, 2000.

Davis, Jefferson. *The Rise and Fall of the Confederate Government.* New York: D. Appleton, 1881. Reprint, New York: Da Capo Press, 1990.

Davis, William C. *The Union That Shaped the Confederacy: Robert Toombs and Alexander H. Stephens.* Lawrence: University Press of Kansas, 2001.

Eaton, Clement. *Jefferson Davis.* New York: Free Press, 1977.

Freeman, Douglas Southall. *Lee.* New York: Scribner, 1997.

Kavanaugh, Jack, and Eugene C. Murdoch. *Robert E. Lee.* New York: Chelsea House, 1994.

Kerby, Mona. *Robert E. Lee: Southern Hero of the Civil War.* Springfield, NJ: Enslow, 1997.

King, Perry Scott. *Jefferson Davis.* Philadelphia: Chelsea House, 1990.

Lee, Fitzhugh. *General Lee: A Biography of Robert E. Lee.* New York: Da Capo Press, 1994.

Marrin, Albert. *Virginia's General: Robert E. Lee and the Civil War.* New York: Atheneum, 1994.

Phillips, Ulrich Bonnell. *The Life of Robert Toombs.* New York: Macmillan, 1913. Reprint, New York: B. Franklin, 1968.

Schott, Thomas Edwin. *Alexander H. Stephens of Georgia: A Biography.* Baton Rouge: Louisiana State University Press, 1988.

Stephens, Alexander Hamilton. *Recollections of Alexander H. Stephens: His Diary Kept When a Prisoner at Fort Warren, Boston Harbour, 1865.* New York: Doubleday, 1910. Reprint, Baton Rouge: Louisiana State University Press, 1998.

Thomas, Emory Morton. *Robert E. Lee: A Biography.* New York: W. W. Norton, 1995.

Thompson, William Y. *Robert Toombs of Georgia.* Baton Rouge: Louisiana State University Press, 1966.

Von Abele, Rudolph. *Alexander H. Stephens: A Biography.* New York: Knopf, 1946. Reprint, Westport, CT: Negro Universities Press, 1971.

Web Sites

Beauvoir, Jefferson Davis Home and Presidential Library. http://www.beauvoir. org (accessed on July 27, 2004).

Brasington, Larry, Jr. *From Revolution to Reconstruction: Robert E. Lee.* http:// odur.let.rug.nl/~usa/B/relee/relee.htm (accessed on July 27, 2004).

"Civil War Biographies." *Shotgun's Home of the Civil War.* http://www. civilwarhome.com/biograph.htm (accessed on July 27, 2004).

Jefferson Davis Memorial Home Page. http://www.pointsouth.com/csanet/ greatmen/davis/davis.htm (accessed on July 27, 2004).

The Papers of Jefferson Davis. http://jeffersondavis.rice.edu/ (accessed on July 27, 2004).

"People of Georgia: Alexander Hamilton Stephens." *Netstate.* http:// www.netstate.com/states/peop/people/ga_ahs.htm (accessed on July 27, 2004).

Robert E. Lee Memorial Association. *Stratford Hall Plantation: The Birthplace of Robert E. Lee.* http://www.stratfordhall.org (accessed on July 27, 2004).

"Robert Toombs House." *Washington, Georgia.* http://www.kudcom.com/www/att03.html (accessed on July 27, 2004).

Jay Cooke. *Photo by Hulton Archive/Getty Images.*

Jay Cooke

Born August 10, 1821
Portland, Ohio

Died February 16, 1905
Philadelphia, Pennsylvania

Banker, investor, war bonds pioneer

"Newspapers and individuals got into the habit of gloomily deploring the [Civil War] and its ruinous expenditure. I offset this by quoting the fact that every dollar raised by the loans went right back into the hands of the people and was new and vigorous blood permeating all through the body of the nation."

Jay Cooke had a dramatic rise and fall during the Civil War (1861–65) and the Reconstruction era (1865–77). He used innovative methods to help the U.S. government finance (pay for) the Civil War, for which he became known as the "financier of the Union." During the Reconstruction era, Cooke invested heavily in railroads. When the national economy faltered in 1873, Cooke's financial empire of banks was wiped out; they had invested too heavily and could not pay back their depositors (people who saved money in the banks). In little over a decade, then, Cooke had gone from being America's foremost banker to a man who lost his entire fortune. By 1880, however, he was back on his way to being a millionaire.

An eye for money

Jay Cooke was born in present-day Sandusky, Ohio, on August 10, 1821. The town was called Portland at the time of his birth, but the name changed to Sandusky City and then simply to Sandusky. He was the third child and second son of Eleutheros and Martha Cooke. They were well-educated Easterners with pioneering spirits. Cooke's parents lived in New York before undertaking a journey to Ohio and settling in a sparsely populated area. Cooke's father was a prominent lawyer and was later elected to the U.S. House of Representatives. The family home was named "Ogontz" in honor of a Native American chief who had lived on the land. Young Cooke soon developed his lifelong passion for hunting and fishing in the sparsely settled area overlooking Lake Erie.

At fourteen, Cooke became a store clerk in Sandusky. The following year, he traveled to St. Louis, Missouri, but lost his job as a clerk there when his employers lost their business in the Panic of 1837. A panic, in economic terms, is a severe downturn in the economy. Cooke then traveled to Philadelphia, Pennsylvania, to work for his brother-in-law, who ran a shipping business. At the age of eighteen, Cooke joined a bank, E. W. Clark & Company.

At the time, Philadelphia was the financial center of the United States. E. W. Clark served financial institutions by buying and selling banknotes. The U.S. government only issued coins until the Civil War era. Before then, private bankers provided paper currency, but the value of the currency was different in different parts of the country. Bankers for E. W. Clark bought those banknotes with coin—making a profit because the value of coin was stable, while the value of currency fluctuated. To perform his work, Cooke had to be able to judge the worth of paper currency. He showed a talent for keeping track of the value of banknotes from various areas of the country and became expert at identifying counterfeit money.

In August 1844, Cooke married Dorothea Elizabeth Allen. They would have two sons and two daughters.

 Cooke's Memories of His Childhood Home

In a speech delivered on October 3, 1900, at the Firelands Historical Society (of Northern Ohio), Jay Cooke reminisced about his childhood days in Sandusky, Ohio (excerpted from the *Jay Cooke Family Website*).

From my earliest boyhood I have roamed the waters of Sandusky Bay, and this island region and every portion of it is most familiar to me. I have explored every hunting and fishing ground. I have camped out for a week at a time, and on occasions in the forests and marshes bordering the lake and bay and upon many of the islands, I have captured every variety of game and fish.

Begins investing

When Cooke reached his thirties during the 1850s, he began to invest in business ventures. He bought land from the U.S. government in Iowa and Minnesota for low prices, speculating (predicting) that it could be sold at a higher price as more people entered the region. Iowa had become a state in 1848, but Minnesota was just beginning to attract settlers and would win statehood in 1858. Cooke bought large tracts of land for little more than $1 per acre. The land was sold to people coming into the area to create farms, usually at $3 or more per acre. Cooke became very wealthy from his land speculation deals and retired from E. W. Clark in 1857, at the age of thirty-six.

Cooke had traveled regularly between Philadelphia and New York for business and pleasure since the late 1830s, and also regularly returned to his hometown of Sandusky. In between stays in Ohio, where Cooke could enjoy the outdoors as a hunter and fisherman, he began planning his own banking business. In 1861, he founded Jay Cooke & Company.

Cooke proved to have excellent timing and good connections. The Civil War had begun and the federal government was in financial trouble. The country had had budget deficits (debts) since 1857, and the expense of a war made the deficit even greater. President Abraham Lincoln (1809–1865; served 1861–65) took office in March 1861; his secretary of the Treasury, Salmon P. Chase (1808–1873), had been governor of Ohio and was acquainted with Cooke's brother, Henry, who was involved in politics in Ohio. Needing to find ways to pay off the deficit and to collect money to spend on the war, Chase turned to Cooke for financial advice.

Cooke and Chase decided that selling bonds would support the war effort. When a consumer purchases a government bond, the money spent goes to the government to be used or invested. Meanwhile, the bond increases in value over an extended period of time; the longer the consumer waits to redeem the bond, the more money he or she will receive. Chase wanted to promote bonds as a way for citizens to support the Union war effort. When the Union army was defeated at the First Battle of Bull Run in July 1861, Northerners began to realize that the Civil War would last for awhile.

Cooke secured $2 million from Philadelphia bankers to begin a bond-selling operation, and he collected another $50 million from a group of New York City banks to back the bonds. The bonds sold by Cooke were an attractive means for people to support the Union effort during the Civil War. Secretary of the Treasury Chase, as the saying goes, used the war to sell the bonds, but used the bonds to sell the war.

The marketing campaign by Cooke and Chase helped inspire over six hundred thousand people to buy war bonds. During one period, more than one million dollars worth of bonds sold daily. By February 1862, Jay Cooke & Company opened an office in Washington, D.C., to better serve its connections with the government. Cooke used the services of twenty-five hundred subagents across the nation to sell bonds. Five hundred

million dollars was raised through bonds by the end of 1863. According to Cooke, "Newspapers and individuals got into the habit of gloomily deploring the [Civil War] and its ruinous expenditure. I offset this by quoting the fact that every dollar raised by the loans went right back into the hands of the people and was new and vigorous blood permeating all through the body of the nation. Thus by using the newspapers and pamphlets and circulars to disseminate [spread] these facts thoroughly and constantly all over the land I soon dispelled all gloom and brought about a more cheerful condition of public opinion."

U.S. secretary of the Treasury Salmon P. Chase provided financial advice for financier Jay Cooke. *The Library of Congress.*

"Jay Cooke invented the bond drive," wrote John Steele Gordon in the *Wall Street Journal Interactive Edition* on October 7, 1998. Gordon added that bonds have been used to secure war funds in most major wars involving the United States since the Civil War. "Cooke sold bonds in denominations as small as $50 to ordinary people, and allowed them to pay on an installment plan," continued Gordon. (An in-

A Long Way from Sandusky

Jay Cooke reached prominent heights during the Abraham Lincoln administration—a long way from his days as a teenaged store clerk in Ohio. One morning while Cooke was conducting business at the Washington, D.C., home of Salmon P. Chase, secretary of the Treasury, a servant announced that Attorney General Edward Bates (1793–1869) and President Abraham Lincoln were outside waiting in a carriage. Cooke and Chase joined them, and the four men met General George B. McClellan (1826–1885) to review his troops, soon bound for battle.

stallment plan allows a buyer to make regular payments over a specified time period.) Cooke persuaded millions of people to take small savings and put them into government bonds. Cooke, Gordon concluded, "made Jay Cooke & Company the most powerful and prestigious bank in the country and himself its most famous banker."

When Chase left the government in 1864, his replacement, William P. Fessenden (1806–1869), began a new sale of bonds, but was able to sell just over $130 million in bonds over seven months. To spur sales, he appointed Cooke to a position in the Treasury Department so that Cooke could administer the program. After Cooke came on board, the government sold another $600 million in bonds in less than six months. When the Civil War ended in April 1865, Cooke had three banking houses—in Philadelphia, New York, and Washington—and each with a separate group of partners.

Meanwhile, in 1864, Cooke purchased Gibraltar Island in Lake Erie and built a home he called "Gibraltar." The Cooke family traveled there often for pleasant vacations. The house, which was later referred to as "Cooke's Castle," was given by the Cooke estate to Ohio State University. The university restored the home to its original form.

In 1866, Cooke purchased a second home, which he called "Ogontz," in honor of his parents' home and the Native American chief for which it was named. The location chosen by Cooke reflected his passion for business and the outdoors: The home was near Philadelphia, as well as a wilderness area with good hunting grounds and good fishing on the Delaware River. Cooke later lost the house, then repurchased it and converted it into a school for girls. A devout Christian, Cooke regularly gave 10 percent of his income for religious and charitable purposes. He donated funds for the building of several Episcopal churches.

An illustration from the October 11, 1873, issue of *Harper's Weekly* shows a crowd of people in front of the New York office of Jay Cooke & Company during the Panic of 1873. *The Library of Congress.*

Reversal of fortune

Following the Civil War, Cooke turned his interest to the booming business of railroads. As an investment banker, Cooke sold loans to banks and small investors. In this capacity, Cooke introduced two new ideas to banking. He established banking syndicates (smaller, local banks that could quickly address financial issues in a certain area) and he took an active, daily role in the operations he was helping to finance. In 1869, Cooke became the banker of the Northern Pacific Railroad, which was building a cross-country line from Duluth, Minnesota, to Tacoma, Washington. Cooke made short-term loans to the railroad from his own banking house. Construction on the railroad reached eastern Montana when disaster struck in 1873.

As the national economy turned downward in early 1873, Cooke could not make money through investments to support the loans he had provided. By summer, Cooke's banks and his banking syndicates could not compensate customers who had deposited their money with them. On September, 18, 1873, the New York office of Jay Cooke & Company and all the syndicate banks were closed for business. The collapse of Cooke's firm started the large-scale financial recession called the Panic of 1873. Stocks quickly lost value. On September 20, 1873, the New York Stock Exchange announced that it would close for the first time in its history and did so for ten days. The Cooke empire quickly collapsed and Cooke's personal fortune was wiped out.

The stunning reversal of fortune was swift. The nation's most prominent banker was bankrupt. After the Panic, industrial plants shut down and over half of the railroads defaulted on their bonds. An economic depression followed. On the morning the offices of Jay Cooke & Company closed, Cooke was entertaining President **Ulysses S. Grant** (1822–1885; served 1869–77; see entry) at his Philadelphia mansion.

Cooke's position as the nation's most powerful banker was quickly assumed by J. P. Morgan (1837–1913). Morgan swiftly merged the Susquehanna Railroad he had recently purchased, stepped in to consolidate and reorganize railroads that had failed in the Panic of 1873, and became the new high financier of the federal government.

Cooke, meanwhile, spent several years sorting out debt. He reemerged in 1880 as an investor in western mines. A small amount of money he staked in a silver mine brought him a new fortune, as the mine struck a huge deposit at a good time. During the 1880s and early 1890s, silver had become more valuable as many small farmers and people of modest income demanded that additional currency be made available in the United States with its value backed by silver. In 1890, the Sherman Silver Purchase Act increased the amount of silver that could be coined. This act was repealed in 1894, but by then Cooke had sold his holdings in the silver mine for over $1 million.

During the last two decades of his life, Cooke lived comfortably in Philadelphia and continued to visit Sandusky. In 1899, he spoke to an Ohio historical society and noted it was the first speech he had given in fifty years. Cooke died in 1905 in Philadelphia.

For More Information

Books and Periodicals

Gordon, John Steele. "History Repeats in Finance Company Bailouts." *Wall Street Journal*(October 7, 1998).

Harnsberger, John L. *Jay Cooke and Minnesota: The Formative Years of the Northern Pacific Railroad, 1868–1873*. New York: Arno Press, 1981.

Josephson, Matthew. *The Robber Barons: The Great American Capitalists, 1861–1901*. New York: Harcourt, Brace and Company, 1934. Reprint, 1995.

Larson, Henrietta M. *Jay Cooke, Private Banker*. New York: Greenwood Press, 1968.

Web Sites

"Cooke Castle: Jay Cooke: The Man." *Ohio State University*. http://www.osu.edu/cookecastle/theman.html (accessed on June 21, 2004).

Jay Cooke Family Website. http://www.jaycooke.com/ (accessed on June 21, 2004).

Kangas, Gene. "Jay Cooke, the Banker from Philadelphia." *Creekside Art Gallery*. http://www.creeksideartgallery.com/articles/jcooke/jcooke.html (accessed on June 21, 2004).

Frederick Douglass

Born c. February 1817
Easton, Maryland

Died February 20, 1895
Washington, D.C.

Writer and activist

"Rebellion has been subdued, slavery abolished, and peace proclaimed, and yet our work is not done.... We are face to face with the same old enemy of liberty and progress."

Frederick Douglass. *The Library of Congress.*

Frederick Douglass was an eloquent spokesperson for abolition (the end of slavery) and equality. He persevered through an early life of slavery to become a celebrated speaker and writer. Relating his experiences as a victim of cruelty, Douglass maintained a strongly moral conviction in undoing the evil of slavery and establishing equality for people of both sexes and all races. He wrote celebrated autobiographical works, beginning with *Narrative of the Life of Frederick Douglass, an American Slave* (1845), and founded newspapers, including the *North Star* in 1847. The masthead of the *North Star* featured the motto, "Right is of no sex. Truth is of no color. God is the Father of us all, and we are all Brethren." During the Reconstruction era (1865–77), Douglass was a leader in supporting passage of the Fifteenth Amendment in 1870, which extended voting rights to African American males, and the efforts of Congress to ensure protection of the rights of freedmen.

Born into slavery

Frederick Douglass was born into slavery with the name Frederick Augustus Washington Bailey. His birth is generally considered to have occurred in February 1817. He took the surname Douglass (after a character in Sir Walter Scott's poem "Lady of the Lake") following his escape from slavery. Born on a farm near Easton, Maryland, Douglass was the son of a slave, Harriet Bailey, and an unidentified white man. He had a difficult childhood, separated from his mother and victimized by the cruelty of a violent slave master, Captain Anthony. Upon Anthony's death, ownership of Douglass fell to Anthony's daughter and son-in-law, Lucretia and Thomas Auld. When he was nine, Douglass was sent to Baltimore, Maryland, to be a house servant to Thomas Auld's brother, Hugh Auld, and his wife Sophia.

Douglass's main responsibility in the Hugh Auld home was to care for their child, Tommy. Sophia Auld read aloud from the Bible, and Douglass asked her to teach him to read. Sophia was enthused about teaching Douglass, but when Hugh Auld learned what his wife was doing he immediately made her stop. It was unlawful to teach a slave to read, and Auld believed that keeping slaves from reading and writing was a way to maintain power over them. Douglass realized that reading and writing was a way to freedom. He continued his education through interaction with people—by questioning and listening to them—and by reading anything he could. Sometimes he traded his food for a newspaper or a book. By age thirteen, he was reading abolitionist newspapers.

Douglass was returned to the farm at age fifteen, and he was again subjected to cruelty and beatings. At sixteen, he fought back against a whipping and earned a measure of power. He plotted an escape with a group of slaves when he was nineteen, but their plans were exposed and the slaves were jailed. Douglass returned to the Auld household in Baltimore, where he trained as a caulker (one who seals the hull of a boat to keep water from seeping in). After Douglass was beaten by white workers, Auld transferred him to his own shipbuilding business, where Douglass earned regular wages.

In his little spare time from work, Douglass met with a group of free and educated African Americans and was admitted by them to the East Baltimore Mental Improvement Society. During meetings of this organization, Douglass learned how to be a political debater and met a free African American woman named Anna Murray. They were engaged in 1838.

Determined to win his freedom above all else, Douglass risked everything he had by traveling in disguise by train from Baltimore to Philadelphia and on to New York City. If caught, he could be jailed, killed, or sold to slave masters. On September 4, 1838, he reached New York City safely.

Famous speaker and writer

After roaming New York City streets for a few days, Douglass met an African American sailor, who introduced him to a member of the Underground Railroad—a secret group of Northerners who helped runaway slaves escape to safety. Anna Murray joined Douglass in New York and they were married on September 15, 1838. They moved to a safe haven in New Bedford, Massachusetts, and lived for a time in the home of a prosperous African American family. Douglass resumed work as a caulker.

Douglass quickly became involved with abolitionist groups and read the *Liberator,* an abolitionist newspaper founded by William Lloyd Garrison (1805–1879). "The paper became my meat and drink," Douglass once recalled. "My soul was set all on fire." He attended a convention of the Massachusetts Antislavery Society, in Nantucket, Massachusetts, in 1841, and was invited to speak. His skills as an orator were so well received that he was invited to become an activist with the group. He met Garrison, who employed him as a speaker to tell his life story and help sell copies of the *Liberator.* In 1843, Douglass participated in the Hundred Conventions project, the American Anti-Slavery Society's six-month tour of meeting halls throughout the west. During travels to towns and cities from Maine to Indiana, Douglass suffered mistreatment and inequality, but persevered to get his message across.

Ironically, Douglass was so eloquent that increasing .numbers of people began to question whether he had actually experienced the incidents he related. Such responses, in part, motivated Douglass to write his autobiography, *Narrative of the Life of Frederick Douglass, an American Slave* (1845). Recounting Douglass's life experiences in a strong moral tone against the evils of slavery on victim and victimizer, the book was an instant sensation. Widely popular in the North and in

NARRATIVE

OF THE

LIFE

OF

FREDERICK DOUGLASS,

AN

AMERICAN SLAVE.

WRITTEN BY HIMSELF.

BOSTON:
PUBLISHED AT THE ANTI-SLAVERY OFFICE.
No. 25 CORNHILL
1845.

Europe, the *Narrative* also put Douglass in danger: As a fugitive slave, he had no legal protection if slave owner Thomas Auld were to seize him as Auld's property. Douglass decided to travel to England, which had emancipated (freed) all slaves within the British Empire.

Douglass enjoyed traveling for nearly two years in Britain. Friends in England collected money to buy him out of slavery from Thomas Auld. Although Douglass did not agree with the action—since he did not believe one man could own another, he should not pay for his freedom—he accepted the offer. He returned to the United States in 1847 to his wife and four children, and the family moved to Rochester, New York, where Douglass bought a house. He set up a printing shop and started his own newspaper, the *North Star*. Featuring articles on abolition and equality, the *North Star* was published under the motto, "Right is of no sex. Truth is of no color. God is the Father of us all, and we are all Brethren." Meanwhile, as a participant of the Underground

Portrait of Frederick Douglass and title page from an early edition of *Narrative of the Life of Frederick Douglass, an American Slave,* **published in 1845.** *© Bettmann/Corbis.*

Railroad, he helped more than four hundred slaves reach freedom through his printing shop.

Douglass also became politically active in his fight for equality and the abolishment of slavery. He campaigned against labor discrimination and racial segregation on public transportation; attended the landmark Women's Rights Convention in Seneca Falls, New York, in 1848, and signed the first Declaration of Women's Rights, which was drafted at the convention; and he angrily opposed the Compromise of 1850, a series of bills that included the Fugitive Slave Law, which provided strong legal support for slave owners to pursue runaway slaves in nonslave states. In 1854, Douglass supported the formation of the Republican Party to oppose frequent compromises made by Congress to powerful Southern legislators on issues related to slavery.

Douglass's increasing activism put him at odds with his longtime friend, William Lloyd Garrison, who preferred a more peaceful means for ending slavery. Douglass met on several occasions with John Brown (1800–1859), an abolitionist who preached violence against slave owners. When Brown and a small band of followers were captured in an assault on an arsenal (collection of weapons) in Harper's Ferry, Virginia (now in West Virginia), hoping to take weapons and use them to arm slaves, Douglass was accused by Virginia governor Henry A. Wise (1806–1876) of being a conspirator. Douglass fled to Canada and then returned to Great Britain, where he enjoyed a successful lecture tour.

After returning to the United States, Douglass threw his support in the election of 1860 to Abraham Lincoln (1809–1865; served 1861–65). When the Civil War (1861–65) began shortly after Lincoln took office, Douglass was disappointed that Lincoln's first priority in ending the war was to save the Union, not to abolish slavery (though Lincoln was against slavery). Douglass's political activism focused on two goals: emancipation of slaves and inclusion of African Americans in the Union army. The Emancipation Proclamation announced by Lincoln in 1863 was a major step toward ending slavery and it opened up military opportunities for African Americans. Douglass's sons, Lewis and Charles, were among the first African Americans to enlist in the Union army, and Douglass actively recruited African Americans for the Union cause. He stopped recruiting, however, because segregation was being practiced by the military.

More battles after the war

The Thirteenth Amendment to the U.S. Constitution, abolishing slavery, became law in 1865, but Douglass's life work was not complete. "Slavery is not abolished," he said, "until the black man has the ballot." He focused on voting rights and civil rights throughout the Reconstruction era, speaking around the country in late 1865 and then again beginning in the spring of 1866. In February 1866, Douglass met with President **Andrew Johnson** (1808–1875; served 1865–69; see entry), but Johnson dominated the discussion by insisting he would not use his federal powers to pursue voting rights or interfere with states in civil rights issues. In 1868, the Fourteenth Amendment to the Constitution was ratified, granting citizenship to all people born in the United States.

In 1870, Douglass and his sons began publishing a weekly newspaper, *New National Era,* that supported President **Ulysses S. Grant** (1822–1885; served 1869–77; see entry) and the aggressive protection of African American rights by many Republicans in Congress. That same year, the Fifteenth Amendment was ratified, extending voting rights to African American males. Section 1 of the amendment stated, "The right of citizens of the United States to vote shall not be denied or abridged by the United States or by any state on account of race, color, or previous condition of servitude."

The following year, Grant appointed Douglass assistant secretary of the commission of inquiry to Santo Domin-

Frederick Douglass was well known for his speaking skills. *Illustration from* Frederick Douglass, *by Helaine Becker. Blackbirch Press Inc., 2001. Illustration © North Wind Picture Archives. Reproduced by permission.*

Frederick Douglass on Reconstruction

The excerpt below is taken from "Reconstruction," an article written by Frederick Douglass and published in the December 1866 issue of *Atlantic Monthly* magazine. The article was timed with the return of Congress to session. Douglass wanted Congress to act on Reconstruction in much more forceful ways than President Andrew Johnson. Johnson is mentioned in the final paragraph of the excerpt.

Slavery, like all other great systems of wrong, founded in the depths of human selfishness, and existing for ages, has not neglected its own conservation. It has steadily exerted an influence upon all around it favorable to its own continuance. And to-day it is so strong that it could exist, not only without law, but even against law. Custom, manners, morals, religion, are all on its side everywhere in the South; and when you add the ignorance and servility of the ex-slave to the intelligence and accustomed authority of the master, you have the conditions, not out of which slavery will again grow, but under which it is impossible for the Federal government to wholly destroy it, unless the Federal government be armed with despotic power, to blot out State authority, and to station a Federal officer at every cross-road. This, of course, cannot be done, and ought not even if it could. The true way and the easiest way is to make our government entirely consistent with itself, and give to every loyal citizen the elective franchise,—a right and power which will be ever present, and will form a wall of fire for his protection....

Spite of the eloquence of the earnest Abolitionists—poured out against slavery during thirty years—even they

go (now Haiti and the Dominican Republic). Douglass toured Santo Domingo from January through March 1871 and defended the president's failed attempt to annex the island. Douglass moved to Washington, D.C., in 1872 after his Rochester home was destroyed by fire. Copies of his newspapers and personal letters were lost in the blaze, and Douglass suspected arson.

In March 1874, Douglass assumed the presidency of the Freedman's Savings and Trust Company. He had been offered the position back in July 1867 by President Johnson, but Douglass was concerned about being associated with Johnson, who showed little interest in causes for which Douglass fought. The Freedman's Bureau was founded to help freedmen with their savings and to provide loans. By 1874, the bank was in financial trouble and Douglass, despite infusing some of his own money, was not able to save it. Douglass returned to the lecture circuit, advocating further support and must confess, that, in all the probabilities of the case, that system of barbarism would have continued its horrors far beyond the limits of the nineteenth century but for the Rebellion, and perhaps only have disappeared at last in a fiery conflict, even more fierce and bloody than that which has now been suppressed.

It is no disparagement to truth, that it can only prevail where reason prevails. War begins where reason ends. The thing worse than rebellion is the thing that causes rebellion. What that thing is, we have been taught to our cost. It remains now to be seen whether we have the needed courage to have that cause entirely removed from the Republic. At any rate, to this grand work of national regeneration and entire purification Congress must now address Itself, with full purpose that the work shall this time be thoroughly done....

If time was at first needed, Congress has now had time. All the requisite materials from which to form an intelligent judgment are now before it. Whether its members look at the origin, the progress, the termination of the war, or at the mockery of a peace now existing, they will find only one unbroken chain of argument in favor of a radical policy of reconstruction. For the omissions of the last session, some excuses may be allowed. A treacherous President stood in the way; and it can be easily seen how reluctant good men might be to admit an apostasy [defection] which involved so much of baseness and ingratitude. It was natural that they should seek to save him by bending to him even when he leaned to the side of error. But all is changed now. Congress knows now that it must go on without his aid, and even against his machinations.

extension of civil rights, campaigning for Republicans, and introducing other topics that interested him, including Scandinavian folklore. He often encountered discrimination in restaurants and while lodging and using mass transportation, and always followed up with a letter of protest to local newspapers describing each incident.

After the Reconstruction era

When **Rutherford B. Hayes** (1822–1893; served 1877–81; see entry) became president in March 1877, he appointed Douglass as U.S. marshal of Washington, D.C., a first for an African American. He enjoyed working in city administration and purchased a 15-acre estate in the area. Douglass called it Cedar Hill and frequently entertained family members and friends. In 1881, Douglass was appointed recorder of deeds for Washington, D.C., by President James A. Garfield (1831–

1881; served 1881). Later that year, Douglass published *The Life and Times of Frederick Douglass,* an expanded version of his autobiography.

Douglass's wife, Anna, died in 1882. Two years later, he married Helen Pitts, his secretary. Pitts was white, and the interracial marriage was controversial to many whites and African Americans. Douglass countered that his marriage was an example that the races could coexist peacefully. The couple went on a lengthy honeymoon in Europe. Douglass campaigned for the election of Benjamin Harrison (1833–1901; served 1889–93) in 1888 and was appointed minister and counsel general to Haiti when Harrison took office. Douglass left the position in 1891 and lived in semiretirement. He still spoke out on causes he believed in and emphasized the power of voting as a means for effective change. After giving a speech on February 20, 1895, at the National Council of Women, Douglass suffered a heart attack later that evening and died at the age of seventy-seven.

Mourners gathered at a church in Washington, D.C., where he lay in state, and black public schools closed for the day. Douglass's body was taken back to Rochester, where he was laid to rest.

For More Information

Books
Blight, David W. *Frederick Douglass' Civil War: Keeping Faith in Jubilee.* Baton Rouge: Louisiana State University Press, 1989.

Douglass, Frederick. *Escape from Slavery.* Edited by Michael McCurdy. New York: Knopf, 1994.

Douglass, Frederick. *The Life and Times of Frederick Douglass.* Hartford, CT: Park Publishing, 1881. Reprint, Grand Rapids, MI: Candace Press, 1996.

Douglass, Frederick. *My Bondage and My Freedom.* New York: Miller, Orton and Mulligan, 1855. Reprint, Urbana: University of Illinois Press, 1987.

Douglass, Frederick. *Narrative of the Life of Frederick Douglass.* Boston: Anti-slavery Office, 1845. Reprint, New Brunswick, NJ: Transaction Publishers, 1997.

McFeeley, William S. *Frederick Douglass.* New York: Norton, 1991.

Russell, Sharman. *Frederick Douglass.* New York: Chelsea House, 1992.

Web Sites

Douglass, Frederick. "Reconstruction." *The Atlantic Online.* http://www. theatlantic.com/unbound/flashbks/black/douglas.htm (accessed on July 19, 2004).

"Frederick Douglass." *Afro-American Almanac: Biographies.* http://www.top-tags. com/aama/bio/men/freddoug.htm (accessed on July 19, 2004).

The Frederick Douglass Museum & Cultural Center. http://www.ggw.org/ freenet/f/fdm/ (accessed on July 19, 2004).

Frederick Douglass National Historic Site. http://www.nps.gov/frdo/freddoug. html (accessed on July 19, 2004).

Thomas Eakins

Born July 25, 1844
Philadelphia, Pennsylvania

Died June 25, 1916
Philadelphia, Pennsylvania

Painter

"Respectability in art
is appalling."

**Self-portrait of Thomas
Eakins.** *Photograph by Al
Fenn/Time Life Pictures/
Getty Images.*

A traveling exhibit of the major paintings of Thomas Eakins in 2001 attracted large crowds and strong critical praise. It was far different for Eakins during his lifetime as an artist working in Philadelphia, Pennsylvania, from the Reconstruction era (1865–77) to the early twentieth century. He sold a little over two dozen paintings and his work received a mild amount of attention during his lifetime. In modern times, however, he is regarded as the classic American painter of the Realist style. "Eakins's art was a monumental achievement," wrote art critic Hilton Kramer in 2001. "He was the first major painter of his period to accept completely the realities of contemporary American life and to create out of them a strong and profound art."

Science and art

Thomas Cowperthwait Eakins was born on July 25, 1844, in Philadelphia. He was the first of five children of Benjamin Eakins and Caroline Cowperthwait Eakins. Benjamin Eakins was a writing master and teacher. A writing master provides artistic penmanship, ornamental script (elegantly decorative lettering), and design services for documents, certificates, and books.

Thomas Eakins would later paint a portrait of his father called *The Writing Master.* Typical of many of Eakins's works, the painting shows a skillful man deeply engaged in his work. Painstaking detail of the hands of the writing master is important in this work. Critics believe such attention to detail is intended to show the character of the person being represented, in this case reflecting the care for craftsmanship that Eakins observed in his father.

At the age of thirteen, Eakins entered Central High School of Philadelphia, which was established twenty years earlier as Pennsylvania's first public high school and provided an advanced curriculum with an emphasis on science. Combining his knowledge of science with his enthusiasm for art, Eakins enrolled at the Pennsylvania Academy of the Fine Arts, America's oldest art academy, after he graduated from high school. He studied there from 1862 to 1866 while the Civil War (1861–65) was being fought. He had paid a bounty to avoid the Civil War draft, part of a law that allowed someone to, in essence, hire a substitute.

At the Academy, Eakins honed his drawing skills. Fascinated with anatomy, especially the construction of bones and muscles, Eakins took courses at Jefferson Medical College in Philadelphia. His experience at the medical college included dissecting human corpses of people who had donated their bodies to science.

At the age of twenty-one, Eakins traveled to Paris to study to become a painter and sculptor. He was accepted into the famous École des Beaux Arts (School of Fine Arts), the leading art academy of its time. Eakins was mentored by Jean-Léon Gérôme (1824–1904), a young teacher who encouraged Eakins to study sculpture and portraiture. To stress the importance of becoming a craftsman, Gérôme emphasized study and firsthand knowledge of subjects an artist plans to depict. Preparing for portraiture, Eakins studied anatomy in class and attended autopsies, where dead human bodies are examined to determine the cause of death. Study and observation prepared Eakins to capture in painting the musculature, structure, and other fine details of the human body.

Eakins spent his last year in Paris working and studying at the private studio of Léon Bonnat (1833–1922), a famous portrait painter. Following a tradition of French portrait artists, Eakins traveled to Spain, as Bonnat had done when he was a budding artist. Several major Spanish artists were renowned for their ability to render realistic human body details in their portrait painting. The style suited Eakins, who emphasized the use of science and the intellect in his painting. Eakins spent seven months in Spain at the age of twenty-five. He painted rarely, spending most of the time carefully studying the works of such master Spanish painters as Diego Velázquez (1599–1660) and Francisco Goya (1746–1828).

Painter of Philadelphia

Eakins returned home to Philadelphia on July 4, 1870. His father created a studio for Eakins on the fourth floor of the family home. Eakins painted scenes and images he experienced in daily life in Philadelphia. He taught painting as well. Eakins became known around Philadelphia for eccentric behavior: Living in a polite and somewhat prudish social scene, he dressed very casually and spoke his mind, often offending respectable society. Dedicated to painting, Eakins worked slowly and methodically.

Eakins enjoyed the outdoors, whether walking around and observing daily life in Philadelphia or pursuing his hobbies as a sportsman—hunting, fishing, boating, and riding. Many of his early paintings were scenes of outdoor life in and around the city, including people sailing and fishing on the Delaware River or hunting in marshes in nearby New Jersey. One of his most famous paintings, *Max Schmitt in the Single Shell* (1871), shows a man rowing on the Schuylkill River. Eakins also painted pictures of his family and friends in their homes.

In 1876, Philadelphia was enjoying the Centennial Celebration, the hundredth anniversary of the signing of the Declaration of Independence in the city. Among the festivities planned was an exhibition of paintings, and artists were invited to submit entries for consideration. Eakins submitted several paintings, including one that eventually became acknowledged as his masterpiece.

One of Thomas Eakins's most famous paintings, *The Gross Clinic.* © *Geoggrey Clements/Corbis.*

Eakins began planning a portrait of Samuel D. Gross (1805–1884), who was known as America's foremost surgeon. Gross worked in Philadelphia and Eakins attended some of the live surgical demonstrations Gross performed while lecturing to students. The painting that resulted, *The Gross Clinic* (1875), shows a chloroformed patient (chloroform was used to induce unconsciousness) on a table attended by four medical assistants, while a man in the center, Dr. Gross, speaks to an audience of medical students. In one hand the doctor holds a scalpel on which there is some blood from an incision he has just made on the thigh of the patient, but Gross is turned away from the patient and talking to the assembly. The doctor dominates the picture and suggests a character of intelligence and mastery.

The painting was placed in a portion of the exhibition dedicated to the medical sciences. Eakins was not able to sell the painting immediately; it eventually sold for $200 and was exhibited in Chicago, Illinois; St. Louis, Missouri; and Buffalo, New York. Now his most famous work, *The Gross Clinic* hangs at the Jefferson Medical Clinic in Philadelphia. The Centennial Exposition accepted other character studies by Eakins represented in *Chess Players* and *Baseball*.

Interest in photography

In 1876, Eakins began teaching at the Pennsylvania Academy of the Fine Arts. He became head of the Academy in 1879. There he met Susan H. Macdowell, an art student. They were married in 1884. The couple lived in a modest home with an art studio in a third-floor room. Eakins installed a blackboard in the dining room so he could sketch out his ideas at any time. He had another studio at the top of an office building.

Eakins began using the developing medium of photography as an aid to painting. He collaborated in 1884 with pioneer photographer Eadweard Muybridge (1830–1904) to capture the motion of humans and animals. From photographs, he could recreate human features with even more precise detail, and he used them as well in his classes. Eakins also pursued his interest in sculpture during this period. He produced several full-scale anatomical casts as well as models of human forms he could recreate in his paintings. Critics generally agree Eakins might have become equally renowned as a sculptor, but he maintained his emphasis on painting.

In 1886, Eakins resigned his position at the Pennsylvania Academy of the Fine Arts over a dispute that reflected his differences with society around him. Eakins insisted on using nude models in his classes. When ordered to stop, Eakins left the Academy and started his own school. A good number of his students at the Academy followed Eakins to the Arts Students League of Philadelphia, where he taught for eight years.

Seeing what is

After leaving the academy, Eakins produced several of his most memorable paintings. He had wanted to paint a portrait of Walt Whitman (1819–1892), the famous American poet, and Whitman obliged. The result was a dynamic portrait of the poet, capturing the essence of Whitman with his grizzly beard and robust face. Of Eakins, Whitman said, "I never knew of but one artist, and this is Tom Eakins, who could resist the temptation to see what they think ought to be rather than what is."

Other famous paintings of this period include *Agnew Clinic* (1889), which recalls *The Gross Clinic*. The subjects are similar—both feature a famous doctor lecturing an audience while surgery is being performed on a patient. The later painting is more relaxed and without some of the artistic embellishments of *The Gross Clinic*. *Miss Amelia Van Buren* (1891), another major work, shows a seated, mature woman looking away, wistfully. Like all of Eakins's work, the character of the person being represented is revealed as much in her hands and posture as in her facial expression.

These paintings helped bring Eakins his first significant public interest. He held an exhibition in Philadelphia in 1896, and in 1902, after having painted for over thirty-five years, Eakins was invited to join the National Academy of Design. To mark the occasion, he painted a self-portrait, which he referred to as his "diploma." The painting shows Eakins as a weary but resolute older man. Of the relative lack of recognition he received during his lifetime, Eakins said, "My honors are misunderstanding, persecution & neglect, enhanced because unsought." When the National Academy of Design awarded him a medal, he had it melted down to extract the gold, which he sold for cash.

During his later years Eakins became overweight and sluggish, whereas in youth he had been slim and athletic. In 1910, he suffered kidney problems and could no longer pay attention to painting. He worked little during the last six years, and died in 1916.

For More Information

Books and Periodicals

Carter, Alice A. *The Essential Thomas Eakins*. New York: Harry N. Abrams, 2001.

Homer, William Innes. *Thomas Eakins: His Life and Art*. New York: Abbeville Press, 2002.

Kramer, Hilton. "Realist Thomas Eakins Back, Still Beloved." *New York Observer* (October 15, 2001): p. 1.

Sewell, Darrell, ed. *Thomas Eakins*. New Haven, CT: Yale University Press, 2001.

Web Sites

"American Masters: Thomas Eakins." *PBS*. http://www.pbs.org/eakins/biography.htm (accessed on June 21, 2004).

"Thomas Eakins: American Realist." *Philadelphia Museum of Art*. http://www.philamuseum.org/exhibitions/exhibits/eakins/index.shtml (accessed on June 21, 2004).

"Thomas Eakins." *Artcyclopedia*. http://www.artcyclopedia.com/artists/eakins_thomas.html (accessed on June 21, 2004).

Harry Fenn

Born September 14, 1837
Richmond, England

Died April 21, 1911
Montclair, New Jersey

Illustrator and painter

Harry Fenn was one of the great illustrators of the nineteenth century. Before photography came into regular use by the end of the century, illustrators created images for books and periodicals. Fenn worked for many of the leading magazines and authors. In addition, he was the major contributor to the highly popular and critically acclaimed "Picturesque America" series that appeared in *Appleton's Journal* and in a book published in 1872. The series showcased the variety of natural wonders in the United States, from mountain scenes of the northeast to lush vegetation and wildlife along the rivers and swamps of Florida. The book proved so popular that Fenn was also commissioned as the main illustrator for *Picturesque Europe* (1876) and *Picturesque Palestine, Sinai, and Egypt* (1883).

Young artist

Harry Fenn was born with the name Henry on September 14, 1837, in Richmond, outside of London, England, to James and Alice Fenn. Fenn's father, who sold dry goods,

"At home I was only a little chap who liked to amuse himself with paints. After the bishop [encouraged] me, I felt myself dedicated to the work of transcribing the beauties of the world."

recognized his son's talent as an artist and wanted to ensure those skills were advanced and could be put to practical use in a professional career. Fenn was working on a painting at age twelve in a local park and drew the attention of a bishop visiting from New Zealand. The bishop was so impressed with Fenn's talent that he bought the boy a box of paints and brushes. Fenn would say later in a magazine interview that the experience transformed him from painting for fun to becoming "dedicated to the work of transcribing the beauties of the world."

Soon after, Fenn's father apprenticed (worked as a student with an experienced adult) the young artist to the Dalziel Brothers, a wood engraving firm in London. As an apprentice, Fenn worked odd jobs in the firm while learning to master the skill of wood engraving. A wood engraver uses a sharp tool (a graver) to cut an illustration into a wooden block. Ink is placed on the illustration, and the block is pressed against paper to reproduce the image created by the engraver. The block can be used to recreate the picture many times in the printing process of books, magazines, and other items.

The Dalziel Brothers firm was engraving for the finest English illustrators, including Birket Foster (1825–1899), a leading watercolor painter of nature scenes. Engravers at the Dalziel Brothers recreated such illustrations so they could be included in print sources. By the time he was eighteen, Fenn was an accomplished engraver and had continued his own creative work by illustrating and painting works of buildings and landscapes.

Off to America

Having established his credentials as an engraver, Fenn set off to the United States at age nineteen with Charles Kingdon, a fellow worker at Dalziel Brothers. Fenn soon found work in New York City as a wood engraver for *Frank Leslie's Illustrated Newspaper* in 1857 and 1858. Since newspapers were only beginning at that time to include multiple and sophisticated illustrations, Fenn's skills were in demand. Periodicals were becoming more picture-oriented, and photography had not yet developed enough for use in mass media. Fenn also found work illustrating mass-produced fiction called dime novels (the name refers to books produced cheaply and quickly that sold for a dime), which were popular at the time.

Fenn attended the Graham Art School in Brooklyn, New York, for further training. Around this time, he met Marian Thompson, the daughter of a Brooklyn silver engraver. Married in 1862, the Fenns would have six children, four daughters and twin sons. One son died in infancy and the other, Walter, would become an illustrator like his father. Shortly after their marriage, the Fenns traveled to Europe, which included a return to England for Fenn and a stay in Italy, where he studied painting.

After the couple returned to the United States in 1863, Fenn established a dual career as an illustrator for publishers and as a creative artist. He enjoyed drawing and painting his own works, including watercolors of landscapes for exhibitions with the American Watercolor Society. The Fenns lived in Brooklyn, but soon settled in Montclair, New Jersey, where several other artists lived. In Montclair, Fenn had closer access to nature but was still close enough to New York City to maintain business relationships. Fenn's work between 1864 and 1868 included illustrations of Trenton Falls for a New Jersey guidebook; images for a book of poems by John Greenleaf Whittier (1807–1892); and pictures for gift books, including depictions of plants, birds, and farm life for *Our Young Folks,* published by the popular firm of Ticknor and Fields.

Fenn also began illustrating from photographs, which were still difficult to reproduce into mass publications at that time. *Beyond the Mississippi* (1867), by Albert D. Richardson, and *A Journey in Brazil* (1868), by Louis and Elizabeth Agassiz, were books that contained Fenn's illustrations made from photographs. By 1868, Fenn was working regularly for Harper and Brothers, New York's largest publishing house.

Picturing the Picturesque

Fenn soon won a commission to work with New York's second-largest publishing firm, D. Appleton and Company, on its new "Picturesque America" series. Through magazines and books, Appleton wanted to provide illustrations of natural wonders that had been previously impossible to publish on a large scale with excellent details. Fenn was commissioned to

travel to the South to create illustrations for *Appleton's Journal*. The choice of the South for the first issue was significant because it "promoted sectional reconciliation, satisfied curiosity, and attempted to expand the market of the magazine" following the Civil War (1861–65), according to Sue Rainey, who wrote a history of the "Picturesque America" series.

The series began in the November 1870 edition of *Appleton's Journal* with Fenn's renditions of river and swamp scenes from Florida. Later issues included Fenn's illustrations of rivers and mountains in the Poconos region of Pennsylvania, the Natural Bridge in Virginia, and ocean side scenes from East Hampton, New York. Many of Fenn's engraving formats were unconventional and innovative. He captured a sense of energy and wonder by careful attention to viewpoint, and he kept up with the latest advances in production of images, from sophisticated engraving techniques to improvements in the printing process. The dynamic quality he achieved kept Fenn's work valuable and popular for another century, and

many of his prints sell as posters in the twenty-first century. A review of his work by the *Art Journal* of London in January 1877 praised Fenn as having "a very happy faculty of seizing upon unconventional points of view in a scene."

In the spring of 1872, the Appleton firm expanded the "Picturesque America" series to book form, available by subscription or sold as individual pages for fifty cents each. Fenn was the most prolific and the first contributor to *Picturesque America*, setting the standard and model for other illustrators to follow. *Picturesque America* was regarded as among the finest productions by an American publisher. That view became an official honor by an esteemed panel at the Centennial Exposition of 1876, a celebration of Americana on the one hundredth anniversary of the Declaration of Independence.

The success of *Picturesque America,* meanwhile, led Appleton to plan a similar series on Europe. Fenn and his family went to England in 1873, where Fenn began his work. After sketching places in England and Ireland, Fenn traveled to

A painting of Cumberland Gap in Kentucky and Virginia by Harry Fenn that appeared in the "Picturesque America" series. *The Library of Congress.*

Spain, Italy, Germany, France, Belgium, and Switzerland on assignments. *Picturesque Europe* (1876) won the same acclaim and success as the *Picturesque America* series. Meanwhile, Fenn had contributed to illustrated editions of *The Song of the Sower* (1871) and *The Story of the Fountain* (1872) by American poet William Cullen Bryant (1794–1878).

Mature artist

From 1878 through 1882, Fenn contributed to a third series on the *Picturesque* theme, this time focused on the Middle East. Fenn collaborated on this assignment with another illustrator, John Douglas Woodward. They combined to produce more than six hundred wood engravings and thirty-eight steel engravings for *Picturesque Palestine, Sinai, and Egypt.* Fenn and Woodward traveled in the lands mentioned in the book title, walking among the ruins and wearing traditional Arabian clothes. In 1879 and 1880, Fenn completed his work on the book in Haslemere, England, working from sketches and photographs. While in England, he became acquainted with poet Alfred, Lord Tennyson (1809–1892), and would provide illustrations for several American editions of Tennyson's poetry.

Returning to the United States in 1881, Fenn found regular and profitable employment with *Century* magazine and continued to compose, exhibit, and sell watercolor paintings. His experience in the Middle East led to commissions for images of Egypt and the holy lands of the Bible for such books as *The Sermon on the Mount* (1886), *Bethlehem to Jerusalem* (1888), and *Out-of-Doors in the Holy Land* (1908). Fenn had become wealthy and built a huge home called the Cedars on Orange Mountain, near Montclair.

In 1890, Fenn made a trip to California to capture the essence of that state's towns, missions, wildlife, and landscapes. However, Fenn's type of illustrations was going out of style by the 1890s, when photography became more commonplace in magazines. Still, he never lacked for work. As he approached the age of seventy, Fenn composed a series of illustrations of insects for *Harper's Monthly* from 1904 to 1907. As late as April 1911, the month he died, Fenn's illustrations of suburban gardens appeared in the April edition of *Harper's Monthly.*

Fenn was active in the American Watercolor Society and the Society of Illustrators until the time of his death. Through these organizations, he helped develop younger artists.

For More Information

Books and Periodicals

Brooks, Sydney. "Harry Fenn: An Appreciation." *Harper's Weekly* (May 13, 1911): p. 10.

Rainey, Sue. *Creating Picturesque America: Monument to the Natural and Cultural Landscape.* Nashville, TN: Vanderbilt University Press, 1994.

Reed, Walt. *The Illustrator in America: 1860–2000.* New York: Harper Design International, 2001.

Ulysses S. Grant

Born April 27, 1822
Point Pleasant, Ohio

Died July 23, 1885
Mount McGregor, New York

U.S. president, Civil War general

"The country having just emerged from a great rebellion, many questions will come before it for settlement in the next four years which preceding Administrations have never had to deal with. In meeting these it is desirable that they should be approached calmly, without prejudice, hate, or sectional pride, remembering that the greatest good to the greatest number is the object to be attained."

Ulysses S. Grant. *The Library of Congress.*

U lysses S. Grant was president for eight of the twelve years of the Reconstruction era (1865–77). The popular Civil War general hoped to help reunify North and South and accepted the Republican nomination for president in 1868 with the statement "Let us have peace," which became his campaign theme. As president, however, Grant became upset at how slow respect for the civil rights of African Americans came, and pursued aggressive action against Black Codes (laws intended to limit the rights of African Americans) and violence in Southern states. Meanwhile, the Grant administration was riddled by several scandals—none of which involved the president, but all of which showed Grant's poor judgment in selecting officials for his administration. A weak economy also plagued the Grant years.

Expert on horses

Grant was born with the name Hiram Ulysses Grant on April 27, 1822. Most often called Ulysses by his family, he was the oldest of six children of Jesse Grant and Hannah Simpson Grant. The family soon moved to a farm in Georgetown, Ohio, to be nearer to the raw materials Grant's father needed for his tanning business. (A tanner produces leather from the hides of horses.) Growing up around horses, Grant quickly learned how to handle and care for them and to appraise their health and value.

Grant attended school in Georgetown and then moved on to the Maysville Academy across the Ohio River in Maysville, Kentucky, when he was fourteen. He studied at the Academy from 1836 to 1837, and the following year he attended the Presbyterian Academy in Ripley, Ohio. As Grant was completing his schooling, his father asked the local U.S. representative, Thomas L. Hamer (1800–1846), to help secure an appointment to the U.S. Military Academy for his son. Hamer agreed and filled out the necessary paperwork. However, Hamer wrote in Grant's first name on the paperwork as Ulysses (instead of Hiram) and his middle name as Simpson (the maiden name of Grant's mother). Grant kept the name change and left for the Military Academy at West Point in 1839.

Although Grant was an average student at West Point, he performed especially well in mathematics and finished first in his class in horsemanship. After graduating in 1843, Grant was assigned to the infantry (where he was trained to fight on foot) and stationed near St. Louis, Missouri. His roommate at West Point, Frederick Tracy Dent (1821–1892), lived near St. Louis and invited Grant to his family's home. Grant met Dent's sister, Julia, during those visits. She shared his love for horseback riding.

The couple was riding in a horse and buggy one day to attend a wedding when they came to a bridge that was nearly flooded over. Julia grabbed hold of Grant's arm and said, "I'll cling to you no matter what happens." After they passed safely over the bridge, Grant proposed to her. He began by saying, "I wonder if you would cling to me all of my life." The couple became engaged in 1844, but did not marry until 1848 because Grant left to fight in the Mexican-American War (1846–48). They would have four children: Frederick, Ulysses Jr., Ellen, and Jesse.

From military hero to hard-luck farmer

Shortly after Grant became engaged, he was sent to serve in Louisiana. When a dispute about the location of the border between Mexico and Texas led to war, Grant served in the Mexican-American War under two distinguished commanders, Zachary Taylor (1784–1850), who would be elected president in 1848, and Winfield Scott (1786–1866), who would lose the presidential election of 1852. Grant fought with distinction and earned several citations for bravery.

After the war, Grant returned to St. Louis and married. Julia Grant joined him on assignments in New York and Michigan. The couple returned to St. Louis in 1850, where their first child was born. Grant was returned to duty in New York in 1851 before being transferred to Fort Vancouver in the Oregon Territory in 1852. (The Oregon Territory comprised the present-day states of Washington, Idaho, and Oregon.) Grant was unhappy in the Northwest and resigned from the army in 1854.

As a civilian, Grant endured a series of failures over the next few years. He tried to make a living as a farmer, but met with poor crop yields on the farm he called "Hardscrabble." He lost the farm altogether in 1857. He was not successful as a real estate agent, either. Finally, in need of money and a job to support his family, Grant began working in his father's store and moved his family to Galena, Illinois, in 1860. He had only ever been professionally successful as a soldier. Grant returned to the military after forces of the Confederate States of America (CSA) fired on Fort Sumter, South Carolina, on April 18, 1861, and the Civil War (1861–65) began.

Civil War leader

As the man with the most military training and experience in Galena, Grant chaired a town meeting to discuss enlistment, then began training recruits. He was appointed colonel and charged with commanding the Twenty-first Volunteer Infantry Regiment by Illinois governor Richard Yates (1815–1873). When President Abraham Lincoln (1809–1865; served 1861–65) expanded the Union army in August 1861, Grant was promoted to brigadier general. His command encompassed Missouri and Illinois, with a base in Cairo, Illinois, a town on the Mississippi River.

While the Union army was performing poorly during the early part of the war, Grant led his troops in successful campaigns in Kentucky, Missouri, and Tennessee. In April 1862,

Grant regrouped his troops to hold their line in the major and bloody battle of Shiloh, Virginia. Some military leaders questioned Grant's preparedness for the battle, but Grant was supported by President Lincoln. Later that summer and early autumn, Grant's forces won battles in Mississippi. Grant was then instructed to overtake the Mississippi town of Vicksburg, the Confederate stronghold on the Mississippi River.

After failing to take Vicksburg during December 1862, Grant moved his forces through back country in the spring of 1863 and took control of Jackson, Mississippi, before laying siege on Vicksburg. After almost two months of fighting, Grant accepted the surrender of Vicksburg on July 4, 1863. That same day, Union forces won a major battle at Gettysburg, Pennsylvania. The two victories helped turn the tide of the war in favor of the Union.

President Lincoln had changed his commanding generals several times during the war, wanting a leader who was

A depiction of the surrender of Vicksburg on July 4, 1863. *The Library of Congress.*

aggressive. In March 1864, Lincoln appointed Grant the supreme commander of Union forces. Grant led the Wilderness Campaign, a large offensive to capture the Confederate capital of Richmond, Virginia, which left nearly thirty thousand dead and ended in a stalemate. More heavy casualties occurred in the Battle of the Bloody Angle as the Union offensive continued from the summer of 1864 to the winter of 1865. Union forces won many battles throughout Tennessee, Virginia, North Carolina, and South Carolina, while Grant besieged the forces of Confederate general **Robert E. Lee** (1807–1870; see Confederate Leaders entry). Finally, on April 9, 1865, General Lee surrendered to Grant at Appomattox Court House, Virginia, effectively ending the Civil War.

Political battles begin

Grant's triumphs during the war made him the most popular man in the United States. He was commissioned by Congress as General of the Army, a position that only former president George Washington (1732–1799; served 1789–97) had held previously. With the approval of President Lincoln, Grant had allowed lenient terms of surrender for the Confederacy. After Lincoln was assassinated days after the end of the war, Congress planned a stricter and more punitive policy toward the Southern states that had seceded. Congress became embroiled in a power struggle with **Andrew Johnson** (1808–1875; served 1865–69; see entry), who succeeded Lincoln as president and proposed an even more lenient program of Reconstruction than Lincoln.

Grant became involved in a tense political battle between the president and Congress. He agreed to serve as secretary of war after President Johnson had fired **Edwin M. Stanton** (1814–1869; see entry) from the position. Congress demanded the right to vote on the removal, and when the president refused, Congress voted to impeach Johnson. Meanwhile, after completing his assignment as secretary of war, Grant decided against continuing in the position, claiming he had only planned to hold it on a temporary basis. Johnson felt betrayed, and Grant began to show his support for powerful Republican leaders in Congress—the so-called Radical Reconstructionists who opposed Johnson and wanted a harsher Reconstruction policy.

In 1868, Republicans nominated Grant as their candidate for president. He easily defeated former New York governor Horatio Seymour (1810–1886) in the November election. In his inaugural address, Grant called for an end to regional conflict, but he would have a troubled administration. The end of the Civil War did not end racial oppression (persecution); the Republican majority in Congress exerted great federal power over the Southern states as they reentered the union; and Grant showed poor judgment in his selection of officials for his administration.

Problems of the Reconstruction

Just prior to Grant's inauguration, Congress proposed the Fifteenth Amendment, which declared that the right to vote could not be denied "on account of race, color, or previous condition of servitude." Within a year, the amendment was accepted by state legislatures and became law. Grant contributed to the passage of the amendment by requesting that Nebraska governor David Butler (1829–1891) call a special session of the state's legislature to quickly debate the amendment.

However, racial problems persisted, and Grant responded to incidents of violence, intimidation, and disorder in the South. The Enforcement Act of 1870 empowered him to use federal troops to protect the voting rights of African Americans. The Ku Klux Klan Act of 1871 was directed specifically toward a white supremacist group that organized violence against African Americans. The law empowered Grant to impose martial law (military control over an area). Despite several uses of federal force, however, little improvement was made in race relations.

During his second term, in 1874, Grant sent federal troops to Vicksburg, following a mass murder of African Americans. Grant supported the Civil Rights Act of 1875, which prohibited racial segregation (separation) in public housing and transportation. The act was later declared unconstitutional by the U.S. Supreme Court in 1883. The Court ruled that the federal government could not force states and local communities to act against segregation.

Grant faced economic crises after taking office in March 1869. During the Civil War, the government had printed money, called "greenbacks," to help farmers and workers pay for the necessities of life. Unlike coins, greenbacks were not backed by gold reserves (valuable gold the government held to represent the value of money it minted) and their value became unstable—sometimes a greenback was equal to a dollar, sometimes two greenbacks equaled a dollar. Grant delayed in addressing the problem.

Meanwhile, two wealthy men, Jay Gould (1836–1892) and Jim Fisk (1834–1872), bought large amounts of gold, making the precious metal even more valuable and making greenbacks even less valuable. The gold purchase created a financial crisis in the stock market. The market closed on September 24, 1869, a day called "Black Friday." Grant acted quickly to authorize the U.S. government to sell some of its gold reserves—making more gold available on the market and helping reduce its value.

Fisk and Gould had wanted to involve the president in their scheme. They were assisted by Abel Rathbone Corbin, who was married to Grant's sister. Corbin provided the financiers with access to the president. Grant not only turned away Fisk and Gould, he quickly and effectively acted against them, but the relationship became the subject of a congressional investigation and some public embarrassment for Grant.

Nevertheless, Grant was a popular president. Economic conditions were improving in 1872, lower taxes on imported goods kept prices downs, and repeal of an income tax that had been instituted during the Civil War all contributed to his easy reelection that year.

The Grant family prospered, meanwhile, while Grant was president. Fred Grant, the couple's oldest son, graduated from West Point; Ulysses Jr. graduated from Harvard and became a presidential secretary; and daughter Nellie enjoyed a lavish, well-publicized White House wedding in 1874.

In foreign affairs, the Grant administration was led by Secretary of State Hamilton Fish (1801–1893) (see box). Fish inherited the controversy over the *Alabama,* a cruiser purchased by the Confederacy in Great Britain and used during the Civil War. The purchase violated British neutrality during the war and contributed to a group in rebellion against the United States. Fish negotiated the Treaty of Washington, signed by

Grant in 1871, where Great Britain acknowledged violations and agreed to arbitration over monetary settlement (in arbitration, two parties in conflict submit claims to an impartial third party that decides on a settlement). The arbitration commission awarded the United States $15.5 million in damages.

Grant became interested in annexing (claiming as U.S. territory) Santo Domingo, a nation in the Caribbean Ocean that had won independence from Spain. Representatives aligned with Santo Domingo president Bonaventura Báez approached Secretary of State Fish with an offer to sell the country to the United States. A treaty of annexation was negotiated. Because all treaties negotiated by the president are subject to approval by the U.S. Senate by a two-thirds majority, the annexation proposal went to a vote; it failed. Grant continued to press for annexation of Santo Domingo after the annexation treaty was rejected in 1871, despite no sign of additional support. At the very end of his second term, Grant raised the issue again in his last message to Congress.

Troubled second term

The economy took a downturn in 1873. The poor business conditions affected financier **Jay Cooke** (1821–1905; see entry), whose system of banks had made loans to the Northern Pacific Railroad, which was building a cross-country line from Duluth, Minnesota, to Tacoma, Washington. Cooke could not make money through investments to support the loans he had provided and could not compensate customers who had deposited their money with Cooke's banks. The collapse on September 18, 1873, of Jay Cooke and Company started a large-scale financial recession called the Panic of 1873. Stocks quickly lost value. Beginning on September 20, 1873, the New York Stock Exchange closed for ten days.

During the first year of Grant's second term, Congress completed an investigation of the Crédit Mobilier scandal that implicated Schuyler Colfax (1823–1885), vice president during Grant's first term, and Henry Wilson (1812–1875), vice president from 1873 to his death in 1875 during Grant's second term. Grant's secretary of the treasury, William A. Richardson (1821–1896), was implicated in a tax fraud scheme. Pressured to remove Richardson from office, Grant

Hamilton Fish

In an administration riddled by scandal, Hamilton Fish served with distinction as secretary of state under President Ulysses S. Grant. Fish was born on August 3, 1808, in New York City. His father, a politician, named his son after his friend, the late statesman Alexander Hamilton (1757–1804). Fish studied at a private school before going to Columbia College, from which he graduated in 1827. After three years of studying in a law office, Fish formed a law partnership with William B. Lawrence. Fish married Julia Kean on December 15, 1836, and the couple had eight children.

After becoming involved in New York politics, Fish won a seat in Congress in 1842. He was not reelected, but in 1848 he was elected governor of New York. His administration helped establish free public schools throughout the state. From 1851 to 1857, Fish served in the U.S. Senate. As a member of the Whig Party, which existed from the mid-1830s to the mid-1850s, he was against the expansion of slavery. Fish joined the Republican Party after it was formed in 1854. The Party was comprised of former Whig Party members as well as former Democrats who were against slavery.

Fish and his family traveled in Europe for two years before returning to the United States in 1860. Fish began campaigning for Abraham Lincoln, the Republi-can nominee for president. During the Civil War, Fish served on the Union defense committee of New York and as a commissioner of the federal government for the relief of prisoners, contributing to the negotiations for an agreement on exchanges of prisoners between the warring sides.

After being elected president in 1868, Ulysses S. Grant wanted Fish in his administration. When Grant offered him the position of secretary of state, Fish refused, but later decided to take the post. Fish was involved in three major foreign policy areas for the Grant administration: the attempt to annex Santo Domingo; the pursuit of war reparations (compensation) from Great Britain for having aided the Confederacy during the Civil War; and tense relations with Spain over its colony of Cuba.

Santo Domingo had won independence from Spain, but a small group wanted to reunify with Spain. Some Grant administration officials envisioned an American naval base in Santo Domingo as a means for more power in the region. Santo Domingo government officials approached Fish with an offer to sell the country to the United States. Fish negotiated a treaty of annexation as a first option and an agreement for a naval station as a second option. But when the proposal was taken to a vote, the U.S. Senate failed to approve the treaty. Previous to the vote, it was revealed that

Hamilton Fish. *The Library of Congress.*

Orville E. Babcock (1835–1884), a secretary to Grant, had offered $100,000 and weapons to assist Santo Domingo president Bonaventura Báez with opposition in his country. Fish was not involved in the situation, which brought embarrassment to the Grant administration.

Fish's most notable achievement as secretary of state was settling a controversy with Great Britain. During the Civil War, Britain had equipped or supplied Confederate boats in British ports, a violation of Britain's neutrality. The boats caused damage to commercial and military vessels of the North. Americans demanded huge reparations and some wanted Great Britain to cede (give) Canada, then a part of the British empire, to the United States. Fish successfully negotiated the Treaty of Washington (1871), which provided for arbitration of U.S. claims. An arbitrator set the amount of damages paid to the United States at $15.5 million.

Fish's other major foreign concern was the Spanish colony of Cuba. A rebellion in Cuba was put down by Spain, and in the process some Americans were injured. In addition to seeking reparations for the injuries, the United States demanded reform in the ways Spain governed the island. Tensions were easing until, in 1873, a ship called the *Virginius* registered as American and, with a mainly American crew, was captured and taken into a Cuban port because the vessel belonged to a Cuban revolutionary group based in New York. Spanish authorities murdered the captain and fifty-three of the crew and passengers. Amid cries for retribution and war with Spain, Fish negotiated a settlement that included reparations for families of the deceased Americans.

After Grant's second term as president ended in 1877, Fish retired to private life in New York. He was sixty-eight at the time. He stayed active in the development of Columbia College (now Columbia University), from which he had graduated in 1827. Fish died in New York on September 6, 1893.

Editorial cartoon showing President Ulysses S. Grant with members of his administration who were involved in various scandals during Grant's time in office.
The Granger Collection, New York. Reproduced by permission.

fired him from his cabinet post and then appointed Richardson as a judge on the U.S. Court of Claims.

Benjamin H. Bristow (1832–1896) replaced Richardson and began an investigation of a conspiracy involving taxes paid on whiskey. More than two hundred people were involved in what became known as the Whiskey Ring. Grant's private secretary, Orville E. Babcock (1835–1884), was among those implicated for misuse of tax collection on the sale of whiskey. Meanwhile, Grant's secretary of war, William W. Belknap (1829–1890), was discovered to have illegally taken money the government earned from sales of forts and trading posts to the public.

Grant entered office in 1869 hoping for improvement in relations with Native Americans. However, Americans continued moving westward and inevitably ran into conflicts over land with Native Americans. Chief Joseph (1840–1904), the famous Native American leader of the Nez Perce, helped convince Grant to issue an Executive Order in 1873 that recognized the Wallowa Valley of Oregon as Nez Perce territory. Two years later, however, Grant rescinded the order after pressure by the U.S. Bureau of Indian Affairs to permit the building of a wagon road that would bring more settlers into the valley. In 1876, Native Americans surprised and defeated the forces of General George A. Custer (1839–1876) at the Battle of Little Big Horn in Montana.

Despite scandals, none of which involved Grant directly, economic hardships, and ongoing sectional and racial problems, Grant remained a popular president. Many Republicans wanted Grant to run for an unprecedented third term, but Grant had enough of the presidency. Instead, the Grant family went on a world tour. Grant was an honored guest at ceremonies in several nations. After visiting Europe, Africa, and Asia, the Grants settled in New York City. In 1880, Republicans again wanted Grant to run for president, but after early support at the party's convention, Grant was passed over.

Grant remained active, serving as president of the Mexican Southern Railroad Company beginning in 1881 (at the age of fifty-nine). He helped negotiate a trade treaty agreement between the United States and Mexico in 1883. However, Grant went bankrupt in 1884. He had invested his life savings in his son's investment firm, but financial scandals drove the firm out of business.

To make some money, Grant contributed articles on his Civil War experiences to *Century* magazine. Grant's friend, writer Mark Twain (1835–1910), urged him to expand his articles into memoirs. For close to a year and in ill health, Grant wrote his autobiography, which was published as *Per-*

sonal Memoirs of U. S. Grant in 1885. He died a few days after completing his memoirs, which went on to be a best-seller.

A crowd of mourners estimated at over one million people lined the streets of New York City to witness Grant's funeral procession. His body was laid in a temporary cemetery until Grant's Tomb was completed in 1897. The tomb bears the inscription, "Let us have peace."

For More Information

Books

Grant, Ulysses S. *Personal Memoirs of Ulysses S. Grant.* New York: C. L. Webster & Co., 1885. Multiple reprints.

Mantell, Martin E. *Johnson, Grant and the Politics of Reconstruction.* New York: Columbia University Press, 1973.

O'Brien, Steven. *Ulysses S. Grant.* New York: Chelsea House, 1991.

Smith, Jean Edward. *Grant.* New York: Simon & Schuster, 2001.

Web Sites

"The American Experience: Ulysses S. Grant." *PBS.* http://www.pbs.org/wgbh/amex/grant/ (accessed on July 13, 2004).

"Ulysses S. Grant Association." *Southern Illinois University.* http://www.lib.siu.edu/projects/usgrant/ (accessed on July 13, 2004).

Ulysses S. Grant Home Page. http://www.mscomm.com/~ulysses/ (accessed on July 13, 2004).

Ulysses S. Grant Network. http://www.css.edu/usgrant/ (accessed on July 13, 2004).

Horace Greeley

Born February 3, 1811
Amherst, New Hampshire

Died November 29, 1872
New York, New York

Newspaper publisher and editor, writer,
and presidential candidate

An influential newspaper publisher and writer, Horace Greeley was a significant public figure for reform from the 1840s to the early 1870s and was affectionately called "Uncle Horace" by admiring readers. He was a leading proponent for abolition (end of slavery) through the Civil War years, supported programs for the poor and working class, and sought to improve society through pacifism (nonviolence) and cooperation. During the Reconstruction era (1865–77), Greeley rallied for civil rights legislation and favored policies of reconciliation toward former members of the Confederacy. The latter view distanced Greeley from many Northern Republicans still bitter over the Civil War (1861–65). Greeley had been a Republican since the party was founded in the mid-1850s, but he ran for president as a Democrat in 1872. That year proved tragic for Greeley: He was heavily criticized during the presidential campaign, endured the death of his wife, lost a landslide election, and lost control of the famous newspaper he had founded over thirty years earlier. Greeley died a broken man less than a month after the 1872 election.

"I am weary of fighting over issues that ought to be dead—that logically *were* dead years ago. When slavery died, I thought that we ought speedily to have ended all that grew out of it by universal amnesty and impartial suffrage."

Horace Greeley. *AP/Wide World Photos. Reproduced by permission.*

New York, New York

Horace Greeley was born in Amherst, New Hampshire, on February 3, 1811. He was the third child of Zaccheus Greeley and Mary Woodburn. The family was poor and Greeley had little education, but he was encouraged to learn to read by his mother. At the age of fourteen, Greeley was apprenticed to Amos Bliss, editor of the *Northern Spectator* in Vermont. (An apprentice learns a trade by assisting a skilled craftsperson.) Greeley learned how to set print for periodicals (magazines, newspapers, and journals). When the *Northern Spectator* ceased publication in 1830, Greeley stayed with his parents for a short while and briefly worked with printers in the area but found little opportunity in small towns of the northeast.

With about $25 in savings and his possessions tied together with a piece of cloth, Greeley set out for New York City at age twenty in 1831. After several weeks, he found a job printing an edition of the New Testament of the Bible. While working on various other printing jobs, Greeley regularly read periodicals for news and to learn how news was reported. He had saved enough money by early 1833, before he turned twenty-two, to take on printing jobs with a partner, Jonas Winchester. The duo also produced two periodicals, *Sylvester's Bank Note and Exchange Manual* and the *Constitutionalist,* both of which combined information on winning lottery numbers with assorted news items.

In March 1834, Greeley and Winchester founded a weekly literary and news journal called the *New Yorker.* (This was not the same publication as the modern day *New Yorker* magazine, which was founded during the 1920s.) The journal contained some original contributions by Greeley and other writers as well as reprinted stories, fiction, reviews, and transcripts of notes from musical compositions from American and foreign newspapers. While Greeley struggled to make a success of the *New Yorker,* his personal life took a happy turn when he met Mary Youngs Cheney, an independent-minded social activist and schoolteacher. They married on July 5, 1836, and would have seven children. However, only two of the children lived into adulthood. The emotional pain of losing so many children contributed to Mary Greeley's increasing isolation and mental and physical ailments.

Success with political writings

To earn extra money, Greeley began writing political articles for the *Daily Whig* and other newspapers. He was a member of the Whig Party, which began in the 1830s and lasted to the 1850s. Most Whigs were against slavery and were more socially reform-minded than their rivals in the Democratic Party. Greeley's political writings and his editorial skills drew the attention of New York's Whig leaders, Thurlow Weed (1797–1882) and William H. Seward (1801–1872). Greeley was picked by them to edit a weekly magazine, the *Jeffersonian*, through which the Whig Party communicated its views to a national audience. Periodicals were the major form of mass media in the United States during the nineteenth century. The *Jeffersonian* ran for one year as a general information magazine and supporter of Whig views.

Preparing for the 1840 presidential campaign, Whig leaders selected Greeley to edit and publish the *Log Cabin*. Immensely popular, the *Log Cabin* reached a circulation of almost one hundred thousand subscribers. Greeley became a public figure through his work on the periodical and was invited to make speeches, sit on committees, and help manage the Whig campaign in New York.

Seeing an opportunity for an inexpensive daily newspaper that represented the views of the Whig Party, Greeley merged the *New Yorker* and the *Log Cabin* and combined his own money and a loan to launch the *New York Tribune* in April 1841. The political activism of the *Tribune* brought quick attention and sales, and it was soon established as the best New York City newspaper at a time when more than twelve daily papers were published.

When Greeley took on a partner, Thomas McElrath (1807–1888), to concentrate on production efficiency, he was freed to focus on writing and shaping the editorial views of the *Tribune*. The paper became known for accurate and lively presentation of news, literary reviews and stories, and for Greeley's progressive views on civil, political, and economic equality. Greeley wrote editorials supporting free distribution of government lands on the frontier to settlers; attacking government land grants to railroads; opposing capital punishment; demanding abolition; and supporting labor unions (in 1850, Greeley became the first president of the New York

The Media Changes Political Campaigns

The *Log Cabin,* edited and published by Horace Greeley, was significant because it helped change the nature of presidential campaigns in the United States. In its one-year existence during the 1840 presidential race, the magazine helped make songs and slogans part of presidential campaigns, alongside issues and speeches. The title of the magazine reflected the Whig Party's portrayal of its candidate, William Henry Harrison (1773–1841; served 1841), as a farmer who lived in a log cabin and drank apple cider. This folksy image was meant to appeal to common people and contrast with that of Harrison's opponent, President Martin Van Buren (1782–1862; served 1837–1841), who was portrayed as an urban political sophisticate and wine drinker, out of touch with the common voter.

Printers' Union). The paper opposed the Mexican-American War (1846–48), viewing it as an offensive action against another country that was intended to expand the United States and spread slavery further.

Public figure

Greeley began traveling widely during the 1850s as a popular speaker and voice at political conferences. After serving briefly as a U.S. representative from New York—he was selected to fill a vacant seat from December 4, 1848, to March 3, 1849—Greeley toured Europe in 1851 and spoke before the English parliament. In 1853, he purchased a fifty-four acre farm in Chappaqua, New York. He spent weekends there and wrote articles on his experiences with farming.

By the mid-1850s, a national version of the *New York Tribune,* called the *Weekly Tribune,* was launched. It quickly became a leading national newspaper. The abolitionist movement was growing stronger and the *Tribune* helped represent it as the nation grew divisive over slavery. Greeley advocated resistance to the Fugitive Slave Act of 1850, which permitted slave owners to pursue fugitive slaves into nonslave states. Greeley joined the Republican Party when it was formed in 1854. The new party appealed to antislavery Whigs and Democrats. He attended the national organization meeting in 1856 when, for the first time, Republicans nominated a presidential candidate, explorer John C. Frémont (1813–1890).

During this period, Greeley published books drawn from his newspaper writings on political issues and his travels. His books included *Hints Toward Reforms* (1850), *Glances at Europe* (1851), and *An Overland Journey from New York to San Francisco in the Summer of 1859* (1860). Greeley also edited

History of the Struggle for Slavery Extension or Restriction in the United States (1856). As a political candidate, Greeley was far less successful: He failed in attempts for Congress in 1850, lieutenant governor of New York in 1854, and the U.S. Senate in 1861 and 1863. He later failed as a candidate for the House of Representatives in 1868 and 1870. Still, Greeley was a respected and popular public figure, beloved to admirers as "Uncle Horace" and seen as somewhat comical to his opponents. Caricatures (exaggerated cartoon drawings) of Greeley appeared frequently, showing the beard that grew around his throat and his habit of wearing a broad-brimmed hat and disheveled clothes.

During the Civil War years, Greeley found difficulty balancing his pacifist views with political activism. While momentum grew strong among abolitionists for viewing the Civil War as a moral cause, Greeley continued advocating peaceful resolution, even though political solutions to end slavery had failed for decades. He challenged President Abra-

A campaign portrait showing 1872 Democratic presidential nominee Horace Greeley as "the Chappaqua farmer" (referring to the name of his farm) riding on a horse towards a stormy Washington, D.C. Campaign slogans are visible. *The Library of Congress.*

A dissheveled Horace Greeley, typical of Greeley caricatures of the day. *The Granger Collection, New York. Reproduced by permission.*

ham Lincoln (1809–1865; served 1861–65) for not immediately emancipating slaves. In 1863, he advocated that the Union and Confederacy should present their cases before an international mediator (someone without bias who settles disputes), and he worked to begin peace negotiations. He did not support reelection of Lincoln as president in 1864 until two months before the election. Greeley had wanted immediate abolishment of slavery, while Lincoln took more gradual steps that would lead to a constitutional amendment that banned slavery.

Controversial Reconstruction figure

Following the Civil War, Greeley supported passage of the Fourteenth Amendment in 1868 (which granted citizenship to all the people born in the United States) and the Fifteenth Amendment (which mandated that voting rights were not to be denied due to race). He advocated reconciliation of the Union, an end to antagonism between the North and South, and amnesty (a free pardon) toward former soldiers of the Confederacy. Greeley was personally involved in the release of **Jefferson Davis** (1808–1889; see Confederate Leaders entry), who had served as president of the Confederacy. Outraged Northerners, who wanted to punish participants in the Confederacy, reacted bitterly to Greeley: The *New York Tribune* lost almost half of its subscribers, and many book buyers cancelled orders for Greeley's two-volume history, *The American Conflict* (1868), which recounts the causes, incidents, and results of the Civil War and opinions on slavery since 1776.

Greeley's Power with Words

As an editorial and feature writer for one of the nation's most popular newspapers of the nineteenth century, Horace Greeley attracted the attention of many readers. Among them was the president of the United States, Abraham Lincoln. Since periodicals were the dominant form of mass media at the time, they carried tremendous influence. On August 19, 1862, Greeley wrote an open letter to Lincoln in the *New York Tribune* titled "The Prayer of Twenty Million." In his letter, Greeley demanded that Lincoln commit himself definitely to emancipation (freedom from slavery). Lincoln's reply was published several days later, addressed "to an old friend, whose heart I have always supposed to be right." In the famous reply, Lincoln explained to the large readership of the *Tribune* that his sole purpose for the Civil War was to preserve the Union. He hoped that slavery would end, but as president his main responsibility was to ensure the United States remained intact.

Another example of Greeley's public power is reflected in the saying he is

Journalist Horace Greeley, newspaper in hand.
© *Bettmann/Corbis.*

most associated with—"Go west, young man." The saying was intended to inspire young men to settle in the western frontier where they would find opportunity, independence, and success through self-reliance. The phrase actually dated back to an Indiana newspaper writer, John Soule, in 1851, but when Greeley repeated it over a decade later, it became popular and remained associated with him.

Greeley supported the impeachment of President **Andrew Johnson** (1808–1875; served 1865–69; see entry) in 1868, referring to him in an editorial as "an aching tooth in the national jaw" for Johnson's refusal to sign civil rights legislation. Greeley supported Civil War hero **Ulysses S. Grant** (1822–1885; served 1869–77; see entry) in his successful run for the presidency in 1868. By 1870, however, Greeley dropped his support for Grant because Greeley believed presi-

Honors for Greeley

The town of Greeley, Colorado, a planned community, was named in honor of Horace Greeley. Another example of Greeley's lasting influence is the Horace Greeley Award, presented by the New England Press Association in honor of Greeley, "one of the greatest and most dedicated journalists in the history of American journalism."

dents should only serve one term and because he disagreed with some of Grant's actions as president. Greeley was concerned that Grant had appointed too many government workers as a way of returning political favors, was against Grant's efforts to annex (claim as U.S. territory) Santo Domingo, and believed some of Grant's policies were harsh towards the South.

In an editorial in a May 1871 edition of the *New York Tribune,* Greeley officially opposed Grant's bid for reelection. He became increasingly distanced from the most powerful members of the Republican Party, which included the president and a group of congressmen responsible for most of the legislation that became law during the Reconstruction era.

Greeley became part of a faction (small group) within the Republican Party that challenged the president and the most powerful congressmen. In March 1872, the members of the faction, called the Liberal Republicans, broke with the Republican Party and nominated Greeley as their candidate for president. The Liberal Republicans formed a coalition with Democrats to support an opponent to Grant in the 1872 campaign. By the time Democrats met in Cincinnati, Ohio, in May 1872 to plan their national convention, Greeley had some support to become the party's presidential nominee. The Democratic national convention held in Philadelphia, Pennsylvania, in July 1872 was divided on several candidates. Many party regulars disliked Greeley because he had supported Republican policies for years. When Greeley won the nomination after hotly contested voting, many Democrats left the convention with no intention of supporting Greeley.

The presidential campaign of 1872 was among the uglier campaigns in American history. Republicans attacked Greeley as a traitor, and he was not treated with seriousness and respect by many major newspapers and commentators. Influential political cartoonist Thomas Nast (1840–1902) regularly lampooned (ridiculed) Greeley.

Emotionally drained by heavy criticism and a long campaign tour, Greeley returned home a few weeks before the election to care for his dying wife. He had little sleep as he sat by her bedside. Mary Greeley died on October 30, 1872. A week later, Greeley was soundly defeated in his bid for the presidency, winning only six states and losing in the electoral college, 286 to 66. When he returned to the office of the *Tribune* later in November, Greeley discovered that daily operations and editorial responsibilities had been permanently taken over by others.

Greeley soon suffered a mental breakdown and was hospitalized. His health declined rapidly and he died on November 29, 1872. Greeley's funeral, held in New York City on December 4, was attended by President Grant and members of his administration as well as a huge number of supporters.

For More Information

Books

Cross, Coy. *Go West Young Man!: Horace Greeley's Vision for America.* Albuquerque: University of New Mexico Press, 1995.

Lunde, Erik S. *Horace Greeley.* Boston: Twayne, 1981.

Parton, James. *Life of Horace Greeley.* Manchester, NH: Ayer Company, 1982.

Web Sites

"Horace Greeley." *Spartacus Educational.* http://www.spartacus.schoolnet.co.uk/USAgreeley.htm (accessed on July 14, 2004).

Bret Harte

Born August 25, 1836
Albany, New York

Died May 5, 1902
Camberley, England

Writer and editor

"The only sure thing about luck is that it will change."

In 1868, Bret Harte burst onto the literary scene as a popular writer of tales set in California mining camps and boomtowns and as the founding editor of a new magazine called *Overland Monthly.* By 1871, he signed the highest paying publishing contract in American history to that time. Harte was known as a satirist (a writer who uses a humorous tone to criticize human characteristics) and a writer who specialized in regional stories. He carefully recreated distinct California settings, speech patterns of people drawn to mining districts, and details of clothing and manners from people of high society to everyday men and women trying to get rich or find work. Harte himself experienced the boom and bust of a gold rush: He went from being the highest-paid and most popular writer in America to experiencing a series of personal and professional failures within five years that would challenge him the rest of his life.

Aspiring writer

Francis Brett Hart was born in Albany, New York, on August 25, 1836, to Henry and Elizabeth Hart. The youngster was called Frank as a child. He had two older siblings, Eliza and Henry; a younger sister, Margaret, was born in 1838. Harte's father added an "e" to the family surname when Harte was a young boy, apparently to distance himself from his father, with whom he did not have a good relationship. Harte's father was a teacher, but many schools closed during financial hard times that began in 1837. The family moved frequently to wherever Henry Harte could find work as a teacher. When he died in 1845, the family was left in dire conditions and moved to New York City. By the time he reached thirteen, Harte quit school to work as a clerk. He later joined a local military company.

Around the time Harte was sixteen and already living on his own, he accompanied his sister on a boat ride from New York to San Francisco, California. The boat sailed from New York to Nicaragua. The Hartes crossed Nicaragua to reach a boat on the Pacific Ocean and sailed to San Francisco. Harte's mother had settled there after marrying Andrew Williams, who became the first mayor of Oakland, California.

Soon after arriving in Oakland, Harte headed north to a mining district near Sonora, California. He started a school, but could not attract enough students, and then turned to mining. Harte moved around the area north of San Francisco during his early twenties, working as an agent and messenger for the Wells, Fargo and Company bank, in an Oakland drugstore, as a tutor for ranching families, and as a typesetter and occasional writer for the *Northern Californian* newspaper in Arcata.

Meanwhile, he pursued his ambition of becoming a writer. Having been an avid reader since he was a boy, Harte long held onto hopes of writing professionally one day. He began contributing poems and tales to local newspapers as well as the national magazine, the *Knickerbocker*. Several stories he wrote for the *Golden Era,* a weekly San Francisco literary paper, including "The Man of No Account" and "High-Water Mark," would appear in his later book, *The Luck of Roaring Camp, and Other Sketches* (1870).

In February 1860, Harte's career with *Northern Californian* came to an abrupt end. He was in charge of the paper on a Sunday when a report came in about a group of whites who killed sixty Native Americans, mostly women and children, at a nearby camp. Harte reported the story and wrote about his outrage in an editorial. Relations between whites and Native Americans in the area were very tense at the time, and Harte's articles met with a strong negative reaction by local residents. After being threatened with violence, Harte returned to San Francisco. He held government jobs during the 1860s as a surveyor, marshal, and in the U.S. mint division based in San Francisco. In 1864, Harte married Anna Griswold, a church singer. They would have four children.

Reaches national audience

Continuing to write, Harte landed a story, "The Legend of Monte del Diablo," in the *Atlantic Monthly* in October 1863 (the magazine still publishes today) and edited a collection of poetry. Meanwhile, he drew attention for parodying (making fun of by imitating) works by famous writers like Charles Dickens (1812–1870) and James Fenimore Cooper (1789–1851). The pieces were collected in *Condensed Novels, and Other Papers* (1867), published in New York. Winning respect in the east for his writing skills, Harte became the California correspondent for two Massachusetts papers, the *Springfield Republican* and the *Boston Christian Register*. In 1868, he was selected by a San Francisco publisher, Anton Roman, to edit a new magazine, *Overland Monthly*.

Roman wanted to produce a magazine that had the flavor of the west but would appeal to a national audience, and Harte delivered on that goal. From the first issue in July 1868, *Overland Monthly* won praise and gained subscriptions across the nation. The second issue a month later featured Harte's story, "The Luck of Roaring Camp," which proved immensely popular. Within a year, *Overland Monthly* sold as many copies in the East as in the states of California, Nevada, and Oregon. Readers admired Harte's portraits of the people who lived and passed through California mining towns.

"The Luck of Roaring Camp" is set around 1850 in an isolated mining settlement. The camp's only female resident dies while giving birth to a child, named Tom Luck, and the miners struggle to raise the child. The mystery of luck, an important subject in Harte's works, is explored in this story and in another popular tale, "The Outcasts of Poker Flat," published in the January 1869 edition of *Overland Monthly*. As that story begins, the town of Poker Flat has just "suffered the loss of several thousand dollars, two valuable horses, and a prominent citizen." The outcasts include a group of characters forced out of Poker Flat and living in a mountainside camp. The tough landscape is carefully evoked and reflects the characters' difficult attempts to survive and make good in an often hostile physical and social environment.

However, even with the immediate success of *Overland Monthly,* Harte ran into conflicts. Roman sold the magazine, believing Harte had made both the magazine and California look rough and unmannered. John H. Carmany, who bought the magazine from Roman for $7,500, found himself competing for Harte's services. Harte was offered contracts to write exclusively for magazines and publishers in the East. He became even more sought after when his stories were collected and published in *The Luck of Roaring Camp and Other Sketches* in 1870 to critical and popular success. In addition, the September 1870 issue of the *Overland Monthly* contained "Plain Language from Truthful James," a sing-song poem that became a national sensation. Telling the story of how two frontier card sharks (professional card players who win by cheating) are outwitted by an unassuming Chinese man, the poem was frequently recited, set to music, and made into a short play.

Illustration of a mountain gold mining camp from *Devil's Ford,* by Bret Harte. © *Bettmann/Corbis.*

Harte decided to leave California, despite generous offers by Carmany and the University of California, which offered to make him a professor of modern literature with an annual salary and freedom to keep writing and editing. Instead, Harte decided to head East: He signed an exclusive con-

An Excerpt from "The Outcasts of Poker Flat"

The following is an excerpt from Bret Harte's "The Outcasts of Poker Flat." Harte presents gambler John Oakhurst's observations.

> As Mr. John Oakhurst, gambler, stepped into the main street of Poker Flat on the morning of the twenty-third of November, 1850, he was conscious of a change in its moral atmosphere since the preceding night. Two or three men, conversing earnestly together, ceased as he approached, and exchanged significant glances. There was a Sabbath lull in the air, which, in a settlement unused to Sabbath influences, looked ominous [threatening].

> Mr. Oakhurst's calm, handsome face betrayed small concern in these indications. Whether he was conscious of any predisposing cause, was another question. "I reckon they're after somebody," he reflected; "likely it's me." He returned to his pocket the handkerchief with which he had been whipping away the red dust of Poker Flat from his neat boots, and quietly discharged his mind of any further conjecture.

> In point of fact, Poker Flat was "after somebody." It had lately suffered the loss of several thousand dollars, two valuable horses, and a prominent citizen. It was experiencing a spasm of virtuous reaction, quite as lawless and ungovernable as any of the acts that had provoked it. A secret committee had determined to rid the town of all improper persons. This was done permanently in regard of two men who were then hanging from the boughs of a sycamore in the gulch, and temporarily in the banishment of certain other objectionable characters. I regret to say that some of these were ladies. It is but due to the sex, however, to state that their impropriety was professional, and it was only in such easily established standards of evil that Poker Flat ventured to sit in judgment.

> Mr. Oakhurst was right in supposing that he was included in this category....

tract to produce twelve poems and stories for one year for *Atlantic Monthly* and *Every Saturday,* magazines owned by Fields, Osgood and Company, which had published *The Luck of Roaring Camp and Other Sketches.* As a literary celebrity, Harte enjoyed publicity all along his cross-country travel. When he arrived in Boston, Massachusetts, he met many of the major writers of the day at a party in his honor.

Reputation suffers

Harte continued writing for another thirty years. He fulfilled his exclusive contract with Fields, Osgood and Company, but none of the pieces he submitted generated the excitement of his previous work. One of the best stories, "How Santa Claus Came to Simpson's Bar," was postponed for three months in favor of works by other writers. Meanwhile, Harte lived lavishly and ran up debts. He went on a lecture tour to make extra money, but many fans who attended the events were disappointed: They expected a rough-looking and sharp-witted man, but Harte was soft-spoken, fashion conscious, and sipped champagne during his lectures.

Harte's reputation suffered further when he took advance payments for story ideas, then worked on other projects, including writing a play for Stuart Robson (1836–1903), a famous actor of the period. The play, *Two Men of Sandy Bar: A Drama* (1876), received awful reviews when performed in Chicago and New York. A critic in the *New York Times* called it "the worst failure witnessed on the boards of our theatres for years." However, Harte's friend and fellow author Mark Twain (1835–1910) enjoyed it and suggested that he and Harte should collaborate on a play. Their comedy of mistaken identity, *Ah Sin* (1877), received modest reviews and closed after a brief tour.

Still in debt in 1877, Harte managed to get a government appointment to work in the American consulate (a government office mandated to oversee specific interests of the home country) in Germany. Thinking he would be away for only a year or two, Harte left his family in their New Jersey home. But he disliked living in Germany, was reappointed to Scotland, and remained there until being dismissed from his position in 1880. He moved to London and began writing and publishing prolifically. He lived in England until his death, never again living with his family. Harte published at least one volume of new fiction every year from 1883 until his death from throat cancer in

A caricature of writer Bret Harte from *Spy Vanity Fair* magazine, 1879. *Hulton Archive/Getty Images.*

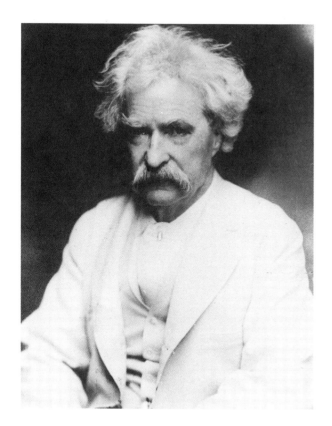

Camberley, England, near London, in 1902. These later works had a steady sales and provided Harte with a regular income, but he was no longer a literary superstar. Harte's literary reputation remains with the stories and poems he published before leaving California.

For More Information

Books

Barnett, Linda. *Bret Harte: A Reference Guide.* Boston: G. K. Hall, 1980.

Harte, Bret. *The Luck of Roaring Camp, and Other Sketches.* Boston: Fields, Osgood, 1870. Multiple reprints.

Nissen, Alex. *Bret Harte: Prince and Pauper.* Jackson: University Press of Mississippi, 2000.

Scharnhorst, Gary. *Bret Harte.* New York: Twayne, 1992.

Scharnhorst, Gary. *Bret Harte: Opening the American Literary West.* Norman: University of Oklahoma Press, 2000.

Mark Twain (above) collaborated with friend Bret Harte on a play, *Ah Sin,* **that closed shortly after it debuted in 1877.** *AP/Wide World Photos. Reproduced by permission.*

Web Sites

"Bret Harte." *California Authors.* http://www.cateweb.org/CA_Authors/harte.html (accessed on July 22, 2004).

"Bret Harte." *San Francisco History Index.* http://www.zpub.com/sf/history/harte.html (accessed on July 22, 2004).

Ferdinand V. Hayden

Born September 7, 1829
Westfield, Massachusetts

Died December 22, 1887
Philadelphia, Pennsylvania

Explorer and geologist

G eologist Ferdinand V. Hayden is best remembered for his 1871 expedition that directly led Congress to pass and President **Ulysses S. Grant** (1822–1885; served 1869-77; see entry) to sign legislation creating Yellowstone National Park. Reports by Hayden and members of his expedition, which included painter Thomas Moran (1837–1926) and photographer William Henry Jackson (1843–1942), thrilled and astounded politicians and the general public about the natural wonders and sublime beauty of the region. As a geologist and explorer, Hayden traveled in and mapped the states of Montana, Colorado, Wyoming, and Idaho. During his early work in the Badlands of South Dakota (then Dakota territory), Hayden was called "the man who picks up stones running" by Native Americans because of his quick method for collecting specimens. Hayden was also the first person on record to discover dinosaur fossils in North America (in 1854 in Montana).

Doctor turned scientist

Ferdinand Vandiveer Hayden was born in Westfield, Massachusetts, on September 7, 1829, to Asa and Melinda

"From the river our path led up the steep sides of the hill for about one mile when we came suddenly and unexpectedly in full view of the [Mammoth Hot Springs of Yellowstone].... Before us arose a high white mountain, looking precisely like a frozen cascade....

Ferdinand V. Hayden. *The Library of Congress.*

Hayden. When Hayden was ten, his father died, and his mother remarried soon afterward. Hayden was sent to live with an uncle who owned a small farm near Rochester, New York. He worked on the farm when not attending school. Hayden started teaching in a local school when he was sixteen. At eighteen, he walked away from the farm with little money but great determination to forge a life of his own. He arrived at Oberlin College in Oberlin, Ohio, where he was befriended by the school's president, Asa Mahan (1800–1889), who helped him enroll at the school in 1847. Hayden graduated in 1850, overcoming hardships of little money and his own shyness.

Following graduation, Hayden returned to New York. Having decided to pursue a career in medicine, he entered Albany Medical College. Hayden received his M.D. from Albany in 1853, but by the time he graduated, his interest had turned to science. He had become a friend of geologist and paleontologist James Hall (1811–1898). Paleontology (the study of the past through fossils) and geology (the study of earth history) were relatively new sciences and methods for scientific understanding of ancient history.

Instead of starting a medical practice, Hayden was sponsored by Hall to join paleontologist Fielding Bradford Meek (1817–1876) on a trip into the Badlands of Dakota territory (present-day South Dakota) in 1853 to collect fossils and rocks. Hayden gained valuable experience on the expedition, learning how to observe and make maps and reports of strata (layers) of rock as a means for understanding the history of a region. The Badlands earned its name for its difficult, rocky terrain of deep gullies and steep hills. As one of the people with some background in science, Hayden often served to retrieve materials or scout adjacent areas. Local Native Americans observing his quick movements nicknamed Hayden "the man who picks up stones running."

Becomes noted explorer and scientist

In 1854, the twenty-five-year-old Hayden returned to the Badlands region to begin an expedition, sponsored by the American Fur Company, to map the Missouri River basin. Traveling mostly by foot for almost two years, Hayden and his fellow expedition members packed light provisions in order to be able to quickly set up and take down camps that served as temporary central locations for their surveys. They followed the Missouri River from Dakota Territory into present-day Montana. Near the end of their journey (in Fort Benton, around the middle of northern Montana), the expedition set up camp at the confluence (where rivers meet) of the Missouri and the Judith Rivers and made a great discovery. Hayden uncovered and collected teeth that were later determined to be those of dinosaurs. Hayden's 1854 expedition, then, was the first on record in North America to uncover the dinosaur remains.

In 1856, Hayden joined an expedition led by Lieutenant Gouverneur K. Warren (1830–1882) of the Topographical Engineers to explore the Yellowstone and Missouri Rivers in Montana, as well as the Black Hills of Dakota Territory. In 1858, Hayden reunited with Meek to explore unsettled areas of Kansas, which was not yet a state, and the following year Hayden returned to Montana and followed the Yellowstone River further south, toward the Wyoming border. Viewing the rugged and sublime natural environment of the area made a significant impression on Hayden as a scientist and lover of nature. Over campfires at night, he began discussing with his traveling companions the possibility that the lands could be set aside to remain in their pristine splendor. Railroads and settlers were already making their way into the region. During winter months, Hayden taught at the University of Pennsylvania.

When the Civil War (1861–65) began, Hayden joined the Union army to utilize the training as a physician he had rarely employed since graduating from college a decade earlier. He remained with the army until after the end of the war, retiring in June 1865 at the age of thirty-six with the rank of lieutenant colonel. Hayden returned to teaching during the

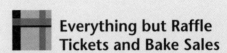

Everything but Raffle Tickets and Bake Sales

To help promote and finance his expeditions, Hayden gave out gifts to sponsors, politicians, and scientists. The gifts included reports, maps, books of photographs, such as *Sun Pictures of Rocky Mountain Scenery* (1870), and specimens. Young scientists wanted to join his groups to gain first-hand experiences they could write about and publish. Hayden made gifts to army officers in exchange for supplies and transportation when needed by his group. Businessmen, especially those with interests in settling the West, took interest in Hayden's work. Among them was railroad man **Jay Cooke** (1821–1905; see entry), who saw Hayden's reports on the spectacular scenery as another promotional opportunity for more westward train travel.

fall of 1865 and the winter of 1865–66 at the University of Pennsylvania before journeying again to the Badlands in the spring of 1866. That expedition was sponsored by the Philadelphia Academy of Natural Sciences.

Meanwhile, the amount of resources used during the Civil War and the increasing industrialization of the northeast led Congress in March 1867 to authorize funding for geological studies of natural resources in the west. Hayden was selected to lead a survey team along the fortieth parallel, the southern border of Nebraska, which became a state that year. Hayden and another scientist, Clarence King (1842–1901), were the first major field leaders of the newly formed U.S. Geological Survey for the Territories.

While pleased with government support for his efforts, Hayden also found himself competing for funds with fellow surveyors: King won a large appropriation to survey routes for railroads, while John Wesley Powell (1834–1902) explored the Colorado basin and Lieutenant George Wheeler (1842–1905) won funds for exploring Nevada and Colorado. Hayden led small, government-funded expeditions to Colorado, Idaho, Montana, Wyoming, and Utah between 1868 and 1869.

Hayden created a system of uniformly scaled maps that made it easier to capture the topography and geology of an area and to easily compare it with other maps. The Department of the Interior adopted the system. Previously, accurate maps of the frontier were rarely available. Meanwhile, on November 9, 1871, Hayden married Emma C. Woodruff, daughter of a Philadelphia merchant. The couple, both in their forties at the time of the marriage, would have no children. After the wedding, Hayden continued to teach at the University of Pennsylvania until the spring of 1872, when he resigned to devote his full attention to government work.

Discovers the glory of Yellowstone

After Hayden lobbied Congress to fund a survey of the Yellowstone territory, Congress appropriated $40,000 in 1871 for an official expedition led by Hayden. His thirty-four-member crew included photographer William Henry Jackson,

painter Thomas Moran, and geologists, mineralogists, topographical artists, botanists, and other scientists. The expedition focused on creating the first accurate maps of the region, capturing the region's geography in words, illustrations, and photographs, observing unusual features, like hot springs and petrified trees, collecting specimens and other data, and making notes on the living creatures they encountered. Among other things, the expedition produced the first list of butterflies inhabiting the area.

An expedition led by Ferdinand V. Hayden travels on a trail between Yellowstone and East Fork Rivers in 1871. *The National Archives and Records Administration.*

When he returned to Washington, D.C., to report on Yellowstone, Hayden so amazed Congress with a description of Yellowstone in his five-hundred-page report, pictures of the region, and Moran's paintings that Congress quickly addressed Hayden's vision for preserving Yellowstone. A bill was introduced to set aside an area encompassing more than two million acres surrounding the Yellowstone River as public land. President Ulysses S. Grant signed the measure into law on March 1, 1872.

Contract with Congress

When Ferdinand Hayden received funding for field work in what is now Yellowstone National Park, the conditions for his work were spelled out in a letter from Secretary of the Interior Columbus Delano (1809–1896) to Hayden, dated May 1, 1871. The excerpt below, from the *ParkNet: National Park Service* Web site, lists those conditions:

In accordance with the act of the third session of the 41st Congress, making appropriations for the continuation of the Geological Survey of the Territories of the United States, dated March 4, 1871, you are appointed U.S. Geologist, to date from the first day of July, 1871, with a salary of four thousand dollars per annum. You will be permitted to select your own assistants who will be entirely subject to your orders, and all your expenditures of the public funds are expected to be made with judicious [careful] economy and care.

The area of your explorations must be, to some extent, discretionary, but in order that you may continue your labors of preceding years, geographically, your explorations of the present season will be confined mostly to the Territories of Idaho and Montana. It is probable that your most available point of departure will be Salt Lake City, proceeding thence north-

ward along the mail route as a base to Helena, Montana, and completing the season's work about the sources of the Missouri and Yellow Stone rivers. You will be required to make such instrumental observations, astronomical and barometrical, as are necessary for the construction of an accurate geographical map of the district explored, upon which the different geological formations may be represented with suitable colors.

As the object of the expedition is to secure as much information as possible, both scientific and practical, you will give your attention to the geological, mineralogical, zoological, botanical, and agricultural resources of the country. You will collect as ample material as possible for the illustration of your final reports, such as sketches, sections, photographs, etc.

Should your route lead you in the vicinity of any of our Indian tribes, you will secure such information in regard to them as will be useful to this Department, or the Country. It is desirable that your collections in all Departments shall be as complete as possible, and you will forward them to the Smithsonian Institution to be arranged according to law.

You will be expected to prepare a preliminary report of your labors, which will be ready for publication by Jan'y 1,1872.

Meanwhile, Hayden had brought images and descriptions of Yellowstone to the American public in magazine articles and lectures. In an article in *Scribners Monthly, an Illustrated Magazine for the People* in February 1872, Hayden described the many wonders of Yellowstone, including the first encounter with the Mammoth Hot Springs: "From the river our path led up the steep sides of the hill for about one mile when we came suddenly and unexpectedly in full view of the [Great Hot Springs of Yellowstone].... Before us arose a high

Ferdinand V. Hayden and painter Walter Paris at their campsite during their expedition of the American West in 1874. © *Corbis.*

white mountain, looking precisely like a frozen cascade.... [No] future tourist in traveling the far west will think of neglecting this most wonderful of the physical phenomena of that most interesting region." Railroads brought visitors to Yellowstone in the 1870s. In the late twentieth and early twenty-first centuries, Yellowstone was being visited by more than three million people annually.

After his triumph with Yellowstone, Hayden continued to lead surveys in Colorado, Idaho, Montana, Wyoming, and Utah for the next decade. His health began failing and he was forced to quit field work in his mid-fifties in 1886. He died the following year. Hayden had been a member of the Academy of Natural Sciences of Philadelphia, the National Academy of Sciences, the Geological Societies of London and Edinburgh, the Geologische Reichsanstalt of Vienna, and the Société Impériale of Moscow. Forty-four species of life, from a moth to a dinosaur fossil, have been named for him, as well as geological features, towns, and lakes.

For More Information

Books

Cassidy, James G. *Ferdinand V. Hayden: Entrepreneur of Science.* Chicago: University of Chicago Press, 2002.

Foster, Mike. *Strange Genius: The Life of Ferdinand Vandeveer Hayden.* Niwot, CO: Roberts Rinehart Publishers, 1994.

Goetzmann, William H. *Exploration and Empire: The Explorer and Scientist in the Winning of the American West.* New York: Alfred A. Knopf, 1966. Reprint, New York: Norton, 1978.

Merrill, Marlene D., ed. *Yellowstone and the Great West: Journals, Letters, and Images from the 1871 Hayden Expedition.* Lincoln: University of Nebraska Press, 1999.

U.S. Geological Survey. *Frederick Vandiveer Hayden and the Founding of the Yellowstone National Park.* Washington, DC: General Publishing Office, 1973.

Web Sites

Hayden, F. V. "The Wonders of the West—II: More about the Yellowstone" (from *Scribners Monthly, an Illustrated Magazine for the People,* February 1872, pp. 388–96). *Making of America; Cornell University Library.* http://cdl.library.cornell.edu/cgi-bin/moa/sgml/moa-idx? notisid=ABP7664-0003-72 (accessed on July 22, 2004).

"Washburn and Hayden Expeditions." *Wyoming Tales and Trails.* http://www.wyomingtalesandtrails.com/photos2.html (accessed on July 22, 2004).

"Yellowstone National Park: Its Exploration and Establishment." *ParkNet: National Park Service.* http://www.cr.nps.gov/history/online_books/haines1/ (accessed on July 22, 2004).

Rutherford B. Hayes

Born October 4, 1822
Delaware, Ohio

Died January 17, 1893
Fremont, Ohio

U.S. president and U.S. general

Rutherford B. Hayes presided over the end of the Recon-struction era (1865–77). During his administration, a poor American economy improved and much needed reform was brought to the federal government. But Hayes had a frustrat-ing presidency. It began with a bitter election dispute that was finally settled more than three months after election day and only two days before Hayes took office. Conflict between North and South, Republican and Democrat, made it impos-sible for Hayes to have a successful administration, even though he proved trustworthy, optimistic, and fair-minded.

"[Here] we are, Republicans, Democrats, colored people, white people, Confederate soldiers, and Union soldiers, all of one mind and one heart today! And why should we not be? What is there to separate us any longer?"

Studies and practices law

Rutherford Birchard Hayes was born on October 4, 1822, in Delaware, Ohio. He was the youngest of three chil-dren of Rutherford and Sophia Hayes, who had moved their family from Vermont to Ohio in 1817 for new opportunities. Hayes's uncle, Sardis Birchard, accompanied the family to Ohio. Hayes's father bought farmland and built a farmhouse while the family lived in the town of Delaware. Hayes's father

Rutherford B. Hayes. *The Library of Congress.*

became a successful farmer, but he died after contracting malaria (an infectious disease transmitted by mosquitoes) two months before Hayes was born. Hayes's mother rented the farm to ensure a steady income.

Meanwhile, Hayes's Uncle Sardis became a wealthy banker and paid for a private education for Hayes beginning at age nine. Before then, Hayes had been a sickly child. An excellent student, Hayes went on to Kenyon College in Ohio, where he graduated first in his class in 1842. He began studying law at a firm in Columbus, Ohio, before moving on to Harvard Law School. After graduating from Harvard in 1845, Hayes returned to Ohio and began a practice in East Sandusky with the help of his uncle.

Hayes was not as dedicated to practicing law as he was to his hobbies. He enjoyed travel and reading, particularly works of literature and natural science, and became a local leader in the successful campaign to change the name of the town from East Sandusky to Fremont. In 1846, at age twenty-four, he became friends with Lucy Webb, a bright fifteen-year-old who was allowed to study at the all-male Wesleyan College (now Ohio Wesleyan University). Her two older brothers attended the school, and Lucy had greatly impressed instructors there during a couple of class visits. Hayes met Lucy at a popular swimming spot on the campus. He later recalled in a diary entry that she was a "bright, sunny-hearted little girl, not quite old enough to fall in love with."

Hayes moved to Cincinnati, Ohio, in 1849 and became more focused on law. He also paid a visit to the Webb family, who had moved to Cincinnati so the brothers could attend medical school and Lucy could complete her education at Wesleyan Female Academy. Hayes began courting Lucy, who by then had turned eighteen. They were married in 1852 and would have eight children.

Becomes politically active

Hayes had a thriving law practice in Cincinnati. He began defending runaway slaves who were pursued into Ohio by slave masters, as allowed by the Fugitive Slave Law that was part of the Compromise of 1850. Hayes joined the Republican Party, which was formed in 1854 to attract those who opposed the expansion of slavery or who wanted the institution completely abolished. Beginning in 1858, Hayes served as a lawyer for the Cincinnati City Council, and in 1860 he worked with the campaign of Republican nominee Abraham Lincoln (1809–1865; served 1861-65), who won the presidential election that year.

When the Civil War (1861–65) began, Hayes organized a small group of men and led them in military drills. He was soon appointed major of the Twenty-third Ohio Infantry (foot soldiers). Hayes proved to be an excellent military leader and a brave soldier. He led nine companies of soldiers to safety after they were overwhelmed in a surprise attack in Parisburg, Virginia. He commanded a military unit that held its ground against an attack led by Confederate War general **Robert E. Lee** (1807–1870; see Confederate Leaders entry). Hayes was severely wounded in the battle and needed several weeks to heal. Lucy Hayes traveled hundreds of miles to be with her husband. She became a nurse for Union soldiers, who commonly called her "Mother Lucy." Hayes was wounded four more times during the war, but he was still fighting when it ended in April 1865. At the end of the war, he was leading an assault on Confederate troops in Lynchburg, Virginia.

Hayes's bravery was well known in Cincinnati from reports in local newspapers. Even while Hayes was on the battlefield, he was nominated by the Ohio Republican Party to run for Congress. He replied to a request to return home for the election by writing, "I have other business just now." Nevertheless, he easily won election in a district that had previously been a stronghold of Democrats.

Hayes took office after the end of the war in 1865. He supported the Republican Reconstruction policy and headed a committee that secured funds to expand the collection of science books in the Library of Congress. After serving two terms in the U.S. House of Representatives, Hayes was elected governor of Ohio, a position for which he also served two terms. During his tenure, Ohio enjoyed prosperity and Ohio State University was established.

Hayes planned to retire from public life after his second term as governor, but he was convinced by Republicans to return to Congress. Hayes lost his election bid in 1872 and retired from politics at the age of fifty. He and his family moved to Fremont, Ohio, to live with his uncle, Sardis Birchard. When Birchard died in 1874, Hayes inherited his uncle's wealth and mansion, called Spiegel Grove.

Controversial election

The growing strength of the Democratic Party in Northern states led Ohio Republicans to urge Hayes to run for governor again in 1875. His victory in the election brought national attention, and many Republicans touted him as a presidential candidate for the 1876 election. As a popular and brave Civil War veteran from a key state and having moderate political views, Hayes was acceptable to all factions (groups) of the party. The Republican Party national convention was held in Cincinnati that summer. Hayes's supporters packed the convention area. U.S. representative James G. Blaine (1830–1893) of Maine was favored to win the nomination, but Hayes became the nominee after seven rounds of balloting.

Hayes was opposed in the election by New York governor **Samuel J. Tilden** (1814–1886; see entry). Tilden had a reputation for fighting corruption, an important quality for a candidate to succeed President **Ulysses S. Grant** (1822–1885; served 1869–77; see entry), whose administration was implicated in many scandals. The election was close: The victor needed 185 electoral votes, and Tilden led Hayes 184–165. However, there were problems with returns from four states, totaling twenty electoral votes; Hayes needed to win all four states, and Tilden only one. The three Southern states—Florida, Louisiana, and South Carolina—were under Reconstruction governments (state governments under federal supervision) administered by Republicans. Those states each sent two sets of election returns to Congress, one with Hayes as the winner, another sent by local officials, all of whom were Democrats, that had Tilden as the winner. The Oregon situation, meanwhile, was complicated by the revelation that a presidential elector held a federal office, which violated the Constitution. (See box for more on the Electoral College).

The controversy over the election of 1876 would drag on for months. Democrats were sure Tilden had won, but Republicans were certain that voter fraud and intimidation had

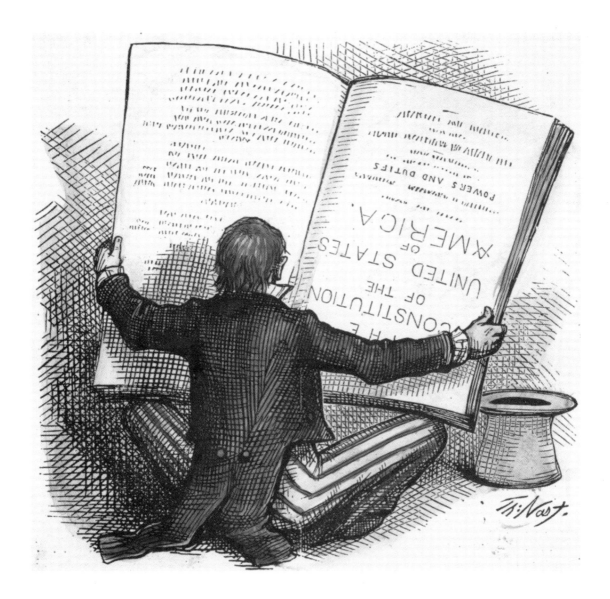

occurred in Louisiana, Florida, and South Carolina. Holding power in those states, Republicans dismissed results counted by Democrats and declared Hayes the winner (and other state Republican candidates were declared winners as well).

Because of the dispute, a bipartisan (neither wholly Democrat nor Republican) majority in Congress voted to create a special electoral commission to determine which sets of votes should count. The commission was intended to be politically balanced: it consisted of five senators (three Republi-

A Thomas Nast editorial cartoon shows a perplexed Uncle Sam trying to read an upside-down copy of the U.S. Constitution in an attempt to resolve the disputed Hayes-Tilden election of 1876. *The Granger Collection, New York. Reproduced by permission.*

How the Electoral College Works

When the U.S. Constitution was being drafted, delegates devised the Electoral College as a way to entrust the responsibility to the people for electing presidents. The delegates agreed that an election based on the popular vote could easily be influenced by partisan politics. They were also concerned that voters in one state might not be well informed about a candidate from another state.

Since 1961, the total of state and District of Columbia electors has been 538; a simple majority of 270 is necessary for election. The presidential candidate who receives the most votes in a particular state wins all of that state's electoral votes (except for Maine and Nebraska, where electoral votes are awarded for winning a congressional district). The number of electors in each state is equal to the total number of senators and representatives it sends to the U.S. Congress.

Presidential electors are designated by each state legislature. Following a general election on the first Tuesday after the first Monday of November every four years, the electors meet to officially record the state's electoral votes. They meet simultaneously in all the states on the first Monday after the second Wednesday in December of presidential election years. On January 6, their votes are counted in the presence of both houses of Congress.

cans and two Democrats), five representatives (two Republicans and three Democrats), four associate justices of the Supreme Court (two Republicans and two Democrats), and one associate judge to be chosen by the four associate judges already selected. It was widely assumed that the fifth judge was to be David Davis (1815–1886), an independent. But he was elected to a vacant U.S. Senate seat in Illinois and turned down the commission appointment. Joseph P. Bradley (1813–1892) was chosen in his place—a Republican, but one whose record was acceptable to Democrats as well.

The controversy lasted three-and-a-half months. The committee's final votes on the winners in the disputed states went strictly along party lines; eight Republicans voted Hayes the winner, and seven Democrats voted Tilden the winner. By taking the electoral votes of the four remaining states, Hayes was officially declared winner of the 1876 presidential election on March 2, 1877, two days before he was to take the oath of office.

Ends Reconstruction

In addition to entering office under a cloud of election controversy and facing the anger of Democrats in Congress, Hayes had limited support within his own party. He had narrowly won the party nomination for president at a divided convention. Nevertheless, Hayes governed effectively. He made strong choices for his cabinet members and immediately tackled the major issue of civil service reform. Government jobs had been routinely awarded to people based on political loyalty, instead of skills. Often, the civil servants spent work time on political causes.

Hayes went after the biggest of these so-called "political machines," the New York Customhouse, which collected huge amounts of tax money. The investigation revealed that the Customhouse was overstaffed, and many of its employees did little work. Hayes was successful in getting mild reforms instituted at the Customhouse.

Hayes then turned his attention to the South, where racial problems and political dominance by Democrats were rampant (numerous and chaotic) a decade since the end of the Civil War and the beginning of the Reconstruction era. Two Southern states, Louisiana and South Carolina, still had Reconstruction governments and federal troops to maintain order. Hayes was able to solve disputes between Republicans and Democrats over the governorships of South Carolina and Louisiana. The Democrat stepped aside in South Carolina, and Hayes responded by removing federal troops and ending Reconstruction in the state. A similar arrangement occurred in Louisiana.

 Victory for Hayes

The election of 1876 was held in November. Nearly four months later, Rutherford B. Hayes was declared the winner. A special election commission made up of fifteen members voted 8-7 that Hayes was entitled to electoral votes not yet counted. Those votes provided Hayes with a one-vote margin over his challenger, Samuel J. Tilden. Hayes won the presidency and earned the nickname "Old 8 to 7."

On Saturday, March 3, 1877, one day before the end of the presidency of Ulysses S. Grant, Hayes attended a dinner with Grant and Supreme Court Chief Justice Morrison R. Waite (1816–1888). The inauguration was set for the next day, a Sunday, but Hayes refused to violate the Sabbath (a religious vow to refrain from work on a holy day), even to be inaugurated president of the United States. After dinner, Hayes was sworn into office by Judge Waite. On Monday, March 5, 1877, Hayes reaffirmed the presidential oath of office in a public ceremony.

Hayes went on a tour in September 1877 to Kentucky, Tennessee, Georgia, and Virginia. He was received warmly by local political and business leaders. In Atlanta, Georgia, he made a public speech on the end of Reconstruction: "[Here] we are, Republicans, Democrats, colored people, white people, Confederate soldiers, and Union soldiers, all of one mind and one heart today! And why should we not be? What is there to separate us any longer?" Despite the hopeful words of the president, racial problems persisted and Democrats dominated the region, in some cases by force and violence.

Meanwhile, Hayes addressed other issues. A weak economy since 1873 had hurt farmers as well as workers in urban areas. Strikes began against the railroad industry, interfering with traffic and construction. The Hayes administration worked as impartially as possible, and strikes were slowly resolved. To help ensure economic stability, Hayes insisted on paying off the national debt. He fought soft money measures passed by the Congress (where money would be printed without its value being backed by gold), which included coining silver as well as gold. Hayes consistently vetoed soft money measures in order to maintain stability in the currency. Congress was only successful once, the 1878 Bland-Allison Act, in overriding Hayes's veto. By then, Hayes's policies had helped turn around economic hard times, and Hayes left behind a good economy when he left office in 1881.

Hayes encountered issues relating to Chinese immigrants and Native Americans. Westerners, particularly in California, feared that Chinese laborers would take jobs away from them. As part of an anti-Chinese backlash in California, a constitutional convention was called to revise the state's constitution. Chinese people, as well as the mentally challenged, mentally ill, and criminals were not allowed to vote, and Chinese were prohibited from public jobs in the state. The laws were struck down, but Congress enacted legislation to limit Chinese immigration. Hayes vetoed the bill. Instead, the Hayes administration negotiated a treaty with China that included a provision through which the United States could regulate, limit, and suspend Chinese immigration, but not prohibit it. In return, the United States pledged not to be a part of the opium (a highly addictive drug) trade into China and prohibited China from importing opium into the United States. The treaty was not approved until Hayes left office, and then Congress moved to suspend Chinese immigration to the United States for ten years anyway.

Relations with Native Americans during Hayes's term were unsettling. The Battle of Little Big Horn, where U.S. general George A. Custer (1839–1876) and his regiment were soundly defeated, occurred in 1876. During Hayes's first year in office, U.S. forces defeated the Sioux and the Nez Percé tribes. Committing to better treatment of Native Americans, the Hayes administration reformed the Indian Bureau (now

A political cartoon from *Puck* magazine shows President Rutherford B. Hayes vetoing a congressional anti-immigration bill limiting Chinese immigration. A vocal supporter of the bill, Denis Kearney, the secretary of the Workingmen's Trade and Labor Union of San Francisco, is shown being symbolically cut from the United States following Hayes's veto. © *Corbis.*

Bureau of Indian Affairs). In general, official relations between the U.S. government and Native American tribes improved, but the Hayes approach of acculturation (encouraging an ethnic group to abandon its conventional behavior to join a larger culture) found little success.

In foreign policy, Hayes faced few issues. Most notably, Hayes made it a policy that the United States would be involved and would police a proposed canal across Central

America. Such a canal had been proposed for decades. In 1881, a French company began working on a canal but stopped because of health problems among the crew and lack of funds. The Panama Canal would finally be built in the first decade of the twentieth century.

Meanwhile, the Hayes family enjoyed life in the White House. The couple had eight children born between 1852 and 1872, five of whom survived to adulthood. Lucy Hayes was known as a good singer, and the family kept many cats, birds, and dogs. The couple celebrated their twenty-fifth wedding anniversary while in the White House. As with all social occasions, however, no alcohol was served. Lucy Hayes was a member of the temperance movement that believed in abstinence from alcohol. She was nicknamed Lemonade Lucy for her antialcohol stance while in the White House.

Legacy

Hayes had promised to serve only one term as president and there was little outcry for him to change his mind. He governed during a period when Congress had assumed political power over the presidency for shaping national policy—the period of Reconstruction onward to 1885. Nevertheless, Hayes had served the nation well, with integrity and quiet accomplishments. He was not successful in securing better race relations, but the problem was more national in scope: Whites were reasserting authority in the South after Reconstruction ended, settlers were eroding Native American territories in the west, and Californians were limiting opportunities to Asians. The economy was strengthened during his term.

Before leaving office, Hayes and his wife took a cross-country journey, visiting New Mexico territory and going on to California, then north to Washington. To make the journey, the Hayeses used railroad, steamship, stagecoach, army ambulance, ferryboat, and yacht. After leaving office at age fifty-eight, Hayes retired to Fremont, Ohio. Hayes and his wife remained active at the local level in issues relating to higher education, prison reform, and assistance to Civil War veterans. Hayes died on January 17, 1893, and is buried alongside his wife at the Rutherford B. Hayes Presidential Center in Fremont.

For More Information

Books

Davison, Kenneth E. *The Presidency of Rutherford B. Hayes.* Westport, CT: Greenwood Press, 1972.

Hoogenboom, Ari Arthur. *The Presidency of Rutherford B. Hayes.* Lawrence: University Press of Kansas, 1988.

Otfinoski, Steven. *Rutherford B. Hayes: America's 19th President.* New York: Children's Press, 2004.

Robbins, Neal E. *Rutherford B. Hayes, 19th President of the United States.* Ada, OK: Garrett Educational Corporation, 1989.

Simpson, Brooks D. *The Reconstruction Presidents.* Lawrence: University Press of Kansas, 1998.

Williams, Charles Richard. *The Life of Rutherford Birchard Hayes.* New York: Da Capo Press, 1971.

Woodward, C. Vann. *Reunion and Reaction: The Compromise of 1877 and the End of Reconstruction.* Boston: Little, Brown, 1951. Reprint, New York: Oxford University Press, 1991.

Web Sites

"Diary and Letters of Rutherford B. Hayes." *Ohio Historical Center.* http://www.ohiohistory.org/onlinedoc/hayes/index.cfm (accessed on July 23, 2004).

The Rutherford B. Hayes Presidential Center. http://www.rbhayes.org/ (accessed on July 23, 2004).

Julia Ward Howe

Born May 27, 1819
New York City, New York

Died October 17, 1910
Newport, Rhode Island

Writer and lecturer; activist for abolition, women's rights, and peace

"The new domain now made clear to me was that of true womanhood—woman no longer in her ancillary relation to her opposite, man, but in her direct relation to the divine plan and purpose, as a free agent, fully sharing with man every human right and every human responsibility."

Julia Ward Howe is perhaps best known as the writer of "The Battle Hymn of the Republic" (1862), which became the unofficial song of the Union army during the American Civil War (1861–65). However, Howe was equally significant during her lifetime as an activist for abolition (ending slavery), women's rights, peace, and prison reform. She was a founding member of the American Woman Suffrage Association, a leading organization for promoting voting rights for women. A noted lecturer and author, Howe was the first woman elected to the prestigious American Academy of Arts and Letters.

From a distinguished family

Born in New York City in 1819, Howe was the second daughter and fourth of seven children of Samuel Ward, a prominent banker, and Julia Rush (Cutler) Ward, a published poet. The Ward family roots included two descendants who served as governor of Rhode Island when it was still a colony. Howe's grandfather was a distinguished officer during the American Revolution (1775–83).

Howe became interested in poetry and art at an early age, thanks in part to a home with an art gallery and a large library. Howe's mother died at the age of twenty-eight shortly after giving birth to her seventh child when Howe was five years old. A witty and loving aunt helped care for the Ward children. Howe was tutored at home and at private schools in Latin, French, literature, science, and mathematics, and she received music and voice training. She began learning Italian at age fourteen, and then studied German and Greek as well. Howe would continue to read literature, history, and philosophy throughout her life. By the time Howe was twenty, she had had literary reviews and essays published anonymously in magazines such as the *Literary and Theological Review* and the *New York Review.*

Howe began attending social gatherings in New York City during her late teens after her brother, Samuel Ward Jr., married Emily Astor of the wealthy Astor family in 1837. Howe was petite—just over five feet tall—with blue eyes and red hair. She enjoyed parties and conversation, but when Howe's father died shortly after she turned twenty, she fell into great sadness. To help ease her grief, she visited friends in Boston in 1841. Among her acquaintances was noted poet Henry Wadsworth Longfellow (1807–1882), a longtime friend of her brother, Samuel. In Boston, Howe also met other significant writers of the day, including Ralph Waldo Emerson (1803–1882) and Margaret Fuller (1810–1850), who had recently begun publishing a major new literary magazine called *The Dial.*

The deepest soul of the writer

Howe accompanied Longfellow and his friend **Charles Sumner** (1811–1874; see entry), who would later become an important U.S. senator from Massachusetts, on a visit to the New England Institute for the Blind to meet Laura Bridgman (1829–1889), an extraordinary blind and deaf student. While the group was out on the grounds of the Institute, the school's director, Dr. Samuel Gridley Howe (1801–1876), rode up on a black horse ("a noble rider on a noble steed," Howe would write later of the encounter in *Memoir of Dr. Samuel Gridley Howe … with Other Memorial Trib-*

Samuel Gridley Howe, husband of Julia Ward Howe and director of the New England Institute for the Blind. © *Bettmann/Corbis.*

utes, 1876). A friend of Longfellow and Sumner, Dr. Howe was a famous educator, physician, and reformer, and had been a military hero in the Greek War for Independence during the 1820s, where he earned the title, "Chevalier of the Order of St. Savior." The twenty-two-year-old Howe was immediately attracted to the tall and handsome forty-year-old bachelor.

The couple first appeared together in public in 1842 at a farewell dinner in Boston for Charles Dickens (1812–1870), the famous English author who had been touring the United States. Shortly after the dinner, the couple announced their engagement. They were married on April 23, 1843, and went on a long honeymoon journey to Europe, visiting England, Germany, and France before making an extended stay in Italy. Their first child was born in 1844 in Rome. The Howes would have six children, one of whom died in early childhood. The Howes' marriage was difficult—some say violent—at times, stemming from the couple's different personalities: Dr. Howe was studious, focused on work, and expected his wife to be content as a homemaker and hostess; Julia Ward Howe was a witty conversationalist who enjoyed writing and a lively social scene. Their Boston home, which Howe named "Green Peace," was part of a social environment of philosophers, writers, and social reformers.

While carrying on domestic duties and bearing five children between 1844 to 1856, Howe began receiving attention as a writer. In 1848, she had poems published in two anthologies (collections of writings by various authors). Though her husband frowned at her writing, he teamed with Howe to publish and edit a newspaper called *The Commonwealth*. The periodical featured stories and editorials that argued for the abolition of slavery, and Howe contributed reviews and essays on books. The newspaper remained in circulation up to the outbreak of the Civil War in 1861. During the late 1850s, the

Howe home was a safe haven for fugitive slaves who were fleeing to freedom in Canada. The Fugitive Slave Law, passed in 1851, allowed slave owners to pursue and apprehend runaway slaves in nonslave states.

Meanwhile, Howe's first volume of poetry, *Passion Flowers,* was published anonymously in 1854. In a review in the *New York Tribune,* George Ripley called the poems "a product wrung with tears and prayer from the deepest soul of the writer." A second collection of Howe's poems, *Words for the Hour,"* was published in 1857. A play, *The World's Own,* was published and performed in 1857, and a collection of Howe's travel sketches, called "A Trip to Cuba," appeared in 1860 in issues of the *New York Tribune* and were published as a book later that year.

"Mine eyes have seen the glory"

Following the outbreak of the Civil War in 1861, Dr. Howe became a leader of the United States Sanitary Commission, which worked to maintain clean living conditions for soldiers in camps and in hospitals. Julia Ward Howe joined the women's auxiliary unit of the commission. During the early part of the war, more soldiers died from disease caused by unsanitary conditions in prisoner of war camps and their own army camps than in battle. The Sanitary Commission successfully curtailed the problems in the camps.

In November 1861, the Howes traveled to Washington, D.C., on duty with the commission. They joined a group that was to tour a Union military camp outside the city, but they had to turn back when the camp was attacked in a Confederate raid. During the return carriage ride, the group sang "John Brown's Body," a popular song of the time. With the song's melody in her mind and inspired by her religious fervor for abolition—Howe viewed slavery as morally wrong—Howe arose from bed the next morning and wrote the verses that would form "The Battle Hymn of the Republic" on stationery of the United States Sanitary Commission. First published as a poem in the February 1862 issue of the *Atlantic Monthly* (for which she was paid $4), "The Battle Hymn of the Republic" soon became famous throughout the Union.

On Composing "The Battle Hymn of the Republic"

Julia Ward Howe remembers how she composed "The Battle Hymn of the Republic" (as noted in her *Reminiscences, 1819–1899*).

> *In spite of the excitement of the day I went to bed and slept as usual, but awoke the next morning in the gray of the early dawn, and to my astonishment found that the wished-for lines were arranging themselves in my brain. I lay quite still until the last verse had completed itself in my thoughts, then hastily arose, saying to myself, I shall lose this if I don't write it down immediately. I searched for an old sheet of paper and an old stub of a pen which I had had the night before, and began to scrawl the lines almost without looking, as I learned to do by often scratching down verses in the darkened room when my little children were sleeping. Having completed this, I lay down again and fell asleep, but not before feeling that something of importance had happened to me.*

Sheet music for Julia Ward Howe's "Battle Hymn of the Republic."

In cadences of a Christian hymn, the poem expresses hope that the Lord will secure a Union victory. The Union army adopted the hymn as its unofficial song. The song endures in association with many causes Howe supported: it was adopted by the women's suffrage movement, by African American civil rights activists (many of whom were ancestors of slaves), and as a dirge (song of mourning) at funerals for civil rights supporters. It was sung at the memorial service for Howe at Symphony Hall in Boston in 1910 and at the funeral of U.S. senator Robert F. Kennedy (1925–1968) of New York, who was assassinated while campaigning for president in 1968 and who had been the leading civil rights proponent in the presidential administration of his brother, John F. Kennedy (1917–1963; served 1961–63).

During the Civil War years, Howe became active as a speaker in the Unitarian church. Unitarians are community-based and tolerant toward those of different faiths. In January 1864, Howe delivered a lecture while wearing a modest, black dress and a white lace cap; this would become her standard dress for lectures she gave in the United States and in Europe over the next thirty years.

Suffragette

Following the end of the Civil War in 1865 and passage of the Thirteenth Amendment to the U.S. Constitution, outlawing slavery that same year, Howe turned her attention to women's suffrage. She spoke before a legislative committee in the Boston State House, helped found in February 1868 the New England Woman's Club, and helped found the New England Woman Suffrage Association, which arranged a national conference in Cleveland, Ohio, in 1869. Howe was also a member of the American Woman Suffrage Association (AWSA) when it was formed.

The AWSA differed from a similar women' suffrage group, the National Woman Suffrage Association (NWSA), which was led by **Susan B. Anthony** (1820–1906; see entry) and Elizabeth Cady Stanton (1815–1902). Members of the NWSA worked on a larger number of social and political issues, but focused only on issues pertaining directly to women; membership was limited to women only. The AWSA encouraged men to join and supported the Fifteenth Amendment to the U.S. Constitution, which allowed African American male landowners the right to vote. Beginning in 1870, Howe contributed to the *Woman's Journal,* a periodical founded by her associate, Lucy Stone (1818–1893).

Howe's activism for women's rights was especially fulfilling for her. As she wrote later in *Reminiscences, 1819–1899,* "During the first two thirds of my life I looked to the masculine idea of character as the only true one. I sought its inspiration, and referred my merits and demerits to its judicial verdict…. The new domain now made clear to me was that of true womanhood—woman no longer in her ancillary relation to her opposite, man, but in her direct relation to the divine plan and purpose, as a free agent, fully sharing with man every human right and every human responsibility. This discovery was like the addition of a new continent to the map of the world, or of a new testament to the old ordinances."

Activist for many causes

During the 1870s, Howe became an advocate for peace, primarily as a lecturer and preacher within the Unitarian church. In September 1870, she issued an "Appeal to Womanhood throughout the World," calling for a general congress of women to promote the alliance of different nationalities. The document was translated and published in French, Spanish, Italian, German, and Swedish. At a December 1870 meeting in New York to arrange for the "World's Congress of Women in behalf of International Peace," Howe made the opening address. The American branch of the Woman's International Peace Association was formed in 1871 with Howe as president. However, she was unsuccessful in the spring of 1872 in her attempts to arrange a peace conference to be held in London, England. Nevertheless, while in England, she served as a delegate at a prison reform congress. In 1872, Howe initiated a Mothers' Peace Day observance on the second Sunday in June, which continued to be an annual event for several years and was a forerunner of Mother's Day. Among other activities, Howe hosted conventions of ministers to bring people of different denominations together, and she traveled with her husband on trips to Santo Domingo in 1873 and 1875 to preach in a small Protestant church.

Howe's husband died in 1876. Shortly before his death, he confessed to a number of adulterous affairs, and the two managed to put aside their differences. Their marriage had often been strained, but Dr. Howe had come to respect his wife's activism, if not actively support it. Howe published a loving biography of her husband, *Memoir of Dr. Samuel Gridley Howe ... with Other Memorial Tributes,* that year. Howe went on an extensive lecture tour through the West and used the money she earned for a two-year trip to Europe and the Middle East with her youngest daughter, Maud. She published *Modern Society,* a collection of essays, in 1881, and the biography, *Margaret Fuller,* in 1883. She continued to preach frequently at her own Church of the Disciples and other Unitarian churches. In an address at the World Parliament of

Religions in Chicago, titled "What Is Religion?" she stated that true religions recognize the equality of men and women as well as people of all faiths.

In 1889, the two branches of the women's suffrage movement finally united, as Stanton and Anthony agreed with Howe to focus specifically on winning the right for women to vote. Together they formed the National American Woman's Suffrage Association. Howe published three more works during the 1890s: *Is Polite Society Polite?* (1895), a collection of essays; *From Sunset Ridge: Poems Old and New* (1898); and an autobiographical collection, *Reminiscences, 1819–1899* (1899).

When Howe died in 1910, her long-time role as an activist and writer was well known. In 1908, she was the first woman elected to the prestigious American Academy of Arts and Letters. Shortly before her death, Howe was awarded an honorary degree by Smith College. At the ceremony, Howe was hailed as "poet and patriot, lover of letters and learning; advocate for over half a century in print and living speech of great causes of human liberty."

For More Information

Books

Grant, Mary H. *Private Woman, Public Person: An Account of the Life of Julia Ward Howe from 1819–1868.* Brooklyn: Carlson Publishers, 1994.

Gray, Janet, ed. *She Wields a Pen: American Women Poets of the Nineteenth Century.* Iowa City: University of Iowa Press, 1997.

Howe, Julia Ward. *Reminiscences, 1819–1899.* Boston: Houghton, Mifflin, 1899.

Raum, Elizabeth. *Julia Ward Howe.* Chicago: Heinemann Library, 2004.

Richards, Laura E., and Maud Howe Elliott. *Julia Ward Howe, 1819 to 1910.* Boston and New York: Houghton Mifflin Company, 1915. Reprint, Atlanta: Cherokee, 1997.

Williams, Gary. *Hungry Heart: The Literary Emergence of Julia Ward Howe.* Amherst: University of Massachusetts Press, 1999.

Web Sites

"Julia Ward Howe." *Dictionary of Unitarian & Universalist Biography.* http://www.uua.org/uuhs/duub/articles/juliawardhowe.html (accessed on June 25, 2004).

"Julia Ward Howe." *Women's History.* http://womenshistory.about.com/library/bio/blbio_howe_julia_ward.htm (accessed on June 14, 2004).

"Julia Ward Howe: It's Time to Recognize This Woman's Extraordinary Deeds." *Seattle Times* (June 30, 2001). http://www.lightwatcher.com/old_lightbytes/howe_greatwoman.html (accessed on June 25, 2004).

Andrew Johnson

Born December 29, 1808
Raleigh, North Carolina

Died July 31, 1875
Carter's Station, Tennessee

President, politician, and tailor

A ndrew Johnson succeeded to the presidency after the assassination of Abraham Lincoln (1809–1865; served 1861–65) in April 1865, just a month into Lincoln's second term as president. Johnson was chosen by Lincoln to be his vice president as a symbolic gesture of uniting the nation during the Civil War (1861–65): Lincoln was a Republican from the North, Johnson a Democrat from the South. Johnson faced great challenges as president; the Civil War was over and the nation needed to be reunified and to respect the freedom of emancipated slaves. But Congress and Johnson held different views on Reconstruction (1865–77), the rebuilding of the United States after the Civil War. Those differences would frustrate Johnson, whose presidential power was overshadowed by Congress and who faced impeachment and removal from office for defying Congress. Johnson survived removal by one vote.

"[Most,] if not all, of our domestic troubles are directly traceable to violations of the organic law and excessive legislation. The most striking illustrations of this fact are furnished by the enactments of the past three years upon the question of reconstruction."

From poverty to shop owner at eighteen

Andrew Johnson was born on December 29, 1808, in a cottage in Raleigh, North Carolina. He was the youngest of

Andrew Johnson. *The Library of Congress.*

two sons of Jacob and Mary Johnson. Johnson's father worked many odd jobs to provide for his family, including porter (one who carries suitcases for guests) and waiter at an inn and janitor at a bank. He served in the local militia (a citizen military force) and as a sexton (a minor church official) of the community's Presbyterian Church. Shortly after Johnson turned three, his father died from complications that began after he dove into a pond to save two men from drowning. Already poor, the family scraped along on the money Mary Johnson earned by sewing, weaving, and washing.

Johnson never attended school and no one in the family could read. By age ten, he began working for a tailor, responsible for cleaning shop and learning the skills of a tailor. By his early teens, Johnson had acquired tailoring skills and had learned the basics of reading and writing. It was common for shop owners to keep their workers entertained by having someone read to them while they worked. A local minister read to the tailors in the shop where Johnson worked, and he spent some extra time teaching Johnson how to read and write.

Johnson and his brother left Raleigh in 1824, when Johnson was fifteen, after being involved in some mischief. They wandered over the state border into Tennessee and found work as tailors in the town of Greeneville. Johnson returned to Raleigh in 1826 to convince his mother and his step-father to join him in Greeneville. Johnson seized an opportunity the following year, at the age of eighteen: The best tailor left town, and Johnson opened up a small shop of his own, called A. Johnson, Tailor.

When Johnson first entered Greeneville, he caught the eye of Eliza McCardle, then fourteen years old. They married three years later, on May 17, 1827. Eliza Johnson helped her husband improve his skills in reading, writing, and math. They would have five children: Martha, Charles, Mary, Robert, and Andrew Jr.

Hangout for political discussions

Johnson worked hard and took pride in his labors. Outspoken for the rights and values of common people, he joined a debating society, and his tailor shop became a lively place for political discussions. With a strong speaking voice and strong opinions on issues of importance to working-class people, Johnson was elected as an alderman (town council position) in 1828. Two years later, he became mayor of Greeneville and served in this capacity until 1833, managing his growing tailor business at the same time.

During the period from 1828 to 1838, political power in the United States shifted from large landowners to people of more humble means. Their national hero was President Andrew Jackson (1767–1845; served 1829–1837), who was also a former U.S. senator and representative from Tennessee. Jackson's Democratic Party came to prominence, and Johnson became a member of the party. He was elected to the Tennessee House of Representatives and served from 1835 to 1837.

Johnson failed to win reelection in 1837 and learned an important lesson. He had voted against a road improvement bill, based on his belief that government should be limited and should resist raising taxes to fund projects. The people of eastern Tennessee whom Johnson represented wanted improved roads. Johnson dropped his ideological opposition (a position based on one's ideals) in order to fight for what was best for the people. He was elected again to the Tennessee House of Representatives in 1839. Johnson fought vigorously for laborers of eastern Tennessee against more wealthy slave owners in the state. He was elected to the state senate in 1841. Johnson failed in efforts to repeal a state law that favored slaveholders over other landowners.

Johnson was elected to the U.S. House of Representatives in 1843 at the age of thirty-four and served for ten years. His most notable action as a congressman came in 1846 when he proposed the nation's first homestead legislation. His homestead bill, which failed to pass in the U.S. Senate, would have set aside inexpensive plots of land on the western frontier where small farmers could establish homes and livelihoods. Though the bill failed at the time, the Homestead Act of 1862 that became law was modeled closely on Johnson's original proposal. Johnson's original proposal failed during the 1840s when there was fear in the U.S. Senate that opening up the West would feed the expansion of slavery to new territories and states. In 1862, the Civil War was being fought and Congress and President Lincoln were anxious to push the legislation under the assumption that expansion of slavery was no longer an issue.

In 1853, Johnson was elected for the first of two terms as governor of Tennessee. He supported and signed into law bills that created the state's first public school system, a state library, and a system of agricultural and mechanical fairs to share information on developments in industry and agriculture. In 1857, Johnson was elected to the U.S. Senate; soon thereafter, he renewed his efforts for a homestead bill. In an argumentative legislature, Southern Democrats opposed the bill as they voted in a bloc against any bill that might undermine their protection of slavery. But Johnson was not a crusader against slavery; he wanted to provide more opportunities for people who could not afford to have slaves.

Johnson supported the Democratic Party in the elections of 1860. When Republican Abraham Lincoln was elected on an antislavery platform, many Southern states seceded (separated) from the Union and formed their own government, called the Confederacy. Tennessee did not secede until the Confederacy fired on the federal government's Fort Sumter in South Carolina, which started the Civil War. As Tennesseans debated whether or not to join the Confederacy, Johnson campaigned against leaving the Union. He was committed to the United States and the Constitution. When citizens voted to join the Confederacy, Johnson had to leave the state, and then Confederate authorities forced his wife and children to leave as well. Johnson was the only Southern senator not to resign his seat in Congress.

Johnson becomes president

In 1862, Johnson was appointed brigadier general by Lincoln to serve as military governor of Tennessee. (A military governor is the head government official of an area that has been taken over in a military action.) Johnson restored order in the state: His administration collected taxes, dismissed officials unwilling to take the federal oath of allegiance, shut down Confederate newspapers, and arrested pro-Confederate ministers and fighters.

When Lincoln ran for reelection in 1864, he wanted to appeal to Northern Democrats and Southern Unionists (those that remained in the Union) as well as Republicans. For the election, the Republican Party's name was changed to the National Union Party, and Johnson, a Southern Unionist Democrat, ran as vice president with Lincoln, a Republican. When the Lincoln-Johnson ticket won, it marked only the second time that the nation's president and vice president came from different parties. (President John Adams [1735–1826] and Vice President Thomas Jefferson [1743–1826] were the first.)

Johnson had a brief, but very difficult, time as vice president. On inauguration day (the day he was sworn in as vice president), he was suffering from a fever and drank some alcohol to fight his fever. When called on to make a speech, his words were slurred and his speech was disorganized. The incident damaged his reputation and led to persistent rumors that Johnson had a drinking problem. However, no historical evidence suggests that Johnson was an alcoholic or that his performance at the inaugural was more than an isolated incident.

As vice president, Johnson only discussed issues with Lincoln on one occasion—briefly, on the day Lincoln was later shot by an assassin. Lincoln died the next morning, only a month into his second term. Johnson was sworn into the office of president on April 15, 1865, by Salmon P. Chase (1808–1873), Chief Justice of the Supreme Court. Johnson faced formidable issues: The Civil War was over and the nation needed to be reunified; Congress was led by a group known as the Radical Republicans, with key U.S. senators **Thaddeus Stevens** (1792–1868; see entry) and **Charles Sumner** (1811–1874), who were intent on punishing the former Confederacy and aggressively pursuing civil rights for freed slaves; and Congress believed it had the authority to set the terms of Reconstruction. Believing the president, not Congress, should lead the Reconstruction effort, Johnson prepared to forge ahead before the next session of Congress began in December.

Believing in a limited federal government, Johnson wanted to reestablish state governments in the South as quickly as possible. After assuming the presidency, Johnson announced his Reconstruction plan: Former Confederate states

Congress in Charge

Passed in 1867 by Congress over President Johnson's veto, the Tenure of Office Act concerned federal officials appointed by the president that required confirmation by the Senate. Under the Tenure of Office Act, such officials could not be removed from their position by the president without the consent of the Senate. If the Senate was not in session, the president could suspend an official, but once the Senate reconvened it had to approve the removal or the official would have to be reinstated by the president.

The Tenure of Office Act was one of several actions by Congress during Johnson's administration that enhanced the authority of Congress at the expense of the presidency. Historians generally regard the period from 1865 to 1885 as an era when Congress was more powerful than the president. The powers of the two branches of government became more balanced in 1885, during the presidency of Grover Cleveland (1837–1908; served 1885–89, 1893–97), when the Tenure of Office Act was repealed. Cleveland won back some of the prestige of the presidency, and two of his successors, William McKinley (1843–1901; served 1897–1901) and Theodore Roosevelt (1858–1919; served 1901–9) were powerful presidents.

had to ratify the Thirteenth Amendment to the Constitution (which included the abolishment, or destruction, of slavery), renounce Confederate debts, and nullify (invalidate) secession ordinances. When states met those conditions, Johnson, as the temporary wartime authority, would recognize their restoration to the Union. Several states quickly met the obligations proposed by Johnson. When Congress returned in December 1865, the battle between the executive and legislative branches over Reconstruction became one of the worst struggles between the executive and legislative branches in the nation's history.

Congress versus Johnson

Congress immediately halted Johnson's Reconstruction plan and refused to seat congressmen who had been elected from former Confederate states. Many in Congress were concerned about protecting the civil rights of freedmen (former slaves now emancipated). Johnson believed that Congress was overstepping its bounds. He vetoed civil rights legislation—citing such legislation as a matter for states, not the federal government—and refused to endorse a new constitutional amendment granting African Americans rights of citizenship. The remainder of Johnson's term was a bitter and losing struggle. Congress succeeded in controlling Reconstruction and passed laws that limited presidential authority, including the Tenure of Office Act (see box).

As Congress continued to lead the Reconstruction policy, Johnson made angry public speeches about the federal

President Andrew Johnson speaks about his Reconstruction plans from a railroad car platform. *The Library of Congress.*

legislature and actively campaigned for congressional candidates who supported his view in 1866. However, Republicans made even more congressional gains in 1866. Congress passed the Reconstruction Act of 1867 that placed military governments in former Confederate states and required those states to pass the Fourteenth Amendment to the Constitution to begin the process of returning to the Union (see box).

Johnson, meanwhile, decided to test the Tenure of Office Act during the summer of 1867, when Congress was not in session. Johnson's secretary of war, **Edwin Stanton** (1814–1869; see entry), supported the Reconstruction policies of Republicans in Congress. Johnson wanted to remove Stanton from office. Since Stanton had been appointed by Abraham Lincoln, had been confirmed by the Senate as a Lincoln appointee, and remained in his position when Johnson succeeded Lincoln, Johnson believed the Tenure of Office Act did not apply since he had not appointed Stanton. In August 1867, Johnson asked for Stanton's resignation. When Stanton

The Fourteenth Amendment to the U.S. Constitution

The Fourteenth Amendment to the Constitution set the terms for former Confederate states being readmitted into the Union. The states had to approve the Fourteenth Amendment as part of the process for reentering the Union. Reprinted below are three sections meant to apply specifically to states that had formerly allowed slavery.

Section 1. All persons born or naturalized in the United States and subject to the jurisdiction thereof, are citizens of the United States and of the State wherein they reside. No State shall make or enforce any law which shall abridge the privileges or immunities of citizens of the United States; nor shall any State deprive any person of life, liberty, or property, without due process of law; nor deny to any person within its jurisdiction the equal protection of the laws....

Section 3. No person shall be a Senator or Representative in Congress, or elector of President and Vice President, or hold any office, civil or military, under the United States, or under any State, who, having previously taken an oath, as a member of Congress, or as an officer of the United States, or as a member of any State legislature, or as an executive or judicial officer of any State, to support the Constitution of the United States, shall have engaged in insurrection or rebellion against the same, or given aid or comfort to the enemies thereof. But Congress may by a vote of two-thirds of each House, remove such disability.

Section 4. The validity of the public debt of the United States, authorized by law, including debts incurred for payment of pensions and bounties for services in suppressing insurrection or rebellion, shall not be questioned. But neither the United States nor any State shall assume or pay any debt or obligation incurred in aid of insurrection or rebellion against the United States, or any claim for the loss or emancipation of any slave; but all such debts, obligations and claims shall be held illegal and void.

refused, Johnson suspended him from office, ordering Stanton to cease all exercise of authority, and transferred his power to **Ulysses S. Grant** (1822–1885; see entry), the Civil War hero whom Johnson wanted as his new secretary of war.

After Congress reconvened in January 1868, the Senate voted 35-16 to overrule Johnson on Stanton's removal. Johnson, in turn, refused to accept the Senate's decision and called the Tenure of Office Act an unconstitutional infringement on the power of the president. The House of Representatives immediately began impeachment hearings against Johnson (see box for a description of the impeachment process).

Hearings on grounds for impeaching Johnson began in a few days. The House of Representatives approved eleven articles of impeachment against Johnson for actions related to

The Impeachment Process

Framers of the Constitution wanted to address actions that warranted removal of a federal official from office. Those actions fall under the category of treason, bribery, and "high crimes and misdemeanors."

Impeachment proceedings against a president begin when the House of Representatives votes to begin an investigation into actions that are considered impeachable as defined by the Constitution. The investigation committee reports its findings and recommendations to the House Judiciary Committee. The Committee drafts and approves Articles of Impeachment: Each article discusses a specific impeachable offense. The entire House of Representatives then votes on whether or not to approve each article. Two-thirds majority is needed to approve impeachment. If the House approves any of the articles, the president is considered impeached and must face trial in the U.S. Senate. Presidents are defended by their lawyers, while cases against presidents are argued by Managers—a group of Representatives that are selected to represent Congress. The Senate trial is presided over in the Senate by the Chief Justice of the Supreme Court.

After House Managers and the president's defense lawyers have argued their cases, the U.S. Senate votes on the guilt or innocence of the president based on the Articles of Impeachment and the definition of impeachable offenses in the Constitution. If two-thirds of the Senate vote guilty, the president is removed from office. If less than two-thirds vote guilty, the president remains in office.

his attempt to remove Secretary of War Stanton from office and for remarks he made in speeches in Cleveland, Ohio, and St. Louis, Missouri, where he defamed Congress. Article X of the Articles of Impeachment describes Johnson's public speeches against Congress: "utterances, declarations, threats and harangues [highly emotional speeches], highly censurable in any, are peculiarly indecent and unbecoming in the Chief Magistrate of the United States, by means whereof the said Andrew Johnson has brought the high office of the President of the United States into contempt, ridicule and disgrace, to the great scandal of all good citizens, whereby said Andrew Johnson, President of the United States, did commit, and was then and there guilty of a high misdemeanor in office."

During Johnson's impeachment trial in the Senate, the president's lawyers argued that Johnson's attempt to remove

U.S. House of Representatives impeachment committee of President Andrew Johnson in 1868: (seated, left to right) Benjamin F. Butler of Massachusetts, Thaddeus Stevens of Pennsylvania, Thomas Williams of Pennsylvania, and John A. Bingham of Ohio; (standing, left to right) James F. Wilson of Iowa, George S. Boutwell of Massachusetts, and John A. Logan of Illinois. *Photograph by Mathew Brady. © Corbis.*

Stanton was a test of the constitutionality of the Tenure of Office Act. They focused on the key issue that since Stanton had been appointed by President Lincoln, the Tenure of Office Act did not apply to Stanton's position under President Johnson.

When arguments were completed in Johnson's impeachment trial, the Senate voted first to determine whether each of the eleven articles were grounds for impeachment. The Senate voted against all but three of the articles. Concerned that they might not have the two-thirds majority to find Johnson guilty (needing 36 of 54 votes), Republican Senate leaders delayed the impeachment vote. When the Senate finally voted on the first of the articles, thirty-five senators voted guilty, one short of the majority needed to convict Johnson and remove him from office. After ten days and intense pressuring of Republicans who voted Johnson not guilty, the final two votes were taken, and they also ended 35-19, one short of the necessary two-thirds majority.

Johnson's legacy

Johnson's battles with Congress over Reconstruction and Congress's impeachment of Johnson are the most frequently reviewed events of Johnson's presidency. Those circumstances lead historians to rank Johnson among the least effective presidents though there were positive events during Johnson's presidency. Johnson's secretary of state, William Seward (1801–1872), negotiated the Alaska Purchase, where the United States bought the territory known then as Russian-America from Russia for just over $7 million. While some Americans ridiculed the purchase as "Seward's Folly" and viewed the area as a vast, icy wasteland, the purchase proved extremely valuable. Johnson was successful in challenging France over that nation's increasing involvement in Mexico. France had helped arm factions (small groups) loyal to a prince whom France wanted to become emperor of Mexico. Johnson sent a warning to France not to interfere with Mexican affairs, and France withdrew a military force.

Caricature of outgoing president Andrew Johnson dressed as a crying king, exclaiming, "Farewell, a long farewell, to all my greatness!" *The Library of Congress.*

Johnson's presidency did not end on a positive note. He was passed over for the Democratic nomination for president in the 1868 election and left office after making an often bitter Annual Address to Congress in December 1868. In the address, he called Reconstruction a failure: "[Most,] if not all, of our domestic troubles are directly traceable to violations of the organic law [laws that are changeable] and excessive legislation. The most striking illustrations of this fact are furnished by the enactments of the past three years upon the question of reconstruction."

After he left office in March 1869, Johnson returned to Tennessee. He remained politically active and won enough support to run for and win election to the U.S. Senate in 1874. He is the only president ever to have been elected senator after his presidency. (Former president John Quincy Adams [1767–1848; served 1825–29] served in the House of Representatives from 1831 to 1848; former president John Tyler [1790–1862; served 1841–45] was elected to the Confederate House of Representatives in 1861, but died before his term began.) Johnson received a standing ovation on his first day as senator but did not serve for long. He suffered a stroke and died on July 31, 1875. He was buried in Greeneville, the town where he had worked himself up from poverty and launched a political career that brought him to the nation's highest office.

For More Information

Books

Dubkowski, Cathy East. *Andrew Johnson: Rebuilding the Union.* Englewood Cliffs, NJ: Silver Burdett Press, 1991.

Hearn, Chester G. *The Impeachment of Andrew Johnson.* Jefferson, NC: McFarland & Co., 2000.

Mantell, Martin E. *Johnson, Grant and the Politics of Reconstruction.* New York: Columbia University Press, 1973.

McKittrick, Eric L. *Andrew Johnson and Reconstruction.* Chicago: University of Chicago Press, 1960. Reprint, New York: Oxford University Press, 1988.

Simpson, Brooks D. *The Reconstruction Presidents.* Lawrence: University Press of Kansas, 1998.

Trefousse, Hans L. *Andrew Johnson: A Biography.* New York: W. W. Norton & Company, 1997.

Trefousse, Hans Louis. *Impeachment of a President: Andrew Johnson, the Blacks, and Reconstruction.* Knoxville: University of Tennessee Press, 1975. Reprint, New York: Fordham University Press, 1999.

Web Sites

"Andrew Johnson National Historic Site." *National Parks Service.* http://www.nps.gov/anjo/ (accessed on June 28, 2004).

"Famous American Trials: The Andrew Johnson Impeachment Trial." *University of Missouri–Kansas City.* http://www.law.umkc.edu/faculty/projects/ftrials/impeach/impeachmt.htm (accessed on July 26, 2004).

"North Carolina Encyclopedia: The Biography of Andrew Johnson." *The State Library of North Carolina.* http://statelibrary.dcr.state.nc.us/nc/bio/public/johnson.htm (accessed on June 28, 2004).

Red Cloud

Born c. September 20, 1822
Nebraska

Died December 10, 1909
Pine Ridge Agency, South Dakota

Native American (Lakota) tribal leader and warrior

"I was born a Lakota and I have lived a Lakota and I shall die a Lakota. Before the white man came to our country, the Lakotas were a free people…. The white men made the laws to suit themselves and they compel us to obey them."

Red Cloud.
© *Bettmann/Corbis*.

Red Cloud was leader of the most successful war involving Native Americans and the United States. His success is not measured in the number of people killed or the amount of territory taken. Instead, Red Cloud is credited for stopping, at least for a few years, the loss of land and way of life of his tribe. From 1866 until the Second Treaty of Fort Laramie in 1868, Red Cloud and his warriors frustrated U.S. government attempts to build a road for miners and settlers that led across Lakota (Sioux) lands and into Montana. The treaty led U.S. troops to abandon three forts built to protect the road, and Sioux sovereignty (authority) over the territory was recognized. The treaty was compromised by the early 1870s, as Red Cloud lobbied in vain to have the agreement honored by the United States. Red Cloud found it increasingly difficult to please his people or the government.

Young warrior

Red Cloud (Makhpiya-Luta) was born in 1822 near the Platte River and what is now North Platte, Nebraska. His

The Lakota and the Sioux

The Native American people who call themselves the Lakota became known to colonizers and then in history books as the Sioux. They were called *Naduesiu* by Father Paul le Jeune, a French missionary, in papers dating back to 1640. Sioux is an abbreviation of the French name for the people. Although the Sioux were comprised of many bands, the Sioux nation, which combines all the bands, was relatively united, and bands spoke the same language in three principal dialects: Santee (spoken by eastern bands located in the Minnesota region); Yankton (spoken by bands located in Iowa and the eastern portions of North and South Dakota); and Teton (spoken by western bands located primarily in Missouri, Nebraska, and Wyoming).

Lakota and Sioux, then, are interchangeable names—they refer to the same, large group of people. When Red Cloud was born, Sioux controlled virtually all of the territory in present-day Minnesota, Iowa, Missouri, Nebraska, North and South Dakota, and Wyoming, and portions of surrounding states. Different bands of the Sioux mentioned in this entry include the Oglalas, the Brulé tribe of Teton Sioux, the Koya Oglalas, and the Eastern Lakota.

father, Lone Man, belonged to the Brulé tribe of Teton Sioux and his mother, Walks as She Thinks, was an Oglala related to Chief Smoke (also called Old Smoke). His father died while Red Cloud was a young boy, so Red Cloud was raised by his mother and Chief Smoke. Tribes in the area were often at war, and Red Cloud became a warrior against the neighboring Pawnee and Crow tribes. During a fight among Oglalas in 1841, he killed one of Chief Smoke's primary rivals, Bull Bear, chief of the Koya Oglalas. Not yet twenty, Red Cloud became a leader of a Sioux band in territorial wars against other tribes. He married Pretty Owl in 1842 and they had at least two children, including a boy named Jack Red Cloud.

Little is known about Red Cloud's life from 1842 to 1851, when he was in his twenties. During that time, Americans increasingly settled in the Plains and passed further west—to cross the Rocky Mountains after the United States acquired western land stretching to the Pacific Ocean. On the Plains where Red Cloud lived, Kansas, Nebraska, North and South Dakota, Montana, and Wyoming were not yet states. As more settlers began arriving in these areas, representatives

Native American leaders gather in 1885. Standing (left) is interpreter Julius Meyer and Red Cloud. Seated are (left to right) Sitting Bull, Swift Bear, and Spotted Tail. *Photo by Hulton Archive/Getty Images.*

from Plains tribes met with U.S. government agents at Fort Laramie in Wyoming in 1851. A treaty was negotiated that allowed settlers to pass through the territory in return for payments to the tribes. The U.S. government attempted to organize the area by assigning territorial boundaries to the tribes, a policy that provoked hostility.

Skirmishes between Native Americans and settlers and military personnel occurred regularly, but full-scale battles broke out during the 1850s. The first major battle between the Sioux and American troops occurred in 1854, near Fort Laramie. In the Grattan Massacre, Lieutenant J. L. Grattan and eighteen of his men were killed. Later that year, U.S. troops killed Conquering Bear, chief of the Sioux, and in 1855, General William S. Harney (1800–1889) attacked a camp of Brulé Sioux near Ash Hollow, Nebraska, and killed nearly a hundred of them. In 1854, Kansas and Nebraska were organized as territories and began the process for becoming states. Minnesota became a state in 1858. So many settlers had traveled across the Plains and Rockies to reach Oregon that it qualified for statehood in 1859.

During the Civil War (1861–65), regular army troops were withdrawn from the Plains and replaced by state and territorial militia. When the state of Minnesota forced the Eastern Lakota out of the area in 1862 and 1863, Red Cloud envisioned a similar fate for his people. The U.S. Army had begun to construct forts along the Bozeman Trail, which ran from the South Platte River in present-day Colorado through Wyoming and into Montana, where gold had been discovered. Caravans of miners and settlers began to cross Sioux land. Late in 1863, the Oglala and Brulé joined forces under Red Cloud and Spotted Tail (a Sioux leader in favor of a nonviolent resolution to the disputes with white settlers), respectively, and allied with the Cheyenne. From 1863 to 1865, while the U.S. military was divided and fighting each other in the Civil War, the coalition of tribes ruled much of the Plains. But in Colorado, militia under Colonel John H. Chivington killed 130 Cheyenne at Sand Creek in 1864.

Red Cloud's War

Under Red Cloud's leadership beginning in 1866, the Sioux and their allies began a series of assaults on forts. Peace negotiations began in the spring of 1866, but Red Cloud refused to participate after more American soldiers arrived in the region. Several tribes signed a treaty with the U.S. government, but their lands were not affected by the Bozeman Trail, which ran through the hunting ground of Red Cloud's Sioux tribe. After engaging in a few assaults on forts, Red Cloud led a devastating attack in December 1866 just outside of Fort Phil Kearny in Wyoming that killed or scattered eighty men. Red Cloud informed the U.S. government that no new roads or posts could be built in Sioux country.

Forts continued to be attacked and soldiers were kept on constant watch in what became known as Red Cloud's War. A peace commission was established and a treaty was negotiated and signed at Fort Laramie during the spring of 1868. Roads running from Wyoming into Montana and three forts built to protect them were to be closed. Red Cloud did not sign the treaty until U.S. troops had withdrawn.

The U.S. government planned to build a new road to Montana west of Fort Laramie and in undisputed lands. By August 1868, the forts along the Bozeman Trail were abandoned and Red Cloud agreed to stop fighting. He settled on a reservation called the Red Cloud Agency in Nebraska.

Red Cloud had signed the treaty after stating several objections, and the Sioux considered his objections part of the treaty. The treaty called for the government to provide building, medical, and other supplies to the Sioux, distributing them from Fort Randall on the Missouri River. Red Cloud objected and wanted Fort Laramie as the base for distribution. The conflict led Red Cloud on a journey to Washington, D.C., to meet with President **Ulysses S. Grant** (1822–1885; served 1869–77; see entry) to negotiate for trading rights at Fort Laramie. While trading rights were granted, settlers contin-

Red Cloud meets with President Ulysses S. Grant at a reception in 1869. *Photo by MPI/Getty Images.*

ued to pour into the region and railroad lines were being constructed to bring more settlers to the frontier.

When several new posts were built to protect the railroad and settlers, Red Cloud led the Teton Sioux in an alliance with the Cheyenne and part of the Arapaho in isolated acts of rebellion. Meanwhile, in 1873, General George Armstrong Custer (1839–1876) was ordered to the region. As hostilities continued, Custer explored the Black Hills of South Dakota and reported that gold was present. A new rush of miners came to the region. Towns were established in land guaranteed by treaty to the Sioux. Red Cloud again traveled to Washington, D.C., and met with President Grant in 1875. Unwilling to try to force settlers to stop moving into the area, Grant offered $25,000 to the Sioux if they would give up their rights to hunt along the Platte River in Dakota Territory. The offer was refused by Red Cloud and two other chiefs representing their people.

In January 1876, Custer began aggressive action against Native Americans found in lands outside the territorial boundaries defined by treaties. On June 25, 1776, Custer discovered an Indian camp of Sioux, Cheyenne, and Arapaho bands at Little Big Horn in Montana. He split his troops into three columns to encircle the camp, with just over two hundred men following him in. Custer and his men were quickly surrounded by well-armed Native Americans, who routed Custer's force—killing all of them. Red Cloud did not participate in the battle, but he was accused of supporting the campaign and was later arrested.

Custer had been under orders to wait for additional troops. Those troops soon arrived and many battles were fought in 1876 and 1877 after the Battle of Little Big Horn, also known as Custer's Last Stand. It was the beginning of the end of Native American power on the Plains and in the far west. Representing his people, Red Cloud negotiated with government officials over relocation of agencies. Red Cloud refused to move his people to a location in Nebraska on the Missouri River and finally compromised in 1877 to a location in southwestern South Dakota named the Pine Ridge Agency.

Losing a way of life

Throughout the 1880s, Red Cloud struggled for autonomy (right to self-governance) with Pine Ridge Indian agents (government supervisors assigned to specific locales). He fought to preserve the authority of chiefs, opposed leasing Lakota lands to whites, and resisted the Dawes Act (1887), which allotted plots of land on Native American reservations to individuals. Much of the land ended up being sold, stolen, or swindled away from Native American control. The 1890 battle at Wounded Knee Creek (commonly called the Wounded Knee Massacre) on the Pine Ridge Agency, in which 150 Lakotas were killed, was effectively the last battle of the frontier and the end of a unique way of life for the Sioux.

By the time of the Wounded Knee Massacre, Red Cloud had lost support for not backing what proved to be a final stand by the Sioux. He lived the rest of his life at Pine Ridge, where he was occasionally visited by historians interested in his life and the events in which he participated. He told Warren K. Moorehead in an interview published in the *Transactions of the Kansas State Historical Society* that the U.S.

government in Washington, D.C., "took our lands and promised to feed and support us. Now I, who used to control 5000 warriors, must tell Washington when I am hungry. I must beg for that which I own."

Red Cloud converted to Roman Catholicism late in life. He died December 10, 1909, and was buried in the cemetery at Holy Rosary Mission with the full rites of the Catholic Church. A simple monument marks his grave.

For More Information

Books

Larson, Robert W. *Red Cloud: Warrior-Statesman of the Lakota Sioux*. Norman: University of Oklahoma Press, 1997.

Paul, R. Eli. *Red Cloud*. Helena: Montana Historical Society, 1997.

Red Cloud. "I Was Born a Lakota." In *Lakota Belief and Ritual,* by James R. Walker. Lincoln: University of Nebraska Press, 1980.

Web Sites

"New Perspectives on the West: Red Cloud." *PBS*. http://www.pbs.org/weta/thewest/people/i_r/redcloud.htm (accessed on July 23, 2004).

Ohiyesa. "Red Cloud." *Big Eagle' Y-Indian Program Medallions*. http://www.y-indianguides.com/pfm_x_redcloud.html (accessed on July 23, 2004).

Hiram Revels

Born September 1822
Fayetteville, North Carolina

Died January 16, 1901
Aberdeen, Mississippi

Minister, educator, and U.S. senator

A religious leader and educator, Hiram Revels traveled as a preacher and missionary throughout the Midwest and the upper South before the Civil War (1861–65). During the war, Revels served the Union army as a chaplain for African American soldiers. After settling in Mississippi, Revels became in 1870 the first African American to serve in the U.S. Senate. He was elected to complete an open term of two years that had been vacant since **Jefferson Davis** (1808–1889; see Confederate Leaders entry) had left the Senate to become president of the Confederate States of America. Revels later served as the first president of Alcorn University (now Alcorn State University), the first land grant college for African American students. Revels was also associated with the African Methodist Episcopal (AME) Church and the Methodist Episcopal Church.

Drawn to the ministry

Hiram Rhoades Revels was born in Fayetteville, North Carolina, in September 1822. Little is known about Revels's parents. They were not slaves and are reported to

"I maintain that the past record of my race is a true index of the feelings which today animate them…. They aim not to elevate themselves by sacrificing one single interest of their white fellow-citizens. They ask but the rights which are theirs by God's universal law…."

Hiram Revels. *The Library of Congress.*

153

have been of mixed African, Croatian, and Indian descent. Revels was intelligent and inquisitive as a youth and attended a small and private elementary school in Fayetteville conducted by a free black woman. In 1842, his family moved to Lincolnton, North Carolina, and Revels began earning money as a barber.

Revels moved north to Indiana in 1844 to continue his education. He enrolled at Beech Grove Seminary, a Quaker school located near Liberty, Indiana. Revels quickly became involved with the African Methodist Episcopal (AME) Church. Planning to become a minister, Revels moved to Ohio in 1845 to study theology at Drake County Seminary at Miami University, and went on to Galesburg, Illinois, where he attended Knox College. Revels received ordination as a minister in the AME Church and became well known as a teacher, lecturer, and preacher from Ohio to Missouri as well as in Kentucky and Maryland.

In the early 1850s, Revels married Phoeba A. Bass of Zanesville, Ohio. The couple raised six daughters. Revels continued traveling as a religious teacher and educator. He was sometimes met with racial hostilities and was imprisoned in Missouri in 1854 "for preaching the gospel to Negroes," as he noted in an autobiographical sketch he wrote for the records of the U.S. Senate. Revels had a conflict with the AME Church in St. Louis, Missouri, in 1854 and for a time became a Presbyterian. He accepted a pastorate at the Madison Street Presbyterian Church in Baltimore, Maryland, and also served as principal of a high school for African Americans. His brother, Willis Revels, was an AME minister and pastor of AME Bethel Church in Baltimore at the time.

The following year, Revels returned to the AME Church and decided to continue his education by enrolling in theology courses at Knox College in Galesburg. Revels remained at Knox College for two years before he returned to Baltimore and accepted a pastorate at an AME church in 1857.

Civil War chaplain

When the Civil War (1861–65) began in 1861, African American communities in the Northern states rallied to support the Union war effort. (The Union consisted of Northern states that remained loyal to the United States during the Civil War.) Baltimore had a particularly large and prosperous community of African Americans. Revels assisted in organizing two regiments of volunteers from Baltimore to assist the Union effort. Returning to St. Louis in 1863, Revels established a school for freedmen (previous slaves). Missouri had been one of the slave states that did not secede from the Union and was subject to the Emancipation Proclamation issued by President Abraham Lincoln (1809–1865; served 1861–65) that freed slaves in all states in the Union. The Proclamation also made it possible for African Americans to serve in the Union army. Revels helped recruit and organize the first African American regiment of soldiers from Missouri. After they completed training, he accompanied them to Vicksburg, Mississippi, where approximately seventy-five thousand soldiers were encamped.

After the war, Revels traveled in Kansas, Missouri, Mississippi, and Louisiana to help the Freedmen's Bureau and other charitable organizations assist African Americans with problems related to health, poverty, and illiteracy. He was appointed presiding elder of the AME Church in Natchez, Mississippi, where he settled with his family.

The Reconstruction Act of 1867 and passage of the Fourteenth and Fifteenth Amendments to the Constitution, which provided and protected voting rights for African American men, created an opportunity to participate in local and national politics. In late 1868, the provisional military governor of Mississippi, Adelbert Ames (1835–1933), appointed Revels for a term on the Natchez Board of Aldermen. (A military governor is appointed by the government of an occupying military force. During the Reconstruction era, from the end of the Civil War in 1865 to the end of Reconstruction in 1877, Southern states that had seceded from the Union were run by military governors to ensure that peace and civil rights were protected.)

The following year, Revels became a candidate for the Mississippi state senate. He won the election and joined thirty-three other African Americans in the 140-member state legislature. The presiding officer invited Revels to open the session with a prayer. Making references to cooperation and

In a Thomas Nast illustration that appeared in the April 9, 1870, issue of *Harper's Weekly,* former Confederate president Jefferson Davis of Mississippi is shown looking in at Hiram Revels, the African American who filled his vacant seat in the U.S. Senate. In a reference to the Shakespeare tragic play *Othello,* Davis is portrayed as Iago; the illustration's caption is: "Time works wonders: 'For that I do suspect the lusty moor hath leap'd into my seat: the thought whereof doth like a poisonous mineral gnaw my inwards.'" *The Library of Congress.*

respect, the prayer, according to John Roy Lynch (1847–1939), one of the more vocal Mississippi state congressmen, was "one of the most impressive and eloquent prayers that had ever been delivered in the Senate chamber. He made a profound impression upon all who heard him."

Revels was impressive enough for the legislature to select him to fill the U.S. Senate seat from Mississippi that had been vacant since senators from Southern states left of-

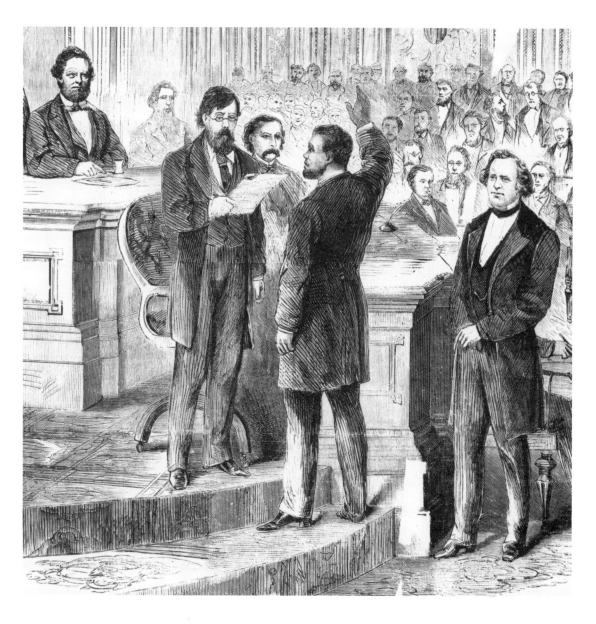

fice when the Confederate States of America was formed in 1861. Without having pursued or expected a high political office, the forty-four-year-old Revels captured the nomination and was elected to fill a seat that had just over a year left in its term. It was the Senate slot that Jefferson Davis had held before becoming the Confederate president. In rapid development, Revels held one of the highest political offices in the nation.

Hiram Revels is sworn into office as a U.S. senator from Mississippi on Janurary 25, 1870. © *Bettmann/Corbis.*

Revels's Early Senate Career

The following excerpt from the February 26, 1870, issue of the *New York Times* describes Hiram Revels's first days as a U.S. senator:

> Mr. Revels, the colored Senator from Mississippi, was sworn in and admitted to his seat this afternoon at 4:40 o'clock. There was not an inch of standing or sitting room in the galleries, so densely were they packed; and to say that the interest was intense gives but a faint idea of the feeling which prevailed throughout the entire proceeding. [U.S. senator George] Vickers, of Maryland, opened the debate to-day, arguing against the admission, on the ground that Revels had not been a citizen for nine years, and therefore was not eligible. [U.S. senator Henry] Wilson [of Massachusetts] followed on the other side, and was succeeded by [U.S. senator Eugene] Casserly [of California], who took a new departure and arraigned the entire reconstruction policy, charging that all the Southern Senators were put in their seats by the force of the bayonets of the regular army [military governors were put in charge of Southern states that had been part of the Confederacy during the Civil War]. This aroused [U.S. senator Charles Daniel] Drake [of Missouri] to a white heat, and provoked him to utter remarks and to make personal allusions to Mr. Casserly which were certainly in bad taste, and in no way pertinent to the subject before the body. [U.S. senator **Charles**] **Sumner** [of Massachusetts; see entry] made the closing speech for the Republican side of the question. It was brief, pithy and eloquent. Then came [U.S. senator John Potter] Stockton [of New Jersey] in deference of his party. He was boisterous and commonplace, and his speech was much better suited to the stump than to the Senate. He argued in favor of his motion to refer the credentials to the Judiciary Committee, which was promptly negatived by a party vote. The question was then put on the admission, which was passed by the same strict drawing of the party lines. Only one thing remained, which was that the first colored Senator elect should advance to the Speaker's desk and be sworn. The Vice-President [Schuyler Colfax] made the announcement to the galleries that all demonstrations of approval or disapproval would be promptly suppressed.... Mr. Revels showed no embarrassment whatever, and his demeanor was as dignified as could be expected under the circumstances. The abuse which had been poured upon him and on his race during the last two days might well have shaken the nerves of any one. The vast throng in the galleries showed no sign of feeling one way or the other, and left very quietly.

Short and memorable Senate term

As a large press contingent reported on the first African American U.S. senator, a debate began immediately on the Senate floor over Revels's credentials and eligibility to serve. Three days of arguments ensued before Revels was accepted by a 48-8 vote. With the Senate galleries packed, Revels delivered a short and self-assured acceptance speech.

As a new senator with a term that lasted a little over a year, Revels was not in a position to accomplish much in the

Senate. He served on the Committee on Education and Labor and the Committee on the District of Columbia, for which he spoke for integration of public schools (the measure did not pass). Emphasizing conciliation, he advocated amnesty (pardon) for former Confederates, provided they pledged loyalty to the government of the United States, and he spoke for readmission of Georgia, which had seceded from the Union in 1861. He used his Senate office to aid African American mechanics who were barred from employment opportunities at the U.S. Navy Yard. When the Senate was not in session, Revels went on lecture tours, traveling throughout New England, New York, and the Midwest.

Political commentators have a mixed view of Revels's effectiveness as senator. While acknowledging the difficulties he faced, some commentators believe he was not aggressive enough. "Revels never offered a more radical plan of action for blacks, other than Republican and later Democratic policies—on white terms," stated biographer Julius E. Thompson. "He did not suggest other approaches to aid blacks in their struggle to solve the economic, political, and social problems facing the community during the years of the emancipation era."

After the Senate

Revels returned to Mississippi following his brief term in the U.S. Senate. He accepted an appointment to become president of the newly established Alcorn University (now Alcorn State University), the first land grant college for African American students. Revels left Alcorn briefly in 1873 to serve as interim (temporary) secretary of state for Mississippi, then resigned his position to avoid being dismissed by Mississippi governor Adelbert Ames, who had become a political enemy. Revels and his family moved to Holly Springs, Mississippi, where Revels became pastor of a Methodist Episcopal church.

Revels and the Republican Party went their separate ways. Revels openly campaigned for several Democrats during the elections of 1875, even though the party was dominated by whites, some of whom were hostile toward the majority black population. Revels returned to the U.S. Senate in a different capacity: He was summoned to appear before the Senate Select Committee investigation of fraudulent practices in

Mississippi during the elections of 1875. Revels testified on behalf of Mississippi Democrats, despite firm evidence that they had used intimidation and violence against African American voters, a large majority of whom favored Republican candidates. Revels lost his Holly Springs pastorate and the support of many African Americans over his testimony. Mississippi's new governor, John M. Stone (1830–1900), reappointed Revels to the presidency of Alcorn University in July 1876.

Revels served as president of Alcorn for nine years in total, and he retired from his position in 1882. Revels and his family returned to Holly Springs, where in semiretirement and failing health Revels taught theology courses and presided as an elder in the Methodist Episcopalian church. He died of a stroke om 1901 while attending a conference of the Methodist Episcopal Church in Aberdeen, Mississippi, and he was buried near his home in Holly Springs.

For More Information

Books and Periodicals

"The Colored Member Admitted to His Seat in the Senate." *New York Times* (February 26, 1870): p. 1.

Lynch, John Roy. *The Facts of Reconstruction.* New York: Neale Publishing Co., 1913. Reprint, Indianapolis: Bobbs-Merrill, 1970.

McFarlin, Annjennette Sophie, ed. *Black Congressional Reconstruction Orators and Their Orations, 1869–1879.* Metuchen, NJ: Scarecrow Press, 1976.

Thompson, Julius E. *Hiram R. Revels, 1827–1901: A Biography.* New York: Ayer Company, 1982.

Ellen H. Richards

Born December 3, 1842
Dunstable, Massachusetts

Died March 30, 1911
Boston, Massachusetts

**Chemist, educator, and founder of the
discipline of home economics**

The first woman admitted to the Massachusetts Institute of Technology (MIT), Ellen Richards was a chemist and the founder of the discipline of home economics, now often called family and consumer sciences. In addition to being a student pioneer at MIT (she was the first American woman to earn a bachelor of chemistry degree) and then as a professor, she helped break barriers and opened more opportunities for women in science professions. In addition to creating methods for analyzing air and water quality, food values, and consumer products, Richards publicized practical ways for Americans to use elements of science to improve their daily lives.

Varied interests and experiences

Born Ellen Henrietta Swallow on December 3, 1842, on the family farm in Dunstable, Massachusetts, Richards was the only child of Peter Swallow and Fanny Gould Taylor. Her parents met while attending New Ipswich Academy in New Hampshire, where they were training to be teachers. Both parents taught, but Peter Swallow also spent time farming.

"I hope in a quiet way I am winning a way which others will keep open. Perhaps the fact that I am not a Radical or a believer in the all powerful ballot for women to right her wrongs and that I do not scorn womanly duties, but claim it as a privilege to clean up and sort of supervise the room and sew things, etc., is winning me stronger allies than anything else."

Ellen H. Richards. *The Library of Congress.*

Richards was educated at home and helped with the farm work and housekeeping from an early age. When she was thirteen, Richards won a sewing award at a local fair for an embroidered handkerchief and a baking award for the best loaf of bread.

When the family moved to Westford, Massachusetts, in 1859, Richards attended Westford Massachusetts Academy, where she studied mathematics, French, and Latin. She worked at the village store her father had purchased and took odd jobs tutoring, housecleaning, cooking, and nursing to help her earn enough money to continue her education. Richards graduated from the academy in 1863.

Later that year, the family moved to nearby Littleton, Massachusetts. Richards spent the next five years waiting for an opportunity to attend college. At the time, no colleges in New England were open to women other than Vassar College, a new women's school in Poughkeepsie, New York, that had only barely begun building a reputation. Frustrated by the seeming impossibility of realizing her goals, and spending long hours at home caring for her ill mother, Richards experienced a period of poor health and deep depression.

Opportunity comes

Finally, at the age of twenty-five in 1868, Richards entered Vassar College. She had had only four years of formal education, yet Richards excelled at Vassar and completed a four-year program in two years. Her interest in science was encouraged by Maria Mitchell (1818–1889), America's first female professor of astronomy and the most significant American woman scientist of the nineteenth century. Another professor, Charles A. Farrar, influenced Richards to pursue studies in chemistry and impressed on her the idea of applied science—that science should be used to help solve everyday, practical problems.

After graduating from Vassar in 1870, Richards was admitted to study at MIT. Up to that point, women had not been admitted to MIT. Viewed as an "experiment," Richards intended to succeed, but she learned later that there was a hidden reason why she had been accepted as a "special stu-

Maria Mitchell

The first famous American woman scientist, Maria Mitchell, made her mark by discovering a comet in 1847 and by opening opportunities to other women in science. As a professor at Vassar College beginning in 1865, she profoundly influenced several young women who became accomplished in their fields, including astronomer Mary Watson Whitney (1847–1921), psychologist Christine Ladd-Franklin (1847–1930), and chemist Ellen Richards, among others.

Born in 1818 on Nantucket Island in Massachusetts, Mitchell was the third of ten children of William and Lydia (Coleman) Mitchell. Her mother was a librarian and her father was a school teacher, bank officer, and amateur astronomer. Mitchell attended private elementary schools from the age of four. By the age of twelve, she was assisting her father with astronomical observations. He taught her to calculate the positions and orbits of celestial bodies. Through her father's connections, she became acquainted with astronomers at the Harvard College Observatory.

On October 1, 1847, the twenty-nine-year-old Mitchell sighted a new comet and was able to calculate its position. With her discovery she became a popular symbol for the professional advancement of women scientists. Louis Agassiz (1807–1873), a renowned biologist and educator, nominated Mitchell for membership in the American

Association for the Advancement of Science (AAAS) in 1850.

When Matthew Vassar (1792–1868) decided to establish a college for women, he wanted it to have an excellent science program. For the astronomy program, which included an observatory, he looked to Mitchell as the director. Mitchell became one of the first faculty members, directing the observatory and introducing young women to the science of observational astronomy. The Women's Educational Association of Boston raised money to ensure Mitchell had one of the best telescopes in the country. Determined to create graduate educational and professional opportunities for women, Mitchell served as a teacher and advisor.

In 1868, Mitchell made the first daily photographic series of sun spots. She recognized that these spots were not clouds above the surface of the sun, as many astronomers believed. She also studied binary, or double, stars and published her observations of Jupiter and Saturn and their satellites. She wrote popular science articles and edited the astronomy section of the popular magazine *Scientific American*. She helped establish the Association for the Advancement of Women, serving as president for two years. At the time of her death in 1889, she was chairing the Association for the Advancement of Women's Committee on Science and still directing the Vassar Observatory.

dent": If administrators or students complained about her, the president of MIT could simply reply that Richards was not a regular student. "Had I realized upon what basis I was taken, I would not have gone," Richards remarked later. But she did succeed, becoming in 1873 the first woman to earn a bachelor of chemistry degree in America. That same year, she submitted a thesis on the presence in iron ore of the chemical element vanadium; her findings resulted in her receiving a masters of arts degree from Vassar.

Richards made a request to begin studying for her doctorate at MIT, but she was rejected—some say because MIT did not want a woman to be the first student to receive a graduate degree in chemistry. Soon after, MIT administrators voted formally against admitting female students. Richards worked as an assistant to MIT professor William R. Nichols, a specialist in water analysis. In 1875, funds to establish a women's laboratory at MIT were secured, and the laboratory opened the following year under the direction of Professor John Ordway, with Richards as his assistant. The Women's Education Association provided money for the laboratory and Richards personally donated $1,000 annually for the seven years of the laboratory's existence. The laboratory was fully operational in 1878, when MIT finally voted to admit female students.

Meanwhile, Richards married Professor Robert Hallowell Richards (1844–1945) on June 4, 1875. He was developing metallurgical and mining engineering laboratories. Professor Richards proposed to her in a chemistry laboratory shortly after she received her MIT degree in 1873. Ellen Richards acted as her husband's chemist on a project where he experimented with methods of concentrating copper ores. At MIT, Ellen Richards provided her students with individual attention, especially since most female students had been restricted from learning laboratory techniques. She also served as an unpaid advisor to female students.

Richards, then, by the force of her success and example, had helped open the doors of academia to women, especially in the sciences. Denied an opportunity to pursue a doctorate, she instead pursued her interests in science, working on important studies and experiments and mentoring a new generation of female students. Her home and laboratory were always open to her students.

More firsts and honors

During the 1880s, Richards became more active in finding practical uses for the results of her laboratory experiments. She published a manual, *The Chemistry of Cooking and Cleaning* (1882), about positive and harmful chemicals in foods and cleaning materials, and a more specific examination of chemicals and food, *Food Materials and Their Adulterations* (1885). When MIT established a chemical laboratory to study problems in sanitation in 1885, Richards was named as assistant, becoming the nation's first female industrial chemist. Her first project was a two-year survey of the ecology of inland waters in Massachusetts. The water survey work and her involvement with environmental chemistry were significant contributions to the new science of ecology. Meanwhile, she taught on the techniques for air, water, and sewage analysis and lobbied leading scientists to recognize a discipline she called "human ecology." The science was recognized a decade later as "home economics."

Ellen H. Richards (far left, back row) with her students at Massachusetts Institute of Technology (MIT), 1888. *Courtesy MIT Museum.*

Richards continued to champion efforts to increase educational opportunities for women. She was a founding member of the Association of Collegiate Alumnae, which later changed its name to the American Association of University Women. She organized a science section for the Society to encourage Studies at Home, a correspondence school (where lessons are mailed to one's home) founded in 1887 by Anna Ticknor. Richards herself benefitted from the correspondence school: As she provided lessons and advice, her correspondences with students provided her insight into daily life problems faced by women in the home. Some of the problems were beyond science, including manners, dress, food preparation, and exercise.

In response to the lack of formal preparation for homemaking, Richards established a series of classes in housekeeping at the Women's Educational and Industrial Union in Boston, Massachusetts, in the early 1890s. The Union was contacted by the Boston School Committee in 1894 to provide information on healthy lunches for school-children. Richards was consulted by other school systems, as well as other institutions, for information regarding food and nutrition. In 1893, Richards ran a kitchen as a featured exhibit in the Chicago World's Fair. Detailed information about the nutritional values of different foods was among the information she began making more readily available to help people live healthy lives. At the exhibit, the cooking area was open to the public. Exhibit-goers could order meals for thirty cents; they received a receipt that included food values—the amount of protein, fat, carbohydrates, and calories in the meal they were eating. Over one hundred years later, such receipts were used again in the United States as the American public became more health conscious.

In 1899, she organized and chaired a summer conference in Lake Placid, New York, where the profession of home economics was established. Conference participants explored methods for applying science, sociology, economics, and other useful disciplines to the home and developed courses for schools and colleges. According to Richards, every person needed to be a kind of sanitation engineer in order for society to overcome problems of waste and unhealthy living. Home economics classes were soon instituted in high schools across the country.

During the first decade of the twentieth century, Richards wrote pamphlets for the U.S. Department of Agriculture on nutrition and food chemistry that were made freely available to the public. In 1908, the American Home Economics Association was formed, with Richards elected as its first president, a position she held until her retirement in 1910. During this time, she helped found and finance the *Journal of Home Economics*. In addition, Richards worked as a consultant, lecturer, and author of books and articles.

In 1910, the National Education Association appointed Richards to supervise the teaching of home economics in public schools. She was awarded an honorary doctorate from Smith College that same year. Four days before her death in 1911, Richards spoke before the Baptist Society Union and finished writing the keynote address (the main speech at a conference) for the first World Congress on Technology. Richards died at her Boston home on March 30, 1911. Numerous home economics schools and clubs, as well as scholarships and fellowships, are named in her honor.

For More Information

Books

Clarke, Robert. *Ellen Swallow: The Woman Who Founded Ecology.* Chicago: Follett, 1973.

Douty, Esther Morris. *America's First Woman Chemist, Ellen Richards.* New York: Messner, 1961.

Hunt, Caroline Louisa. *The Life of Ellen H. Richards, 1842–1911.* Washington, DC: American Home Economics Association, 1980.

Vare, Ethlie Ann. *Adventurous Spirit: A Story about Ellen Swallow Richards.* Minneapolis: Carolrhoda Books, 1992.

Web Sites

"Chemical Achievers: Ellen Swallow Richards." *Chemical Heritage Foundation.* http://www.chemheritage.org/EducationalServices/chemach/hnec/esr.html (accessed on June 23, 2004).

"Ellen Swallow Richards." *National Women's Hall of Fame.* http://www.greatwomen.org/women.php?action=viewone&id=123 (accessed on June 23, 2004).

"MIT Institute Archives & Special Collections: Ellen Swallow Richards." *Massachusetts Institute of Technology.* http://libraries.mit.edu/archives/exhibits/esr/index.html (accessed on June 23, 2004).

Edwin Stanton

Born December 19, 1814
Steubenville, Ohio

Died December 24, 1869
Washington, D.C.

Attorney general, secretary of war, and lawyer

"Now he belongs to the ages." (on the death of Abraham Lincoln)

Edwin Stanton was one of the nation's best-known attorneys during the 1850s, an extremely effective secretary of war under President Abraham Lincoln (1809–1865; served 1861–65) during most of the Civil War (1861–65), and a controversial figure in the administration of President **Andrew Johnson** (1808–1875; served 1865–69; see entry). As Johnson struggled with Congress over control of Reconstruction, the program through which states that joined the Confederacy would reenter the Union, Stanton openly sided with the views of congressional leaders. Johnson hesitated to fire Stanton; when he finally demanded Stanton's resignation, Congress began the first-ever impeachment (formal accusation of wrongdoing) case against a U.S. president. Known for his quick temper and penetrating questions, Stanton overcame personal tragedies and used boundless energy and close attention to detail to achieve remarkable success. He died just days after turning fifty-five and having been confirmed to an appointment as a justice on the Supreme Court.

Edwin McMasters Stanton was born on December 19, 1814, in Steubenville, Ohio. He was the eldest of four chil-

Edwin Stanton. *The Library of Congress.*

dren of Dr. David and Lucy (Norman) Stanton. When Stanton's father, a physician, died in 1827, the family was left in difficult financial circumstances. Not yet fourteen, Stanton left school to work in a local bookstore to help support his mother and three siblings. He continued his studies in his spare time and was admitted to Kenyon College in Ohio in 1831. After two years of college, however, he ran out of money and returned to work in a bookstore.

After moving to Columbus, Ohio, Stanton began studying law in an office and passed his bar exam (a test for certification as a lawyer) in 1836. Later that year, on December 31, 1836, Stanton married Mary Ann Lamson of Columbus, Ohio. They would have two children.

Stanton established a law practice in Cadiz, Ohio. He moved back to his home town of Steubenville in late 1838 to become a partner of Benjamin Tappan (1773–1857), who was elected to the U.S. Senate that year. Stanton succeeded quickly as a lawyer and also served as a legal reporter on decisions by the Ohio State Supreme Court beginning in 1842.

Stanton's contented and prosperous life, however, met with tragedies. First came the death of his daughter, Lucy, and then in March 1844 Stanton's wife, Mary Ann, died. Only thirty years old at the time, Stanton suffered emotional traumas. Two years later, in 1846, Stanton's brother Darwin committed suicide. Stanton had paid Darwin's way through medical school.

Becomes famous lawyer

After deep grieving, Stanton wanted to start a new life and find new opportunities as a lawyer. He moved to Pittsburgh, Pennsylvania, in 1847. Stanton's law practice thrived in Pittsburgh and he earned a national reputation for his handling of a case where he represented the state of Pennsylvania against a bridge-building company. The company, Wheeling and Belmont Bridge Company, won a bid to build a bridge across the Ohio River, but the bridge was too low for steamboats to pass under and reach Pittsburgh. The State of Pennsylvania sued to stop construction and force the company to build a higher bridge. Stanton won the case after hiring a steamboat to run a normal route on the Ohio River. The steamboat's smokestack hit the bridge and was destroyed.

The success of the case brought Stanton regular work as a counsel for the state of Pennsylvania from 1849 to 1856, and he became a highly sought-after lawyer. Stanton's personal life was on an upswing as well. On June 25, 1856, he married Ellen Hutchinson of Pittsburgh. The couple moved to Washington, D.C. The marriage would produce four children.

In Washington, Stanton frequently argued cases before the U.S. Supreme Court. He was selected as a special U.S. attorney to represent the government in fraudulent land claims in California. The problems dated back to the 1840s when California was not yet a state and was being disputed in the Mexican-American War (1846–48). Stanton spent almost a year in California reconstructing records to separate legal and illegal claims. His work helped the U.S. government save millions, perhaps hundreds of millions of dollars it would otherwise have paid on false claims.

As a famous lawyer, Stanton served a variety of clients. Among them was Daniel E. Sickles (1819–1914), whose 1859 trial for murder became one of the most sensational and publicized stories of its time and a groundbreaking case in American legal history. Sickles, a thirty-nine-year-old New York congressman known for his fiery temper and many romances, discovered that his twenty-two-year-old wife was having an affair with his friend, Barton Key. Key was the district attorney for Washington, D.C., and son of Francis Scott Key (1779–1843), who wrote the "Star-Spangled Banner" during the War of 1812 (1812–15). Sickles shot and killed Key in broad daylight on a Sunday afternoon in Lafayette Park, very near the White House. The story made national news and the trial was widely covered by the leading periodicals of the time.

As part of the defense team, Stanton brought in witnesses to testify that Key was a known adulterer and that Sickles had been suffering over his wife's unfaithfulness. Stanton argued that Sickles was in such anguish that he was temporarily insane when he committed the act. It was the first time a plea of temporary insanity was used effectively for a criminal defendant. The jury rendered a not-guilty verdict.

In and out of cabinets

When Abraham Lincoln was elected president in November 1860, outgoing president James Buchanan (1791–

FRANK LESLIE'S
ILLUSTRATED
NEWSPAPER

Entered, according to Act of Congress, in the year 1859, by FRANK LESLIE, in the Clerk's Office of the District Court for the Southern District of New York. (Copyrighted March 7, 1859.)

No. 171—VOL. VII.]   NEW YORK, SATURDAY, MARCH 12, 1859.   [PRICE 6 CENTS.

NEW TALE!

WE desire to call the attention of our readers to the new and deeply interesting tale commenced in our last number, which will be continued from week to week until concluded. The name of the author from whose pen it emanates—PIERCE EGAN, Esq., author of "The Flower of the Flock," "The Snake in the Grass," &c., is of itself a guarantee, that

ADA LEIGH; OR, THE LOVE TEST,

will be found a tale of absorbing interest; and our readers will soon discover for themselves that in accurate delineation of human character, the portrayal of sentiment and the development of a finely constructed plot, ADA LEIGH is a tale that has seldom been surpassed in interest. Let everybody read it. A synopsis of the chapters published in our last is given in this number.

THE WASHINGTON TRAGEDY.

Crime and Bloodshed in the Federal Capital.

SHOOTING OF PHILIP BARTON KEY BY HON. DANIEL E. SICKLES, OF NEW YORK.

(With the only correct Illustrations published; made from sketches by our Special Artist.)

ON the afternoon of Sunday, February 27th, the city of Washington was suddenly thrown into a state of intense excitement on learning

Depiction of U.S. representative Daniel E. Sickles (right) of New York shooting Barton Key in the March 12, 1859, edition of *Frank Leslie's Illustrated Newspaper.* **Edwin Stanton successfully defended Sickles; the jury issued a not-guilty verdict, by virtue of temporary insanity.** *The Library of Congress.*

Abraham Lincoln's first secretary of war, Simon Cameron. *The Library of Congress.*

1868; served 1857–61) reorganized his cabinet (top-ranking advisors of the president). Lincoln's election was viewed with disfavor in the South because of Lincoln's antislavery sentiments. Buchanan wanted to ensure the Union remained together. Buchanan chose Stanton to be his attorney general for the short but significant four months remaining in the president's term in office. Stanton helped convince Buchanan not to abandon the federally owned Fort Sumter in South Carolina. The state had seceded (separated) from the Union and demanded that federal troops be removed from the fort.

Stanton's brief time as attorney general ended with the conclusion of the Buchanan presidency in March 1861. In April, Confederate troops fired on Fort Sumter and the Civil War was underway. Later in 1861, Stanton became a friend and confidential legal adviser of George B. McClellan (1826– 1885), the general in charge of the Union army. Stanton also served as a legal adviser to Secretary of War Simon Cameron (1799–1899). He provided advice on Cameron's proposal to supply arms to slaves in the South to fight the Confederacy. Lincoln was so appalled at the suggestion that he fired Cameron. Oddly enough, Lincoln chose Stanton to replace Cameron. After his appointment was confirmed by the Senate on January 15, 1862, Stanton took office.

Stanton reorganized the War Department (now called the Defense Department). He carefully examined contracts for war supplies and demanded that supplies arrive on time. Stanton's dedication ensured that Union armies were always well supplied with materials and food. To better manage the war effort, Stanton worked through Congress to take control of telegraph lines: all information on the lines was directed through Stanton's office, enabling him to manage news reports and to remove any items Confederates

Stanton and Lincoln

Edwin Stanton did not support Abraham Lincoln's bid for the presidency in 1860. Putting his concern for maintaining the Union above all else, Stanton believed that other candidates were better prepared to work with legislators from the North and South to avoid the secession of Southern states and a possible war. Stanton also questioned Lincoln's leadership abilities. In spite of his views on Lincoln, Stanton accepted the president's offer to become secretary of war after Simon Cameron was fired.

Though Stanton had a quick temper, Lincoln appreciated Stanton's skills and found effective ways to deal with him, according to Colonel William H. Crook in his book, *Through Five Administrations: Reminiscences of Colonel William H. Crook.* Crook recalls a meeting between Lincoln and Stanton:

On one occasion, I have heard, Secretary Stanton was particularly angry with one of the generals. He was eloquent about him. "I would like to tell him what I think of him!" he stormed.

"Why don't you?" Mr. Lincoln agreed. "Write it all down—do."

Mr. Stanton wrote his letter. When it was finished he took it to the President. The President listened to it all.

"All right. Capital!" he nodded. "And now, Stanton, what are you going to do with it?"

"Do with it? Why, send it, of course!"

"I wouldn't," said the President. "Throw it in the waste-paper basket."

"But it took me two days to write—"

"Yes, yes, and it did you ever so much good. You feel better now. That is all that is necessary. Just throw it in the basket."

After a little more expostulation [discussion], into the basket it went.

might find valuable. Stanton also took control of railway lines: He ensured trains were available for troop movement and shipping of supplies, and he hired crews to build and repair railroads to keep the important transportation lines operating. Stanton remained in close touch with military commanders and with the congressional Committee on the Conduct of the War.

Stanton and Lincoln quickly developed a strong personal and working relationship. Stanton supported Lincoln as he changed battlefield commanders several times, including when Lincoln replaced Stanton's friend, George B. McClellan. After Major General Ulysses S. Grant succeeded in taking key

Confederate strongholds at Vicksburg, Mississippi, and Chattanooga, Tennessee, in 1863, Lincoln and Stanton agreed that Grant was the leader they needed to defeat the Confederacy. Stanton worked effectively with Grant, delivering the supplies Grant needed for a long and sustained military offensive during the last year of the war.

Confederate general **Robert E. Lee** (1807–1870; see Confederate Leaders entry) surrendered to Grant at Appomattox Court House, Virginia, on April 9, 1865. Lincoln was assassinated five days later, an event that emotionally shattered Stanton. He worked to uphold the fair and lenient surrender terms that Lincoln demanded his generals negotiate with Confederate leaders. When Major General William Tecumseh Sherman (1820–1891) negotiated a harsher surrender agreement with Confederate general Joseph E. Johnston (1807–1891) in North Carolina, two weeks after Appomattox, Stanton led a cabinet meeting that resulted in General Grant traveling to North Carolina to supervise new terms. Following Lincoln's assassination, Stanton took charge of funeral arrangements. He also uttered the memorable phrase of Lincoln's death: "Now he belongs to the ages."

Stanton's grief and anger over Lincoln's death probably motivated him to take part in accusations and trials of several people involved in the conspiracy to assassinate the president and other government officials. Among them was Mary Surratt (1823–1865), who was accused of complicity (guilty as an accomplice) in Lincoln's assassination. Surratt owned a boardinghouse in Washington, D.C., frequented by Lincoln's assassin, John Wilkes Booth (1838–1865), and Surratt's son, John Surratt Jr. (1844–1916), who had been a Confederate spy and was a friend of Booth's. Another of the conspirators, Lewis Paine, arrived at the boardinghouse just as Mary Surratt was being arrested. Surratt claimed innocence throughout her trial, but her faulty memory and her relations to the conspirators, even though several claimed she was completely innocent, led to her conviction. The jury sentenced her to the death penalty but recommended life in prison due to her "sex and age." President Andrew Johnson, who succeeded Lincoln, claimed he was never shown the jury's plea for mercy. Surratt was executed by hanging on July 7, 1865.

Stanton also attempted to implicate **Jefferson Davis** (1808–1889; see Confederate Leaders entry), president of the Confederacy, in Lincoln's assassination. The case went nowhere and probably reflects Stanton's anger against the Confederacy. Following the end of the Civil War, Stanton quickly and effectively demobilized (took apart) the Union armies.

Warring with Johnson

When Johnson became president upon Lincoln's assassination, he asked Stanton to remain in his cabinet as secretary of war. Stanton showed initial support for Johnson's Reconstruction plan for bringing the former Confederate states back into the Union and resuming normal state governments. As president, Johnson believed he should lead the Reconstruction program. Congress differed. By the time Congress came back in session in December 1865, some former Confederate states had already met Johnson's obligations for readmittance and had elected congressmen. Those officials were refused their seats by Congress, and the Republican-dominated legislative body began passing laws to set the terms of Reconstruction. A bitter battle emerged between the president and Congress: Johnson vetoed legislation, but Congress overrode the vetoes and effectively took control of the Reconstruction program.

Stanton had established good relations with the most powerful congressmen during the Civil War through his frequent communication with the congressional Committee on the Conduct of the War. Beginning as early as the summer of 1865, Stanton supported views on Reconstruction similar to those of powerful politicians known as "Radical Republicans" or "Radical Reconstructionists," including U.S. representative **Thaddeus Stevens** (1792–1868; see entry) of Pennsylvania and U.S. senator **Charles Sumner** (1811–1874; see entry) of Massachusetts. They supported a more demanding program for seceded states to reenter the Union and demanded civil rights and voting rights bills that would protect freedmen.

The first conflict over Reconstruction concerned a plan by Johnson for residents of North Carolina to elect delegates to a state convention that would frame a new state constitution. Cabinet members were spilt over the issue of

Johnson's "Blunder" on Stanton

Historians view President Andrew Johnson's hesitation to fire Edwin Stanton as a fatal error by the president. Even fellow cabinet members expected Johnson to fire Stanton. "The failure of the President to exercise his undoubted right to rid himself of a minister who differed with him upon very important questions, who had become personally obnoxious to him, and whom he regarded as an enemy and a spy, was a blunder for which there was no excuse, " wrote Hugh McCulloch (1808–1895), Johnson's secretary of the treasury, in his autobiography, *Men and Measures.*

whether African American men could vote in the election of delegates. Johnson decided to restrict voters to those qualified to vote (whites only) under state law at the time of North Carolina's secession. As noted on the "Famous American Trials: The Andrew Johnson Impeachment Trial" Web site, Stanton reported to Sumner that "the opposition of the President to throwing the franchise open to the colored people appeared to be fixed." Congress rejected the plan.

As Johnson fought a continuous losing battle with Congress, he began to express displeasure with Stanton but did not try to fire him. Meanwhile, in early 1867, Congress passed the Tenure of Office Act as another step towards gaining more power over the presidency. The Tenure of Office Act concerned federal officials appointed by the president that required confirmation by the Senate. Such officials could not be removed from their position by the president without the consent of the Senate under the Tenure of Office Act. If the Senate was not in session, the president could suspend an official, but once the Senate reconvened it had to approve the removal or the official would have to be reinstated by the president. Johnson vetoed the measure, but Congress overrode his veto on March 2, 1867, and the Tenure of Office Act became law.

Johnson finally had had enough of Stanton by the summer of 1867. Though Stanton was protected by the Tenure of Office Act, Johnson wanted to remove Stanton and simultaneously challenge the Act. Since Stanton had been appointed by Lincoln to his cabinet, Johnson argued, the Tenure of Office Act did not apply to Johnson's decision to fire Stanton. In August 1867, Johnson sent Stanton a letter that stated, "Public considerations of high character constrain me to say that your resignation as Secretary of War will be accepted." When Stanton refused to resign (replying to Johnson that "public considerations of a high character … constrain

me not to resign"), Johnson was forced to send Stanton a second letter announcing he had been suspended from office, ordering him to cease all exercise of authority, and transferring his power to **Ulysses S. Grant** (1822–1885; see entry), Johnson's choice as an interim secretary of war.

Five months later, on January 3, 1868, the new Congress convened and the Senate refused to approve Stanton's removal by a vote of 35 to 16. Johnson, in turn, refused to accept the Senate's decision and called the Tenure of Office Act an unconstitutional infringement on the power of the executive. Impeachment hearings began a few days later. During the hearings, Johnson's actions as president, public speeches he made denouncing Congress, and his violation of the Tenure of Office Act were all approved as articles (specific charges) of impeachment.

Johnson's impeachment trial began on March 28, 1868, and ended in May. Before the trial, on February 21, 1868,

Editorial cartoon showing Secretary of War Edwin Stanton preparing to load and fire a congressional cannon at President Andrew Johnson (far right) and his choice as Stanton's replacement, Lorenzo Thomas. *The Granger Collection, New York. Reproduced by permission.*

Johnson named a new secretary of war (Grant had chosen not to continue in the position), Major General Lorenzo Thomas (1804–1875), despite the fact that Congress had not recognized his removal of Stanton. Stanton notified his allies in Congress of a presidential order to vacate his office. He received a one-word telegram in reply from Senator Sumner: "Stick."

Stanton did stick; he remained in his office in the War Department building with a guard posted to protect him and to ensure department records were not seized from February 21 until the end of the impeachment votes against Johnson in May. The president was impeached, but the vote to remove him from office fell one short. As a result, on May 26, 1868, Stanton resigned from office and went home for the first time in three months.

A private citizen once again at the age of fifty-three, Stanton took a period of rest after years of having devoted himself to the war effort and then the battles of Reconstruction. He reemerged on the public scene in the fall of 1868 to support Ulysses S. Grant's candidacy for the presidency. Stanton also resumed his law practice. He refused requests that he run for Congress, but accepted an appointment by President Grant to the U.S. Supreme Court. Stanton's nomination was confirmed by the Senate on December 20, 1869. However, Stanton died just four days later and never took his seat on the court.

For More Information

Books

Allison, Amy. *Edwin Stanton: Secretary of War.* New York: Chelsea House, 2001.

Barney, William L. *The Civil War and Reconstruction: A Student Companion.* New York: Oxford University Press, 2001.

Crook, William H. *Through Five Administrations: Reminiscences of Colonel William H. Crook.* New York: Harper & Brothers, 1910.

McCulloch, Hugh. *Men and Measures of Half a Century: Sketches and Comments.* New York: C. Scribner's Sons, 1888. Reprint, New York: Da Capo Press, 1970.

Pratt, Fletcher. *Stanton, Lincoln's Secretary of War.* New York: Norton, 1953. Reprint, Westport, CT: Greenwood Press, 1970.

Thomas, Benjamin Platt, and Harold Melvin Hymans. *Stanton: The Life and Times of Lincoln's Secretary of War.* Westport, CT: Greenwood Press, 1980.

Web Sites

"Edwin M. Stanton (1814–1869)." *Mr. Lincoln's White House.* http://www. mrlincolnswhitehouse.org/templates/index.cfm?ID=96 (accessed on July 30, 2004).

"Famous American Trials: The Andrew Johnson Impeachment Trial." *University of Missouri–Kansas City.* http://www.law.umkc.edu/faculty/ projects/ftrials/impeach/impeachmt.htm (accessed on July 26, 2004).

"The Impeachment of Andrew Johnson." *Harp Week.* http://www.impeach-andrewjohnson.com/11BiographiesKeyIndividuals/EdwinMStanton. htm (accessed on July 30, 2004).

Thaddeus Stevens

Born April 4, 1792
Danville, Vermont

Died August 11, 1868
Washington, D.C.

U.S. congressman, lawyer, and mill owner

> "We have turned, or are about to turn, loose four million slaves without a hut to shelter them or a cent in their pockets. The infernal laws of slavery have prevented them from acquiring an education, understanding the common laws of contract, or of managing the ordinary business of life. This Congress is bound to provide for them until they can take care of themselves."

Thaddeus Stevens. *The Library of Congress.*

A powerful congressman who fought for the abolition (end) of slavery and for civil rights legislation for freedmen, Thaddeus Stevens was a leading "Radical Reconstructionist." This term describes congressmen who favored strict terms and a carefully supervised program for allowing former Confederate states to reenter the Union after the Civil War (1861–65). Stevens led the battle against President **Andrew Johnson** (1808–1875; served 1865–69; see entry), who wanted a speedier and more lenient program for reunification. Stevens led the attempt to impeach (formally accuse of wrongdoing) Johnson and remove him as president; impeachment was successful, but the effort to rid him from office failed by one vote. Throughout his political, legal, and professional careers, Stevens was a champion of people of humble means.

Overcomes hardships

Thaddeus Stevens was born in Danville, Vermont, the youngest of four sons of Joshua and Sally (Morrill) Stevens. Stevens's father was a shoemaker who spent his earnings and then left the family. Some reports suggested he fought and died in the War of 1812 (1812–15). His sudden disappearance left his family in severe poverty. Stevens's mother earned money as a maid and housekeeper. Stevens was sickly as an infant, but his mother raised him into health and worked to ensure he was educated. The family moved to Peacham, Vermont, in 1795. The area was rugged and sparsely settled, but was near an excellent school, Peacham Academy.

Stevens began working at an early age and attended and performed well at the academy. He entered Dartmouth College as a sophomore in 1811, spent one term at the University of Vermont, and graduated from Dartmouth in 1814. Stevens was trained in Greek and Latin, mathematics, and ethics, and wrote and performed with drama clubs. His language and theater skills were evident later when he entered politics and became known as an excellent public speaker.

After graduation, Stevens took a teaching position at a school in York, Pennsylvania, and began studying law. Soon, he crossed the border to Maryland to take his bar exam (a test prospective lawyers must pass to become certified to practice law). Pennsylvania required a specified period of study before one could take the bar exam, but Maryland left it up to the individual. Stevens passed the exam and settled in Gettysburg, Pennsylvania, in 1816 at the age of twenty-four to practice law. He never married.

Stevens struggled to make a living as a lawyer for several years. In 1821, his successful defense of a man accused of murder made him the most sought-after lawyer in the county. He won numerous appeals to the state Supreme Court (the losing side in a court case can often appeal the verdict to a higher court). Stevens also defended runaway slaves from neighboring Maryland, winning freedom for many of them.

With money earned from his successful law practice, Stevens became a partner in 1826 at the James D. Paxton & Company, a builder of stoves. Unable to obtain quality metal, the company bought property near Chambersburg, Pennsylvania, and built a forge (metal shop). The company, which became known as Stevens & Paxton in 1828, was never very profitable. Although dwarfed by competing firms, the company was kept alive by Stevens and continued to provide work for the surrounding community.

Enters politics

Stevens entered politics in the early 1830s. He became a member of the Anti-Masonic Party, which championed the rights of common people. The party derived its name and purpose from distrust of freemasonry—fraternal organizations (brotherhoods) often based in secrecy that many people believed were exerting too much authority in American society. Many of the early presidents, for example, were freemasons, including Andrew Jackson (1767–1845; served 1829–37). Stevens became a political force during the 1831 Anti-Masonic Convention in Baltimore, Maryland, where the party's first presidential candidate, William Wirt (1772–1834), was nominated. Stevens gave an impassioned speech about the dangers of secret societies. In 1833, Stevens was elected to the Pennsylvania House of Representatives as an Anti-Masonic and went on to serve four terms in the Pennsylvania congress. In addition to having mixed success at investigating and legislating against freemasons, Stevens supported legislation in 1834 that expanded the free public school system of Philadelphia across the state, then made an impassioned defense of free education the following year when taxes supporting the system were threatened to be cut. Stevens's advocacy for state support of education extended to colleges as well.

Stevens was a delegate to the Pennsylvania constitutional convention of 1837, where the state constitution was reviewed by delegates representing citizens of the state. Stevens fought for a resolution to abolish slavery in Washington, D.C., through a constitutional amendment that Pennsylvania would be first to support. The resolution failed, but Stevens emerged as a leading abolitionist as well as a defender of working-class citizens. Stevens joined the Whig Party in the mid-1830s; the Whigs and the Democratic Party were the two major political organizations from the early 1830s to the early 1850s. Stevens campaigned for William Henry Harrison (1773–1841; served 1841) for president in 1836 and 1840.

Stevens retired from politics in 1841. He had hoped to be appointed to a position in Harrison's administration after Harrison won the election of 1840. Meanwhile, Stevens faced huge debts from his failed business. He settled as a lawyer in Lancaster, Pennsylvania, in 1842. Stevens rebuilt his finances and returned to politics in 1848, when he was elected to the

U.S. Congress. Stevens immediately joined a group of free-soilers—those against expansion of slavery into territories that had not yet become states. Stevens was fiercely against slavery, criticizing slave owners in Congress and those who defended the institution as an issue for states to decide.

Becomes powerful congressman

Stevens was a leading opponent of the Compromise of 1850, which allowed several prospective new states to decide for themselves whether or not to permit slavery. He was especially angry about the Fugitive Slave Law, which provided federal recognition of the right of slave owners to pursue runaway slaves into nonslave states. In an era when Congress was shaken by loud and angry debates and the country was growing more divided, Stevens was among the harshest critics of slavery.

Along with many Whigs in the early 1850s, Stevens became disgusted with members of his party who continued to support slavery as a states' rights issue. He quit Congress in 1853 and joined the growing movement to establish a new political organization, the Republican Party, made up of Whigs and Democrats against slavery. Stevens helped establish the Republican Party of Pennsylvania. He was a speaker at the Republican National Convention in 1856 and was reelected to Congress as a Republican in 1858. Back in Congress, he railed against Southerners who threatened to secede (separate) from the Union and welcomed the Civil War when it began in 1861.

Following the secession of Southern states that joined the Confederacy and the empty seats in Congress left behind by representatives for those states, Stevens became the most powerful man in Congress. He was chairman of the ways and means committee, a position that oversees all financial bills and, during times of war, all congressional measures relating to the war. Stevens disagreed with President Abraham Lincoln (1809–1865; served 1861–65), a fellow Republican, on many issues. He was one of the two House members who voted against a resolution Lincoln supported that declared that the Civil War was not fought to conquer or to interfere with the established institutions of the South. Stevens instead urged that Confederate property should be seized, slaves should be armed, and that arrests and convictions of Confederates should be quick and punishments should be harsh. Nevertheless, Stevens supported important measures for the Lincoln administration to fight the war, including raising money through taxes, loans, bonds, and the printing of greenbacks (named for their color), the first national paper currency in the United States.

Stevens disagreed with Lincoln's plan for Reconstruction. Called the Ten Percent Plan, Lincoln's program included pardon and amnesty to Confederates who would swear loyalty to the Union. Control of local governments would return to former Confederate states when 10 percent of the 1860 voting population participated in elections. Instead, Stevens wanted more difficult and challenging rules for readmission and believed Congress should set the terms for Reconstruction. The state of Louisiana met the requirements proposed by Lincoln and he supported readmitting the state. When Congress reassembled in December 1864, just after Lincoln was reelected, it pressured Lincoln to drop his support to readmit Louisiana. Reconstruction policy was still being debated when the Civil War ended in April 1865 and Lincoln was assassinated.

Congress battles the president

Vice President Andrew Johnson succeeded to the presidency following Lincoln's assassination in April 1865, just days after the Confederacy surrendered. Congress was not in session, and Johnson believed he should be in charge of Reconstruction. Favoring a limited federal government and wanting to reestablish state governments in the South as quickly as possible, Johnson modified Lincoln's Ten Percent Plan to include a requirement that states ratify the Thirteenth Amendment (which includes the abolishment of slavery). If states met Johnson's demands, the president would recognize their restoration to the Union.

As soon as Congress convened in December 1865, Stevens led Congress in appointing a joint committee (a committee comprising members of the House and the Senate) on Reconstruction. Stevens was named chairman of the House

Editorial cartoon shows President Andrew Johnson (left) and U.S. senator Thaddeus Stevens of Pennsylvania facing off each other. *The Library of Congress.*

side of the committee. On December 18, 1865, he gave a rousing speech declaring that it was the duty of Congress to supervise Reconstruction and demand tough terms of the former Confederate states ("they must come in as new states or remain as conquered provinces"). Stevens also insisted that Congress protect the rights and help provide opportunities for freedmen (see box) and rejected Johnson's authority to define the terms of Reconstruction.

An Excerpt from Stevens's Address to Congress on December 18, 1865

In a stirring speech on December 18, 1865, Thaddeus Stevens forcefully spoke out in favor of Congress taking charge of the Reconstruction efforts. The following is an excerpt taken from the *From Revolution to Reconstruction* Web site:

> Nobody, I believe, pretends that with their old constitutions and frames of government [the former Confederate states] can be permitted to claim their old rights under the Constitution. They have torn their constitutional States into atoms, and built on their foundations fabrics of a totally different character. Dead men cannot raise themselves. Dead States cannot restore their existence "as it was." Whose especial duty is it to do it? In whom does the Constitution place the power? Not in the judicial branch of Government, for it only adjudicates [judges] and does not prescribe laws. Not in the Executive, for he only executes and cannot make laws. Not in the Commander-in-Chief of the armies, for he can only hold them under military rule until the sovereign legislative power of the conqueror shall give them law. Unless the law of nations is a dead letter, the late war between two acknowledged belligerents severed their original compacts and broke all the ties that bound them together. The future condition of the conquered power depends on the will of the conqueror. They must come in as new states or remain as conquered provinces. Congress ... is the only power that can act in the matter....

> But this is not all that we ought to do before inveterate [habitual] rebels are invited to participate in our legislation. We have turned, or are about to turn, loose four million slaves without a hut to shelter them or a cent in their pockets. The infernal laws of slavery have prevented them from acquiring an education, understanding the common laws of contract, or of managing the ordinary business of life. This Congress is bound to provide for them until they can take care of themselves. If we do not furnish them with homesteads, and hedge them around with protective laws; if we leave them to the legislation of their late masters, we had better have left them in bondage.

> If we fail in this great duty now, when we have the power, we shall deserve and receive the execration [curse] of history and of all future ages.

In February 1866, Congress and the president began clashing over legislation when Johnson vetoed the Freedmen's Bureau Bill, which intended to establish an organization to supervise relief and educational activities relating to war refugees and freedmen. After Stevens and Johnson made speeches attacking one another, Stevens helped push through Congress a civil rights bill and a revised Freedmen's Bureau bill over Johnson's vetoes.

When more Republicans won congressional seats in the election of 1866, Congress came to dominate the president. Stevens tried twice to begin impeachment hearings against Johnson, but neither attempt succeeded. Stevens was further in-

censed after a riot in New Orleans, Louisiana, on July 30, 1866. A mob attacked a meeting of Republicans and killed thirty-eight people, including thirty-four African Americans, and many more were injured. New Orleans mayor John T. Monroe (1823–1871) and members of the police and fire forces encouraged the attack. A congressional committee investigating the riots suggested that President Johnson knew of the planned attack and did nothing to stop it. Meanwhile, Johnson made fiery speeches against Congress as he campaigned for Democratic candidates before the congressional elections of 1866.

When Johnson attempted to fire his secretary of war, **Edwin Stanton** (1814–1869; see entry), in violation of the Tenure of Office Act Congress passed in 1867, Stevens pushed and won a resolution from Congress to begin impeachment hearings. (The Tenure of Office Act concerned federal officials appointed by the president that required confirmation by the Senate. These officials could not be removed from their position by the president without the approval of the Senate under

Thaddeus Stevens closes the House debate on the proposed impeachment of President Andrew Johnson on March 2, 1868. *Wood engraving by Theodore R. Davis. The Library of Congress.*

the Tenure of Office Act. If the Senate was in recess, the president could suspend an official, but once the Senate returned to session, it had to approve the removal or the president would would be required to reinstate the official.) Stevens was a member of the committee that drafted articles (charges) of impeachment, but his health began to fail. He took little part in the impeachment trial of Johnson that occurred in March 1868. Johnson avoided removal from office by one vote.

Stevens was too ill to leave Washington, D.C., to return home, and he died on August 11, 1868. Stevens was buried in a small graveyard in Lancaster, Pennsylvania. His tombstone bears an epitaph he wrote for himself: "I repose in this quiet and secluded spot, not from any natural preference for solitude, but, finding other cemeteries limited by charter rules as to race, I have chosen this, that I might illustrate in my death the principles which I advocated through a long life—Equality of Man before his Creator."

For More Information

Books

Brodie, Fawn McKay. *Thaddeus Stevens: Scourge of the South.* New York: W. W. Norton, 1959.

Palmer, Beverly Wilson, ed. *The Selected Papers of Thaddeus Stevens.* Pittsburgh: University of Pittsburgh Press, 1997.

Trefousse, Hans L. *Thaddeus Stevens: Nineteenth-Century Egalitarian.* Chapel Hill: University of North Carolina Press, 1997.

Web Sites

"The Impeachment of Andrew Johnson." *HarpWeek.* http://www.impeach-andrewjohnson.com/11BiographiesKeyIndividuals/ThaddeusStevens.htm (accessed on July 30, 2004).

"Thaddeus Stevens' Legacy." *Thaddeus Stevens College of Technology.* http://www.stevenscollege.edu/about/history.htm (accessed on July 30, 2004).

"Thaddeus Stevens: Speech of December 18, 1865." *From Revolution to Reconstruction.* http://odur.let.rug.nl/~usa/D/1851-1875/reconstruction/steven.htm (accessed on July 30, 2004).

Charles Sumner

Born January 6, 1811
Boston, Massachusetts

Died March 11, 1874
Washington, D.C.

U.S. senator

Charles Sumner led the causes of abolition (ending slavery) and civil rights for over two decades in the U.S. Senate. Uncompromising and often intolerant of opinions different than his own—Sumner once stated, "Nothing against slavery can be unconstitutional!"—he pursued immediate and absolute human equality. During the Reconstruction era (1865-77), Sumner was the Senate leader of the Radical Reconstructionists. These congressmen advocated an aggressive policy for securing the social and economic equality for freedmen (former slaves) and sought to set the terms by which Confederate states and their supporters would return to the Union. Radical Reconstructionists ensured that Congress, not the president, would lead the Reconstruction program, and when they were challenged by President **Andrew Johnson** (1808–1875; served 1865–69; see entry), the Radical Reconstructionists impeached the president and tried to remove him from office. Sumner clashed as well with the administration of President **Ulysses S. Grant** (1822–1885; served 1869–77; see entry). When Sumner died in office in 1874, the influence of the Radical Reconstructionists passed as well.

"This is one of the last great battles with slavery. Driven from the legislative chambers [and] the field of war, this monstrous power has found a refuge in the executive mansion, where, in utter disregard of the Constitution and laws, it seeks to exercise its ancient, far-reaching sway.... Andrew Johnson is the impersonation of the tyrannical slave power. In him it lives again."

Charles Sumner. *The Library of Congress.*

Slowly finding his way

Charles Sumner was born in Boston, Massachusetts, on January 6, 1811, to Charles Pinckney Sumner and Relief (Jacob) Sumner. Sumner's father, a graduate of Harvard College (later called Harvard University), was a lawyer and served briefly as county sheriff. Independent-minded and outspoken, especially against slavery, Sumner's father promoted equal rights and racially integrated schools and opposed a law prohibiting intermarriage of blacks and whites. Sumner attended the Boston Latin School from ages ten to fifteen, then tried but was unsuccessful in securing an appointment to enter the West Point Military Academy. He went instead to Harvard College, excelling in history and literature.

After graduating from college, Sumner attended Harvard Law School from 1831 to 1833. He was mentored (advised) by the law school's distinguished professor, Joseph Story (1779–1845), a Supreme Court justice who encouraged Sumner to take a teaching position at the college following the completion of his studies. Sumner preferred to begin a law practice, but first traveled to Washington, D.C., to attend sessions of the Supreme Court.

As a respected student of Story, Sumner enjoyed many privileges in Washington, D.C. He had conversations with the justices, including Chief Justice John Marshall (1755–1835); he heard a case in which the opposing attorneys were the famed Massachusetts congressman Daniel Webster (1782–1852) and Francis Scott Key (1799–1843), the writer of the "Star-Spangled Banner" and leader of a flourishing law practice. Sumner also attended sessions in the U.S. Senate.

Upon returning to Boston, Sumner soon felt uninspired by the daily routine of practicing law. He returned to Harvard Law School as a lecturer, wrote essays for *American Jurist,* a law journal, and reviewed and revised textbooks used in law classes. He was friends with William Ellery Channing (1780–1842), a Unitarian clergyman who organized groups to eliminate slavery and promote temperance. Sumner was in a social circle that included famous poets Henry Wadsworth Longfellow (1807–1882) and Ralph Waldo Emerson (1803–1882).

Feeling restless and making little progress in his profession, Sumner borrowed money in 1836 and traveled to Europe. He spent two years, primarily in England, France, and Germany, observing and studying politics and law and meeting famous leaders and writers of the day. Upon his return, he maintained a lively social life, but was again miserable in the daily practice of law. After failing to secure a position as reporter of the Supreme Court, he spent long hours adding notes to a twenty-volume collection on law, *Reports of Cases … in the High Court of Chancery,* published in 1844.

The speech that changed Sumner's life

A major turning point in Sumner's life occurred on July 4, 1845. Sumner had been chosen to be the main speaker at an Independence Day celebration in Boston. Facing a large crowd for the first time, Sumner gave an impassioned address on peace, demanding, "Can there be in our age any peace that is not honorable, any war that is not dishonorable?" The speech was controversial, occurring on Independence Day and in front of a crowd that included military personnel. But the power in his voice and his words, and his animated appearance (especially since he stood six-feet, four inches), made Sumner a lively and commanding orator. He was quickly inundated with invitations to speak at other venues.

During that time, many New Englanders were concerned about war and the spread of slavery. Texas was entering the Union as a slave state, and the Mexican-American War (1846–48) was viewed by some Americans as an aggressive action against a weaker nation. Sumner railed against slavery and war, winning over supportive crowds, but also drawing criticism for his unsparing attacks and uncompromising approach to what he believed was right.

In 1848, Sumner called a convention in Massachusetts to oppose the two presidential candidates, Democrat Lewis Cass (1782–1866) and Whig Zachary Taylor (1784–1850; served 1849–50), neither of whom pledged to abolish slavery. Sumner was among many in the Whig Party who left their party to back the Free Soil Party in the 1848 election ("Free Soil" referred to a position against expanding slavery to new states). Sumner was unsuccessful in his bid for Congress that year, but he was nominated in 1850 as a candidate for the U.S. Senate and won the office (see box).

Sumner Becomes Senator

Until passage of the Seventeenth Amendment to the Constitution in 1912, U.S. senators were voted into office by their state congress. The state legislatures were charged with acting on the will of the people but did not always elect the candidate who had received the most votes. In 1850, Sumner did not have enough support in the state congress to be elected, but no other candidate was able to win the two-thirds vote necessary to become senator. Town meetings were called in several communities in Massachusetts, where the law legally authorized communities to call for a vote and then instruct the local representative to support the candidate who received the most votes. Sumner won the popular support needed to overcome reluctance by the Massachusetts state legislature to elect him to the U.S. Senate. The state congress was concerned about Sumner's brash outspokenness.

Firebrand senator

Sumner entered the Senate at an especially turbulent time. The Compromise of 1850, intended to settle national unrest about the spread of slavery, was being debated. As part of the compromise, California was admitted to the Union as a free state; the territories of New Mexico and Utah (encompassing present-day Utah and Nevada) would determine for themselves whether or not to permit slavery; and the Fugitive Slave Law permitted slave owners to enter nonslave states to pursue, capture, and return fugitive (runaway) slaves. With only five days before the end of a nine-month session of Congress, Sumner earned the right to speak after having proposed an amendment to the Compromise. He used the occasion to lecture for more than three hours about the evils of the Fugitive Slave Law. Many Southern senators expressed their anger toward Sumner, and only four senators voted for Sumner's amendment. Sumner had entered the debate too late, but he became a notable new voice in the Senate to speak for those unwilling to accept anything less than the abolishment of slavery.

The Compromise of 1850 only increased national disruption over slavery. With abolition sentiments spreading quickly and impatience with the Whig Party's willingness to compromise, many Whigs and Northern Democrats left their parties to join the Republican Party, formed in 1854. Sumner played an important part in the organization of the party.

Meanwhile, the Kansas-Nebraska bill of 1854 came up for debate in Congress. The bill prepared those territories to petition for statehood and allowed them to decide by popular sovereignty whether or not to be free or slave states. This potential expansion of slavery brought more wrath from Sumn-

ASSAULT ON SENATOR SUMNER, BY P. S. BROOKS.

er, who even threatened to support a Northern antislavery sentiment for seceding from (leaving) the Union. Sumner outraged supporters of the Kansas-Nebraska bill, many of whom urged his expulsion (ejection) from the Senate.

Sumner only became more vocal. He made his impassioned Senate speech, "The Crime against Kansas," at a time when many feared violence would erupt between pro- and antislavery factions in Kansas. Sumner abandoned all politeness in his speech: He singled out supporters of the bill and

U.S. representative Preston S. Brooks of South Carolina attacks U.S. senator Charles Sumner of Massachusetts in the Senate chamber on May 22, 1856. *The Granger Collection, New York. Reproduced by permission.*

An Excerpt from Sumner's "Crimes Against Kansas" Speech

Charles Sumner's speech "Crimes Against Kansas" led to a violent incident in which Sumner was attacked with a cane by U.S. representative Preston Brooks of South Carolina. Sumner had made inflammatory remarks about Brooks's uncle, U.S. senator Andrew Butler of South Carolina. Brooks was present for Sumner's speech; Butler was not.

[The] Senator in the unrestrained chivalry of his nature, has undertaken to apply opprobrious [insulting] words to those who differ from him on this floor. He calls them "sectional and fanatical"; and opposition to the usurpation [seizure by force] in Kansas he denounces as "an uncalculating fanaticism." To be sure these charges lack all grace of originality, and all sentiment of truth; but the adventurous Senator does not hesitate. He is the uncompromising, unblushing representative on this floor of a flagrant sectionalism, which now domineers over the Republic, and yet with a ludicrous ignorance of his own position unable to see himself as others see him—or with an effrontery [boldness] which even his white head ought not to protect from rebuke, he applies to those here who resist his sectionalism the very epithet which designates himself....

The Senator from South Carolina has read many books of chivalry, and believes himself a chivalrous knight, with sentiments of honor and courage. Of course he has chosen a mistress to whom he has made his vows, and who, though ugly to others, is always lovely to him; though polluted in the sight of the world, is chaste in his sight, I mean the harlot, Slavery.

insulted them. Some abolitionists praised the speech, and within a few weeks over a million copies of it were distributed. Some of the interest, however, was spurred by news about violence—not in Kansas, but in the U.S. Senate instead. Two days after his speech, Sumner was brutally attacked by U.S. representative Preston S. Brooks (1819–1857) of South Carolina, who beat Sumner with a cane. In his speech, Sumner mocked Brooks's uncle, proslavery U.S. senator Andrew Butler (1796–1857) of South Carolina, accusing him of taking "a mistress ... who, though ugly to others, is always lovely to him; though polluted in the sight of the world, is chaste in his sight. I mean, the harlot [prostitute], Slavery."

Sumner's wounds left him unable, despite two attempts, to return to his work in the Senate. He tried powerful and painful cures and traveled to spas in Europe, but he did not return to regular duty in the Senate for over three years. Meanwhile, he was reelected by the almost unanimous (unopposed) vote of the Massachusetts legislature.

Sumner resumed work just as the Union began to dissolve. Southern leaders were being even more aggressive: Congress easily passed resolutions introduced by U.S. senator **Jefferson Davis** (1808–1889; see Confederate Leaders entry) of Mississippi to approve slaves as property in territories not yet states. Sumner responded by a complete assault on the institution of slavery. As Abraham Lincoln (1809–1865; served 1861–65) took office and the Civil War (1861–65) began, Sumner urged complete abolishment of slavery and expressed frustration, respectfully, as Lincoln pursued a more gradual policy of emancipation (freedom).

When the Republicans took control of the Senate for the first time after the elections of 1860, Sumner became chairman of the committee on foreign relations, a position he filled admirably during the war and in the early years of the Reconstruction era. He helped ensure that there would be no significant international interference with the Union's war effort.

By 1862, he began the struggle to secure for all citizens of the United States, regardless of race or color, absolute equality of civil rights. He was insistent that the initiation and the control of postwar America should be by Congress, not by the president. Meanwhile, on October 17, 1866, at the age of fifty-five, Sumner married Alice (Mason) Hooper, a young widow. They separated within a year and were later divorced.

Radical Reconstructionist

Following the end of the Civil War in 1865, Sumner and U.S. representative **Thaddeus Stevens** (1792–1868; see entry) of Pennsylvania, became the Senate and House leaders, respectively, of opposition to President Andrew Johnson's Reconstruction policies. The congressional leaders and their supporters are known, historically, as Radical Republicans or Radical Reconstructionists because their policies were both more progressive and punishing than those proposed by President Lincoln and pursued by his successor, President Johnson. Sumner fought for immediate enfranchisement (freedom) for freemen as well as free schools and farmsteads for African Americans. He vigorously supported Republican legislative proposals for establishing the Freedmen's Bureau, passage of the Thirteenth Amendment that abolished slavery,

An illustration portraying Charles Sumner as the modern Moses to African Americans, due to his fight for black rights. © *Corbis.*

and civil rights legislation to protect freed slaves from Black Codes (laws that placed severe restrictions on freed slaves).

Sumner's more progressive proposals were not enacted, but the Radical Reconstructionists were successful in controlling the Reconstruction program. A struggle between Congress and President Johnson ensued, and when Johnson attempted to exert his power it led to angry confrontations that culminated in a vote for impeachment (dismissal from office). Impeachment proceedings begin in the House of Representatives, where a committee considers charges and votes whether or not to present an impeachment proposal to the entire House. If the House votes by two-thirds majority that the president has committed impeachable acts, based on committee evidence and recommendations, an impeachment trial is conducted in the Senate. The Senate then votes on whether or not to remove the president from office.

President Johnson's impeachment trial began on March 30, 1868. Sumner led the prosecution, as noted on the

"Famous American Trials: The Andrew Johnson Impeachment Trial" Web site: "This is one of the last great battles with slavery. Driven from the legislative chambers, driven from the field of war, this monstrous power has found a refuge in the executive mansion, where, in utter disregard of the Constitution and laws, it seeks to exercise its ancient, far-reaching sway. All this is very plain. Nobody can question it."

However, impeachment was questionable and seemed politically motivated to doubters. The impeachment of Andrew Johnson failed in the Senate. There were fifty-four senators at the time, and thirty-six votes were needed to remove Johnson. The Senate voted 35–19 to impeach Johnson. The measure failed by one vote.

Sumner also failed to get along with President Ulysses S. Grant, who succeeded Johnson, though Sumner and Grant were from the same party. Grant wanted to annex (make part of U.S. territory) Santo Domingo, and Sumner led the opposition. The Sumner-Grant relationship became so strained that Sumner lost his chairmanship of the Senate Foreign Relations committee. Sumner's criticism of Grant's civil rights policies, which Sumner judged as too little and too ineffective, contributed to his loss of the chairmanship. Fellow Republicans had become wary of Sumner's attacks on Grant and were fearful of losing control of the presidency to Democrats.

In the presidential election of 1872, in fact, Sumner supported Grant's rival, newspaper editor **Horace Greeley** (1811–1872; see entry). Grant won reelection easily. By this time, the Republican Party had grown more conservative, and

Sumner vs. Presidents

Charles Sumner clashed with all six presidents who served while he was senator. Three preceded Abraham Lincoln—Millard Fillmore (1800–1874; served 1850–53), Franklin Pierce (1804–1869; served 1853–57), and James Buchanan 1791–1868; served 1857–61). They were vilified (talked and written about negatively) by Sumner because they allowed states to decide the issue of slavery. Presidents Johnson and Grant, according to Sumner, proceeded too slowly on civil rights legislation. Sumner also clashed with Lincoln, although much more respectfully, over the president's gradual approach to emancipation.

In August 1861, John C. Frémont (1813–1890), commander of the Union army in Missouri, proclaimed freedom for all slaves owned by Confederates in Missouri. Lincoln asked Frémont to pursue gradual emancipation, freeing only those slaves owned by Missourians actively working for the Confederacy. When Frémont refused, Lincoln replaced him. Sumner wrote a protest letter to Lincoln over his gradual emancipation policy, stating how sad it was "to have the power of a god and not use it godlike."

Radical Republicans were on the wane. Sumner continued to fight for the interests of Southern freedmen, but legislation and federal action in their favor always proved to be weaker than Sumner advocated.

Sumner fell ill in 1874 and was advised against continuing his Senate work. Nevertheless, he attended the Senate session of March 10, 1874. That evening, he suffered a heart attack; Sumner died the next day. His body lay in state in the rotunda of the Capitol, and the funeral services were held in Cambridge, Massachusetts.

For More Information

Books

Blue, Frederick J. *Charles Sumner and the Conscience of the North.* Arlington Heights, IL: Harlan Davidson, 1994.

Donald, David Herbert. *Charles Sumner.* New York: Da Capo Press, 1996.

Web Sites

"The Caning of Charles Sumner." *U.S. Senate.* http://www.senate.gov/artandhistory/history/minute/The_Caning_of_Senator_Charles_Sumner.htm (accessed on June 25, 2004).

"Charles Sumner." *Spartacus Schoolnet.* http://www.spartacus.schoolnet.co.uk/USASsumner.htm (accessed on June 25, 2004).

Linder, Douglas O. "Famous American Trials: The Andrew Johnson Impeachment Trial." *University of Missouri–Kansas School of Law.* http://www.law.umkc.edu/faculty/projects/ftrials/impeach/impeachmt. htm (accessed on June 25, 2004).

Samuel J. Tilden

Born February 9, 1814
New Lebanon, New York

Died August 4, 1886
Yonkers, New York

Governor of New York, presidential candidate, and lawyer

S amuel J. Tilden was a popular national figure during the 1870s as he successfully fought against political corruption in New York and became the Democratic presidential candidate in the 1876 election. Tilden lost one of the most controversial presidential elections in American history. Despite finishing with 250,000 more popular votes than his opponent, **Rutherford B. Hayes** (1822–1893; served 1877–81; see entry), Tilden fell one electoral vote shy of becoming president. A newly created election commission ruled that disputed electoral votes from four states should all go to Hayes. Tilden retired to private life after the election. Following his death, Tilden's fortune, as directed in his will, supported the founding of the New York Public Library.

"If my voice could reach throughout our country and be heard in its remotest hamlet I would say, 'Be of good cheer. The Republic will live. The institutions of our fathers are not to expire in shame. The sovereignty of the people shall be rescued from this peril and be reestablished.'"

Samuel J. Tilden. *The Library of Congress.*

Political teen

Born in New Lebanon, New York, on February 9, 1814, Samuel Jones Tilden was the fifth child of Elam and Polly Tilden. Tilden's father, who owned a store and held the job of postmaster, was an important political figure in the state. He met regularly with elected officials and candidates from around the state. Among them was Martin Van Buren (1782–1862), a New York congressman and governor, a founding member of the Democratic Party in the late 1820s, and a future U.S. vice president and president. By growing up and being encouraged to participate in a lively political environment, Tilden was groomed for a political career.

Tilden suffered health problems while growing up, and they may have been worsened by his father's constant attention and home remedies. Unable to attend school regularly, he received tutoring at home. In his teens, Tilden attended an academy at Williamstown, Massachusetts, but returned home for health reasons. Finally, at age eighteen in 1832, he went to New York City to continue his schooling and to receive more professional medical attention. Living with an aunt who owned a boarding house, Tilden ended up spending most of his time running her business as well as handling political errands for his father.

Tilden's interest in politics motivated him to write an article on a highly controversial political topic: the veto of a bill by President Andrew Jackson (1767–1845; served 1829–37) that would have renewed the charter (contract) of the national bank of the United States. Jackson believed that the bank concentrated too much power in the federal government and wealthy people of the North at the expense of states. Tilden's defense of Jackson's veto was published by the Democratic Party and distributed throughout New York State.

Tilden entered Yale University in June 1834, but left after one term. He returned to New York City, occasionally took classes at the University of the City of New York (later New York University), and focused primarily on writing about politics. Using the pseudonym (name used by an author to conceal true identity) Jacksonis Amicus, he wrote a series of articles for the *New York Times* during the spring of 1837 in which he defended President Martin Van Buren's threat to veto bills that would abolish (end) slavery in Washington, D.C. Democrats of the time believed that states, not the federal government, should decide whether or not to permit slavery. Meanwhile, Tilden entered the law school of the University of the City of New York in 1838 and went on to complete a three-year course. He served as a clerk in a law office, passed the bar exam that certified him as a lawyer, and began a law practice in 1841 in New York City at the age of twenty-seven.

High-profile lawyer

Tilden prospered as a lawyer, working with sustained energy and health that he had never enjoyed previously in his life. He quickly became a key attorney representing New York City and a leading figure in the New York Democratic Party. Democrats during the 1840s became a split party. One group, nicknamed the "Hunkers" and then the "Hardshells," was closely aligned with Southern Democrats and defended slavery. Tilden was part of an opposing faction called "Barn-burners" and then the "Softshells," who opposed the expansion of slavery as settlers moved westward to new territories and states. In 1845, there were thirty states, and only six west of the Mississippi River.

Tilden's political activity during this period included a term in the New York state legislature, serving as a delegate in a state constitutional convention (where a state's constitution is revised) in 1846, and making an unsuccessful bid for the position of attorney general of New York in 1855. Tilden turned his attention back to his law practice in 1855 and won recognition for his work on a voting fraud case. In 1857, he was involved in a high-profile murder trial. Meanwhile, he fought corruption and began advising railroad companies on legal ways to finance operations and reorganize their businesses to maximize profits. Tilden became so popular as a legal adviser to railroads that he made a fortune during the boom in railroad building from the 1850s to the 1870s.

Tilden opposed the election of Abraham Lincoln (1809–1865; served 1861–65) in 1860, believing that it would result in a separation between North and South. When the Civil War (1861–65) broke out, Tilden expected the North to use its superior manpower and industrial might to crush the rebellion. When the war progressed more slowly, Tilden turned his attention to maintaining the strength of the Democratic Party. Democrats were a decided minority in Congress during and immediately after the Civil War because

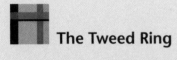

The Tweed Ring

The Tweed Ring was the most notorious of corrupt political machines that dominated politics in several cities and states, as well as on the national level, from the 1860s through the 1880s. Millions of dollars collected in New York City was diverted from the city treasury to political friends through the administration of William Marcy "Boss" Tweed. Tweed was born in New York City on April 3, 1823. He left school at age eleven to work with his father making chairs and later worked as a saddle maker and bookkeeper in a brush business during his teens.

Tweed enjoyed working in New York's volunteer fire department. At age twenty-seven in 1850, he became foreman of a fire department popular in the community. The following year, he was elected as an alderman. Tweed was then elected to the U.S. Congress for a term, 1853–55, but he missed New York politics and returned in 1855 with his mind set on gaining

power in the Democratic Party and the city. As he accumulated power during the 1860s through such positions as membership on the city board of supervisors, state senator, chairman of the state finance committee, school commissioner, deputy street commissioner, and commissioner of public works, Tweed used his political influence to open a law office to dispense legal services to large corporations—services that were often illegal or that benefited Tweed and corporations at the expense of taxpayers. By 1867, Tweed was a millionaire.

The Tweed Ring began in 1866 when "Boss" Tweed and several other New York City officials arranged to have a portion of monies collected for each city contract diverted to members of the ring. By 1869, over 50 percent of all money in the contracts was directed to the Tweed Ring. For example, the cost of building a county courthouse was $12 million, but more than half of the cost

many of their members were from Southern states that had seceded (separated) from the Union.

National prominence during the Reconstruction era

Tilden supported the policies of President **Andrew Johnson** (1808–1875; served 1865–69; see entry), who became president in April 1865 after the war ended and President Lincoln was assassinated. Johnson favored the quick reinstatement of former Confederate states and little federal management of them. Johnson's program for Reconstruction

William M. "Boss" Tweed. © *Bettmann/Corbis.*

"Elegant Oakey"; City Comptroller Richard B. Connolly, also known as "Slippery Dick"; City Chamberlain Peter Barr Sweeny (1825–1911), also called "Brains"; and Tweed, who at the time was president of the Board of Supervisors and leader of Tammany Hall, the city office of New York.

The Tweed Ring was exposed in 1870. A coalition of reformers, including lawyer and state Democratic party leader Samuel J. Tilden, reporters for the *New York Times,* and political enemies of Tweed publicized the crimes and prosecuted members of the ring. Tweed and several associates ended up in prison. Tweed was initially sentenced to twelve years in prison, but was set free in 1875, then was arrested again when previously unknown criminal activities were revealed. Tweed avoided arrest and escaped to Spain, but he ended up back in New York and in jail. He died in jail on April 12, 1878.

came from overcharges for services, building materials, and permits, and that money went to the Tweed Ring. Between 1866 and 1871, the city lost between $40 and $100 million to the Tweed Ring. The ring members were Mayor A. Oakey Hall (1826–1898), known as

was opposed by congressional Republicans, who wanted more difficult requirements for Confederate states to rejoin the Union as well as federal supervision of state governments and civil rights legislation that extended voting rights and legal protection for newly emancipated slaves.

Tilden became chairman of the New York Democratic Party in 1866 and was elected a delegate to the state constitutional convention of 1867. Tilden's major activity during the Reconstruction era involved exposing and undermining the "Tweed Ring" in New York City. Led by an unethical city official, William M. Tweed (1823-1878; see box), the Tweed Ring exerted absolute control of city politics and finances. In 1872,

Tilden worked with the state legislature to create laws that broke the power of the ring. Using his talents as a lawyer, he fought appeals by members of the ring and used legal means for bringing those involved in criminal activities to trial, and then worked to win convictions and remove them from city positions. For evidence of fraud, Tilden developed a system that tracked how municipal funds were diverted into private bank accounts of members of the Tweed Ring. In addition to smashing the Tweed Ring, Tilden led reform efforts of the state judiciary.

Tilden earned a national reputation as a reformer and was immensely popular in New York, where his work against the Tweed Ring was regularly reported in newspapers. Tilden was elected governor of New York in 1874 as a champion of reform. He swiftly improved the financial situation in the state during a period when the nation was experiencing an economic depression. He cut state taxes and expenditures and saved the state millions of dollars by eliminating fraud and wasteful spending. He busted the "Canal Ring," a group of politicians who had become wealthy by controlling construction and repair of the state's extensive system of canals.

Tilden's high-profile success as a reformer during the first half of the 1870s occurred at a time of much corruption in the federal government. Many government officials in the administration of President **Ulysses S. Grant** (1822–1885; served 1869–77; see entry) were implicated in scandals, as were members of Congress. During a period of economic hardship for the country, Congress voted and cashed in on a large, retroactive (covering a specified period of the past) pay raise. When the National Democratic Convention met at St. Louis, Missouri, in June 1876 to nominate a presidential candidate, Tilden was a popular choice along with Thomas A. Hendricks (1819–1885), a well-liked congressman from Indiana. Tilden won the nomination on the second round of voting, and Hendricks became his running mate.

Almost president

The presidential campaign of 1876 was ugly. Democrats were unrelenting in their criticism of the Grant administration and Congress, even though the Republican candidate,

A campaign broadside showing the 1876 Democratic ticket of Samuel J. Tilden and Thomas A. Hendricks.
The Library of Congress.

Thomas Nast illustration referring to the controversial presidential election of 1876 between Republican Rutherford B. Hayes and Democrat Samuel J. Tilden. One hand stops another hand from picking up a gun, suggesting a truce is preferable to violence; "Tilden or Blood" headline is on paper beneath hands. *The Library of Congress.*

Rutherford B. Hayes, had been governor of Ohio and had little association with events in Washington, D.C. Republicans called Tilden a sympathizer of the South and implied that his long association with railroad companies was a form of corruption that had made him rich. Tilden, meanwhile, did not run a spirited campaign; he continued to devote his energy to his role as governor of New York. In addition, poor health reclaimed Tilden, now sixty-two years old.

The election of 1876 became one of the most controversial in American history. Nearly 250,000 more voters cast their ballot for Tilden over Hayes, but disputes in election returns in four states (Louisiana, South Carolina, Florida, and Oregon) left the Electoral College vote in limbo. (See "How the Electoral College Works" in Rutherford B. Hayes entry.) A total of 185 electoral votes were needed for victory: Tilden led Hayes 184 to 163, with 22 electoral votes in dispute.

The election results would not be finalized until four months after the election itself, in early March 1877, days before the inauguration of the new president. (For more on the disputed election of 1876, see the Rutherford B. Hayes entry). Hayes and Tilden remained on the sidelines while a bitter dispute raged in Congress; the dispute was resolved by the creation of the Electoral Commission. The purpose of the commission was to examine the voting irregularities that had occurred in the four states, make judgments on each, and, based on the judgment, allocate the electoral votes to the candidates. The fifteen-member commission was supposed to be bipartisan (made up of members from both political parties), with an even split of Republicans, Democrats, and independents. The one independent member resigned, however, and was replaced by a Republican. Eventually, when the commission voted on rewarding the electoral votes for each state based on their findings, the votes ran strictly along party lines, 8-7, in each case, for Hayes. Hayes took the remaining 22 electoral votes and won, 185-184 over Tilden.

Tilden was understandably angry and bitter at the results, including the long process used to declare a winner and rumors of a deal—nicknamed the Compromise of 1877—where Hayes would win the election if he promised to bring about an end to Reconstruction. Tilden would always be convinced he was unjustly deprived of the presidency, but he did not press matters. Even a decade after the Civil War, the nation was still divided, and Tilden believed he would cause more harm by continuing to press his cause rather than accepting the resolution offered by the Electoral Commission. In his concession speech, Tilden stated, "If my voice could reach throughout our country and be heard in its remotest hamlet I would say, 'Be of good cheer. The Republic will live. The institutions of our fathers are not to expire in shame. The sovereignty of the people shall be rescued from this peril and be re-established.'"

After taking a trip to England in 1877, Tilden endured a long investigation into his tax records, the results of which showed nothing irregular. Meanwhile, in 1879, he purchased an estate in Yonkers, New York, where he quietly lived the rest of his life. Tilden died in August 1886 at the age of seventy-two. Never married, Tilden left most of his estimated $6 million estate to the Tilden Trust with the goal of establishing a public library for New York City. That goal was realized a few years after his death.

For More Information

Books and Periodicals

Flick, Alexander Clarence, and Gustav S. Lobrano. *Samuel Jones Tilden: A Study in Political Sagacity.* New York, Dodd, Mead & Company, 1939. Reprint, Westport, CT: Greenwood Press, 1973.

Goldman, David J. *Presidential Losers.* Minneapolis: Lerner Publications, 2004.

Morris, Roy, Jr. *Fraud of the Century: Rutherford B. Hayes, Samuel Tilden, and the Stolen Election of 1876.* New York: Simon & Schuster, 2003.

Rehnquist, William H. *Centennial Crisis: The Disputed Election of 1876.* New York: Alfred A. Knopf, 2004.

"Samuel Tilden's Speech to the Manhattan Club Conceding the Election of 1876." *New York Herald* (June 13, 1877): p. 3.

Zebulon Vance

Born May 13, 1830
Buncombe County, North Carolina

Died April 15, 1894
Washington, D.C.

Politician and lawyer

Z ebulon Vance was an important political force for North Carolina for over thirty years. He attempted to ease the growing unrest between North and South in the years leading up to the Civil War (1861–65). He was a Confederate military leader during the war, but he had key differences with Confederate leaders over their policy of forced conscription (mandatory military service for all young men) and their harsh treatment of deserters (those who leave military service without permission). Following the war, Vance was a voice for reconciliation. As the Reconstruction era (1865–77) was ending, Vance served as governor of North Carolina and helped ensure the state was strong economically. From 1880 to 1894, he was a U.S. senator, promoting local self-government, individual liberty (freedom), and national unity.

Family tradition of service

Zebulon Baird Vance was born in Buncombe County, North Carolina, on May 13, 1830. He was one of eight children of David Vance, a farmer and merchant, and Mira Mar-

"I do not, altogether, share the general alarm that pervades the Southern mind. The taunts, the gibes, the sneers and the vulgar triumphs of ignoble spirits, which so annoy and mortify, were to be expected…. Happily it is not in the nature of man always to hate; and the reign of the bad passions is short-lived."

Zebulon Vance. *The Library of Congress.*

garet Baird. His grandfather served in the American Revolution (1775–83), fighting in several key battles, including the Battle of Brandywine Creek and the battle at Germantown, both in 1777 in Pennsylvania. He was one of about eleven thousand men who barely survived a frigid winter at Valley Forge in Pennsylvania under General George Washington (1732–1799). Vance's father was a captain during the War of (1812–15), and his uncle, Robert Brank Vance (1793–1827), was a congressman from North Carolina during the mid-1820s. Vance's older brother, also named Robert Brank Vance (1828–1899), became a brigadier general in the Confederate army and served in the U.S. Congress and the North Carolina House of Representatives. The Vance family lived in a large, two-story log home in a fertile farming valley.

Vance attended local schools until he was twelve, and then went on to Washington College in eastern Tennessee. He returned home at fourteen in 1844 upon the death of his father to help his large family.

When he was twenty-one, Vance began studying law at the University of North Carolina. He received his license to practice at the county court in 1852 and settled in Asheville, North Carolina. Having an easy conversational manner and a sincere interest in the lives of small farmers of the area, Vance was quickly elected county solicitor (a lawyer who represents a county). His easygoing manner, wit, and eloquence contributed to his success in engaging jurors and winning his cases.

In 1853, Vance married Harriet Espy. They would have four sons. Vance was having success as a lawyer, but soon after marriage he began pursuing his interest in politics.

Attempts to overcome conflicts

The 1850s was a dynamic and controversial period of American politics. The Whig Party, which had existed for two decades, dissolved when most members joined the newly formed Republican Party in 1854. Other members joined the short-lived American Party, including Vance. The Republican Party was Northern-based and antislavery. The Democratic Party wanted states to decide the issue of slavery for themselves. Vance believed both parties were consumed with self

interest. He ran and was elected to the North Carolina House of Commons in 1854 as a member of the American Party.

As the major parties became more at odds, Vance was elected to the U.S. Congress in 1858 and again in 1860. At the age of twenty-eight in 1858, he was the youngest congressman. Vance supported attempts by President James Buchanan (1791–1868; served 1857–61) to secure the Union, trying to keep in check those who wanted federal legislation to stop the spread of slavery or to abolish it, and battling against growing sentiment for secession (withdrawal) by Southern states. In the presidential election of 1860, Vance supported the Constitutional Union Party candidate, John Bell (1797–1869), a U.S. senator from Tennessee. Vance was a popular speaker in North Carolina for the Bell campaign. Among those who hoped to avoid secession, Vance called for a state constitutional convention that he hoped would keep North Carolina and other states from seceding while demanding that Northern states either support the rights of states or submit legislation for a binding vote.

Shortly after the election of Abraham Lincoln (1809–1865; served 1861–65) as president in 1860, South Carolina seceded from the Union. North Carolina seceded during the spring of 1861, after military actions had begun and the Civil War had started. Congress was adjourned at the time. When it returned to session, Vance no longer had a seat, since the state he represented had left the Union. When President Lincoln responded to a Confederate attack on Fort Sumter by calling for troops to defend the Union against aggression, Vance reversed his opposition to secession.

Military leader

Back in Asheville, Vance organized a company of "Rough and Ready Guards" and was elected its captain. Two weeks later, a North Carolina state convention, called by the legislature, adopted an ordinance of secession on May 20, 1861. During the summer of 1861, Vance and his company patrolled the North Carolina coast. In August, he was elected colonel of the Twenty-sixth North Carolina Regiment and led it successfully in battles in Virginia, including the Seven Days' battle near Richmond, Virginia.

In 1862, Vance was nominated as a candidate for governor of North Carolina. Despite insisting he would continue the Confederate war effort, Vance was portrayed as being loyal to the Union by his more hard-line, clearly secessionist opponent. Nevertheless, Vance won in a landslide and pledged in his inaugural address to pursue a vigorous war policy.

Vance's Thoughts on the War

The following is a section from a speech entitled *The Duties of Defeat*, delivered at the University of North Carolina at Chapel Hill on June 7, 1866, excerpted from the *Documenting the American South* Web site. Vance gave his thoughts on the Civil War, and the future of the South.

During the course of the recent war it was often a subject of remark that each side was grievously deceived in its estimate of the other. And especially was it a favorite opinion at the North, that we of the South were not capable of sustaining for a protracted period the rigors of war. It was said that our climate, and more especially the system of slavery, had unmanned us, and sunk us into effeminacy [unmanliness], and rendered us totally unfit to grapple with the hardier and more robust races of the North.—How they were undeceived by four years of the most desperate strife against overwhelming numbers and resources, it is the province of history to tell. Nor need we fear to let them write that history; for a denial of the full and glorious import of our deeds would be a confession of their own shame and inferiority. It will be our duty now, in better ways, and under happier auspices, still further to undeceive them, by the vigor and energy with which we shall clear away the wreck of our fallen fortunes, adapt ourselves to circumstances under changed in-stitutions and new systems of labor, and the rapidity with which we shall travel in those ways which lead to the rebuilding and adorning a State. Nor will it admit of a doubt that the same courage, constancy and skill, which led our slender battalions through so many pitched fields of glory, will, when directed into the peaceful channels of national prosperity and quickened by the sharp lessons of adversity, be sufficient to place the Southern States of the American Union side by side with the richest and the mightiest....

With regard to current political events and speculations of the future, of which we are permitted to be only quiet, though deeply interested spectators, I do not, altogether, share the general alarm that pervades the Southern mind. The taunts, the gibes, the sneers and the vulgar triumphs of ignoble spirits, which so annoy and mortify, were to be expected. Their brief day will soon pass. They were born of the license of victory, and will endure no longer than the excitements of the occasion serve to render good men ungenerous. Happily it is not in the nature of man always to hate; and the reign of the bad passions is short-lived. It is hardly possible that hatred will long continue between two communities brought into daily, familiar intercourse [discussion], when the subjects of contention have been removed, and when mutual interests and common associations invite to good will.

Still, Vance was soon at odds with the Confederate leadership. He battled against the Confederate policy of forced conscription and military policies that included imprisoning alleged Union sympathizers without formal charges and trying them by military tribunal (where military officers serve as judges) instead of trial by jury. Vance did not interfere with the conscription policy.

Vance again disagreed with the Confederate leadership in regard to thousands of men who left the army and hid in the North Carolina mountains. Confederate authorities considered these men deserters who had to either rejoin their unit or face prison. Vance considered them absentees. By proclamation, he offered to pardon North Carolina soldiers if they returned to their regiments.

Vance helped equip the North Carolina military by trading cotton for military supplies from Europe and organizing a fleet of steamers to guard ships bringing the supplies to North Carolina ports. But by the summer of 1863, the tide of battle had turned in favor of the North and sentiment began building for a peaceful resolution to the conflict. Vance favored a continuation of war, however, and campaigned vigorously, winning another landslide election in spite of a strong sentiment for peace among voters.

Union momentum continued in the war, and in April 1865 the Civil War was effectively over with the surrender of Confederate general **Robert E. Lee** (1807–1870; see Confederate Leaders entry). On May 2, 1865, Vance surrendered in Greensboro, North Carolina. He was directed to join his family in Statesville, North Carolina, and await further orders.

On his thirty-fifth birthday, Vance learned that he was under arrest by the order of President **Andrew Johnson** (1808–1875; served 1865–69; see entry), who succeeded to the presidency after Abraham Lincoln was assassinated in April 1865. Vance was sent to Washington, imprisoned, and held for two months before being paroled (set free, but with restrictions). He was never told why he was arrested or released.

Reconstructing his life

Vance returned to his family in the state capital of Charlotte and resumed practicing law. Drawing on his reputation as an engaging speaker, he went on lecture tours. President Johnson offered pardons for former members of the Confederacy provided they filled out an application that included renouncing their past activities. Vance's application for a pardon was granted on March 11, 1867.

In 1870, Vance was elected to the U.S. Senate. However, he was not allowed to serve. The Fourteenth Amendment,

The Fourteenth Amendment Disables Vance

The Fourteenth Amendment to the Constitution, passed in 1868, reflected the harsh Reconstruction policies pursued by congressmen called the "Radical Republicans." Unlike the policies proposed by President Abraham Lincoln and continued by his successor, Andrew Johnson, Radical Republicans wanted to punish Southern states that had seceded from the Union and those people who had been loyal to the Confederacy. Article 3 of the Fourteenth Amendment made it difficult for former members of the Confederacy to hold federal office. Zebulon Vance was elected to Congress in 1870, but was not allowed to serve because of Article 3 of the Fourteenth Amendment. That the article served the political purposes of Radical Republicans became evident when Vance officially surrendered his elected seat. Congress then moved quickly to authorize him to serve, but it was too late for Vance.

[Article] 3. No person shall be a Senator or Representative in Congress, or elector of President and Vice-President, or hold any office, civil or military, under the United States, or under any State, who, having previously taken an oath, as a member of Congress, or as an officer of the United States, or as a member of any State legislature, or as an executive or judicial officer of any State, to support the Constitution of the United States, shall have engaged in insurrection or rebellion against the same, or given aid or comfort to the enemies thereof. But Congress may by a vote of two-thirds of each House, remove such disability.

passed in 1868, included a provision against former members of the Confederacy that made it illegal for them to serve in the federal legislature or executive branch unless the "disability" was removed by a vote of two-thirds majority in both houses of Congress. After trying unsuccessfully for two years, Vance gave up his certificate of election (an official document that names a person certified by a state authority as having won a position by election). Reflecting the political climate of the times, Congress removed Vance's disabilities after he surrendered his certificate of election. Vance ran again for Congress in 1872, but was defeated.

In 1876, Democrats in North Carolina were determined to replace the state's Republican leadership and their support for Reconstruction policies. They turned to Vance as their gubernatorial nominee, and he won a close election against Thomas Settle (1831–1888).

North Carolina quickly prospered under Vance's leadership. He revived construction of railroads. The new and repaired train lines helped stimulate agriculture and industry by transporting supplies into farms and factories and then transporting goods out to market. Vance supported improvements to public education and he restructured the state's finances to quickly pay off debts. By the time the Reconstruction era ended in 1877, North Carolina was experiencing solid growth.

Back in the Senate

Vance served only two of the four years of his gubernatorial term. In 1878, his wife, Harriet, died. The following year, Vance won election to the U.S. Senate. This time, he was not barred from his Senate seat. In 1880, he married Florence Steele Martin. At the time, Vance was only fifty years old. Reelected to the Senate in 1885 and in 1891, Vance proved to be a uniting force in a Congress still hampered by divisiveness between North and South. By the mid-1880s, the divisiveness began to ease. During his Senate terms, Vance chaired several committees and was famed as a debater who was both eloquent and fair.

Vance's final term was impaired by health problems. He had an eye removed in 1891 and never fully recovered. After an extended period of winter rest in Florida in 1894, he returned to work in the Senate at the beginning of April, but died at his home in Washington, D.C., two weeks later. Funeral services were held in the chamber of the U.S. Senate. Vance's body was then returned to North Carolina, and he was buried in Asheville.

For More Information

Books

McKinney, Gordon B. *Zeb Vance: North Carolina's Civil War Governor and Gilded Age Political Leader.* Chapel Hill: University of North Carolina Press, 2004.

Shirley, Franklin Ray. *Zebulon Vance: Tarheel Spokesman.* Charlotte, NC: McNally and Loftin, 1962.

Tucker, Glenn. *Zeb Vance: Champion of Personal Freedom.* Indianapolis: Bobbs-Merrill, 1965.

Web Sites

"The Duties of Defeat: An Address Delivered before the Two Literary Societies of the University of North Carolina, June 7th, 1866, by Ex-Gov. Zebulon Baird Vance." *University of North Carolina at Chapel Hill Libraries: Documenting the American South.* http://docsouth.unc.edu/nc/vance/vance.html (accessed on July 30, 2004).

"Vance Birthplace." *North Carolina Historic Sites.* http://www.ah.dcr.state.nc.us/sections/hs/vance/vance.htm (accessed on July 30, 2004).

"Zebulon Baird Vance." *Know Southern History.* http://www.knowsouthernhistory.net/Biographies/Zebulon_Vance/ (accessed on July 30, 2004).

Harry Wright

Born January 10, 1835
Sheffield, England

Died October 3, 1895
Atlantic City, New Jersey

Baseball player

"The spectators all arise between halves of the seventh inning, extend their legs and arms and sometimes walk about. In so doing they enjoy the relief afforded by relaxation from a long posture upon hard benches."

Harry Wright. *The Library of Congress.*

H arry Wright organized, managed, and played on the first all-professional baseball team, the Cincinnati Red Stockings of 1869. Baseball had been played since the 1840s under many rules still in effect today, and some teams or bettors had occasionally paid players, but the Red Stockings paid all their players and influenced the development of organized, professional baseball. The Red Stockings traveled the country and won their first 130 games (89 against certified opponents). During the 1870s, Wright played and managed in the first two professional baseball leagues, the National Association of Baseball Clubs (1871–75) and the National League of Professional Baseball Clubs (still in existence today as Major League Baseball's National League). For his pioneering efforts as an organizer, player, baseball strategist, and umpire, Wright was elected to the National Baseball Hall of Fame in 1953.

From bowler to pitcher

Harry Wright was born in Sheffield, England, on January 10, 1835, the eldest of five children of Samuel and Ann

Scene from a baseball game, circa 1866. *The Granger Collection, New York. Reproduced by permission.*

Wright. His father, who played the sport of cricket professionally, moved the family to the United States in 1836 after being hired by the St. George Cricket Club in New York. Wright attended elementary schools in New York City before beginning work with a jewelry manufacturer. As a youngster, he learned the game of cricket from his father. Baseball had recently emerged as a sport in the United States and was being played in New York. Wright took up the sport, but concentrated primarily on cricket. Cricket has some similarities to baseball: action begins with a player throwing a ball (called a bowler in cricket, a pitcher in baseball) to a batter, but the similarities end there.

At age twenty-one in 1856, Wright became a bowler for his father's team, the St. George Cricket Club. Two years later, Wright played organized baseball as an outfielder with a team sponsored by the Knickerbocker Club of Hoboken, New Jersey. While cricket was popular and competitive enough to employ professionals, baseball was still developing. Wright made

The Origins of Baseball

Until 1938, Abner Doubleday was credited with inventing American baseball. Doubleday was born in Ballston Spa, New York, in 1819 and attended school in Cooperstown, which was the site chosen for the Baseball Hall of Fame. The Hall opened in 1936. Two years later, baseball history began being rewritten when evidence surfaced that Alexander Cartwright had created and written down many of the rules baseball still uses today.

A longtime myth claimed that Doubleday had invented baseball in Cooperstown in 1838. But Doubleday himself never made that claim. He was a military man, serving in the Mexican-American War (1846–48) and the Civil War. Doubleday was credited with being the father of baseball when baseball promoters wanted "America's pastime" to have clear American origins. Baseball, in fact, was similar to an older English game called rounders, but games involving a ball hit with a stick date back to ancient times. Baseball is unique in its rules and features, and much of the credit for them can be attributed to Cartwright.

Cartwright, a New York bank teller, suggested to his buddies in the Knickerbocker Base Ball Club in 1845 that they change some of the rules they had been following. They introduced the concept of foul territory, established the distance between bases at 90 feet, decided on three outs per inning, and eliminated the practice of retiring base runners by hitting them with the baseball. The number of players was not specified in the first rules, but by 1846 clubs were playing with nine to a side. The first recorded baseball game under these rules occurred in 1846 when Cartwright's Knickerbockers lost to the New York Baseball Club. The game was held at the Elysian Fields, in Hoboken, New Jersey. In 1858, the National Association of Base Ball Players, the first organized baseball league, was formed.

money as a jeweler and cricket player, and played baseball for fun. A decade earlier, the Knickerbocker Club team had created many of the rules and features baseball retains to this day.

Wright continued to work professionally as a jeweler and cricket player while playing baseball in his spare time. He was recognized, nevertheless, as a team leader and an excellent player. During the Civil War (1861–65), baseball gained in popularity. Soldiers on both sides of the war learned how to play the game during breaks in the fighting. After the war, they took it home with them. Meanwhile, some players had been receiving money from sponsors and bettors to play for certain teams prior to and during the war. Organized professional baseball came into existence during the Reconstruction era (1865–77).

Alexander Cartwright, inventor of baseball.
AP/Wide World Photos. Reproduced by permission.

Evidence of Cartwright's rules, found in his diaries and journals, was brought to the attention of baseball officials in 1938. By then, the Abner Doubleday baseball creation myth had become commonplace. The writ-ten evidence of Cartwright's contributions changed that. The National Baseball Hall of Fame recognizes September 1845 as the time when the rules of the game now known as baseball were first set down.

Cartwright left New York in 1849 with a group of friends to seek gold in California. He took along a baseball and the Knickerbocker rules and demonstrated the game with his friends along the way. After the long journey to California, Cartwright became ill, gave up his pursuit of gold, and traveled as far as Hawaii to recuperate. In 1851, he was joined there by his wife and three children. He introduced baseball to Hawaii in 1852.

Cartwright became a leading businessman and banker in Honolulu. He founded the city library and fire department, and served as fire chief for ten years. Cartwright died on July 12, 1892, but his legend was reborn in 1938.

Play ball!

In 1866, at the age of thirty-one, Wright moved to Cincinnati to serve as an instructor and bowler for the Union Cricket Club. In his spare time, he organized and captained the Cincinnati Baseball Club, which quickly became his main interest. Baseball was growing quickly in popularity, and Wright was a star. He was a pitcher during 1867 and 1868, and a formidable hitter: He was credited with hitting seven home runs in a game in Newport, Kentucky, in 1867. In September 1868, Wright married Mary Fraser of New York City. They would have four children.

In 1869, Wright organized the Cincinnati Red Stockings, the first full professional team in baseball history. Some

An illustration showing members of the Cincinnati Red Stockings, including player-manager Harry Wright (upper right), in 1869. © *Bettmann/Corbis.*

The Wright Brothers: Pioneers of Baseball

George Wright was born on January 28, 1847, in Yonkers, New York. A few months earlier, what is considered the first-ever baseball game was played, using many of the rules still in existence today. During his childhood, Wright began playing baseball with his older brothers, Harry and David. He would later join his brother Harry as a player on the Cincinnati Red Stockings, baseball's first all-professional team. Harry Wright was the manager as well as a star pitcher and outfielder. George Wright was the star shortstop, a feared slugger and excellent fielder. Just as his brother Harry was a pioneer of baseball strategy, George revolutionized the position of shortstop.

After the 1870 season, George Wright followed his brother to Boston, where Harry organized the Boston Red Stockings in 1871. George was captain of the team as it finished in first place four seasons in a row (1872–75) in the National Association of Baseball Clubs. Success continued in the National League of Professional Baseball Clubs, which began in 1876 and continues today as Major League Baseball's National League. George Wright led Boston to National League championships in 1877 and 1878. He continued playing until 1882. He was elected to Baseball's Hall of Fame in 1937, and his brother Harry followed in 1953. After retiring from baseball, George Wright founded a sporting goods company and is credited with having built in 1890 the first nine-hole golf course in New England.

players had been paid before that time, but baseball was still considered an amateur sport. Wright changed that. He was paid an annual salary of $1,200 to manage the team and play center field. His brother, George Wright (1847– 1937), considered the finest shortstop of the time, was paid $1,400. Most of the regulars earned $800.

In 1869 and 1870, the Red Stockings toured the country, traveling more than twelve thousand miles and drawing more than two hundred thousand spectators who paid up to fifty cents per game. In the first game ever played by professional baseball teams (all paid players, no amateurs), the Cincinnati Red Stockings beat the Mansfield Independents, 48-14. The Red Stockings won all sixty-nine of their games in 1869, and the streak reached 130 games the next season before they would lose a game. (Since Harry Wright would only acknowledge victories that came against sanctioned teams— those that paid and registered their players—he counted the

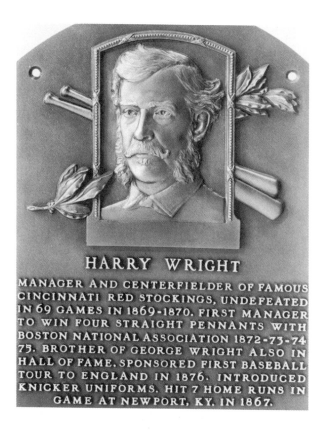

HARRY WRIGHT

MANAGER AND CENTERFIELDER OF FAMOUS
CINCINNATI RED STOCKINGS, UNDEFEATED
IN 69 GAMES IN 1869-1870. FIRST MANAGER
TO WIN FOUR STRAIGHT PENNANTS WITH
BOSTON NATIONAL ASSOCIATION 1872-73-74-
75. BROTHER OF GEORGE WRIGHT ALSO IN
HALL OF FAME. SPONSORED FIRST BASEBALL
TOUR TO ENGLAND IN 1876. INTRODUCED
KNICKER UNIFORMS. HIT 7 HOME RUNS IN
GAME AT NEWPORT, KY. IN 1867.

Harry Wright's National Baseball Hall of Fame plaque. *AP/Wide World Photos. Reproduced by permission.*

Red Stockings' winning streak as 87.) Their first loss came against the Brooklyn Atlantics by an 8-7 score.

The success of the Cincinnati Red Stockings inspired more teams to become entirely professional. But hometown fans in Cincinnati were not as supportive as those in other cities and towns, and the team folded in 1870. Wright moved to Boston, Massachusetts, where he helped form the Boston Red Stockings as part of the National Association of Baseball Clubs, the first professional baseball league. The league was unstable—each year some teams folded and new teams joined. The Boston Red Stockings, however, were consistent. Managed by Wright, Boston finished first in the National Association every year from 1872 to 1875. At the end of the 1874 season, the team demonstrated baseball in a tour of England.

A new league, with a constitution that regulated club activities, required players to honor their contracts, and banned gambling completely, was formed in 1876. The National League of Professional Baseball Clubs, still in existence today as Major League Baseball's National League, began with eight baseball clubs representing the cities of Boston, Massachusetts; Chicago, Illinois; Cincinnati, Ohio; Hartford, Connecticut; Louisville, Kentucky; Philadelphia, Pennsylvania; New York City; and St. Louis, Missouri. At age forty-one, Wright no longer played, but he was manager of the Boston team until the end of the 1881 season. The team won two championships in that span. Wright managed two other teams, including Philadelphia from the 1884 to 1893 season. Before he died in 1895, Wright was chief of umpires of the National League in 1894 and 1895. He was survived by his third wife and seven of his eight children.

Wright's contributions to the game were enormous. In addition to helping popularize baseball, Wright is credited with some of baseball's unique strategies as well. He was the first manager to shift his fielders based on the hitting tendencies of individual batters; he also put his fielders in motion as soon as the ball was in play—by backing each other up and shortening throwing distances between fielders during relays, more base runners advancing on a play were thrown out. Wright attained baseball's highest honor in 1953 when he was elected to the National Baseball Hall of Fame.

For More Information

Books

Devine, Christopher. *Harry Wright: The Father of Professional Baseball.* Jefferson, NC: McFarland & Company, 2003.

Rhodes, Greg, and John Erardi. *The First Boys of Summer: The 1869–1870 Cincinnati Red Stockings, Baseball's First Professional Team.* Cincinnati: Road West Publishing, 1994.

Rosenburg, John M. *They Gave Us Baseball: The 12 Extraordinary Men Who Shaped the Major Leagues.* Harrisburg, PA: Stackpole Books, 1989.

Ryczek, William J. *Blackguards and Red Stockings: A History of Baseball's National Association, 1871–1875.* Jefferson, NC: McFarland & Co., 1992.

Web Sites

"Harry Wright." *Baseball Library.* http://www.baseballlibrary.com/baseballlibrary/ballplayers/W/Wright_Harry.stm (accessed on July 30, 2004).

"Harry Wright." *National Baseball Hall of Fame.* http://www.baseballhalloffame.org/hofers_and_honorees/hofer_bios/wright_harry.htm (accessed on July 30, 2004).

"Red Stockings of Cincinnati." *Cincy Sports.* http://cincysports.net/1866to1875.htm (accessed on July 30, 2004).

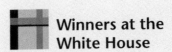

Winners at the White House

One of the traditional rewards in contemporary times for winning baseball's World Series or a championship in other sports is a visit to the White House and a meeting with the president for the championship team. That modern tradition actually dates back to the Reconstruction era. After completing a cross-country, undefeated season in 1869, the Cincinnati Red Stockings were rewarded with a private audience in Washington, D.C., with President Ulysses S. Grant. The president complimented what he called "the western Cinderella club" for its skills and winning ways.

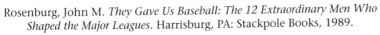

Where to Learn More

Books

Anthony, Susan B., Elizabeth Cady Stanton, and Matilda Joslyn Gage, eds. *History of Woman Suffrage*. New York: Fowler & Wells, 1881–1922. Reprint, Salem, NH: Ayer Co., 1985.

Appiah, Kwame Anthony, and Henry Louis Gates Jr., eds. *Africana: The Encyclopedia of the African and African American Experience*. New York: Basic Civitas Books, 1999.

Archer, Jules. *A House Divided: The Lives of Ulysses S. Grant and Robert E. Lee*. New York: Scholastic, 1995.

Ayers, Edward L. *The Promise of the New South: Life After Reconstruction*. New York: Oxford University Press, 1992.

Barney, William L. *The Civil War and Reconstruction: A Student Companion*. New York: Oxford University Press, 2001.

Benedict, Michael Les. *A Compromise of Principle: Congressional Republicans and Reconstruction, 1863–1869*. New York: Norton, 1974.

Berlin, Ira A., et al., eds. *Freedmen: A Documentary History of Emancipation, 1861–1867*. New York: Cambridge University Press, 1982.

Blassingame, John W., ed. *Slave Testimony*. Baton Rouge: Louisiana State University Press, 1977.

Cox, LaWanda C., and Cox, John H., eds. *Reconstruction, the Negro, and the New South*. New York: Harper & Row, 1973.

Crook, William H. *Through Five Administrations: Reminiscences of Colonel William H. Crook*. New York: Harper & Brothers, 1910.

Cruden, Robert. *The Negro in Reconstruction*. Englewood Cliffs, NJ: Prentice Hall, 1969.

Davis, Jefferson. *The Rise and Fall of the Confederate Government*. New York: D. Appleton, 1881. Reprint, New York: Da Capo Press, 1990.

Douglass, Frederick. *Escape from Slavery*. Edited by Michael McCurdy. New York: Knopf, 1994.

Douglass, Frederick. *My Bondage and My Freedom*. New York: Miller, Orton and Mulligan, 1855. Reprint, Urbana: University of Illinois Press, 1987.

Foner, Eric. *Reconstruction: America's Unfinished Revolution, 1863–1877*. New York: Harper & Row, 1988.

Foner, Eric. *A Short History of Reconstruction*. New York: Harper & Row, 1990.

Franklin, John Hope. *Reconstruction After the Civil War*. Chicago: University of Chicago Press, 1961.

Golay, Michael. *Reconstruction and Reaction: The Emancipation of Slaves, 1861–1913*. New York: Facts on File, 1996.

Jenkins, Wilbert L. *Climbing Up to Glory: A Short History of African Americans During the Civil War and Reconstruction*. Wilmington, DE: Scholarly Resources, 2002.

Josephson, Matthew. *The Robber Barons: The Great American Capitalists, 1861–1901*. New York: Harcourt, Brace and Company, 1934. Reprint, 1995.

Kirchberger, Joe H. *The Civil War and Reconstruction*. New York: Facts on File, 1991.

Litwack, Leon F. *Been in the Storm So Long: The Aftermath of Slavery*. New York: Vintage Books, 1979.

Litwack, Leon F., and August Meier, eds. *Black Leaders of the Nineteenth Century*. Urbana: University of Illinois Press, 1988.

Lynch, John Roy. *The Facts of Reconstruction*. New York: Neale Publishing Co., 1913. Reprint, Indianapolis: Bobbs-Merrill, 1970.

Mantell, Martin E. *Johnson, Grant and the Politics of Reconstruction*. New York: Columbia University Press, 1973.

McCulloch, Hugh. *Men and Measures of Half a Century: Sketches and Comments*. New York: C. Scribner's Sons, 1888. Reprint, New York: Da Capo Press, 1970.

McFarlin, Annjennette Sophie, ed. *Black Congressional Reconstruction Orators and Their Orations, 1869–1879*. Metuchen, NJ: Scarecrow Press, 1976.

McKittrick, Eric. L. *Andrew Johnson and Reconstruction*. Chicago: University of Chicago Press, 1960. Reprint, New York: Oxford University Press, 1988.

McPherson, James M. *The Struggle for Equality: Abolitionists and the Negro in the Civil War and Reconstruction*. Princeton, NJ: Princeton University Press, 1965.

Morris, Roy, Jr. *Fraud of the Century: Rutherford B. Hayes, Samuel Tilden, and the Stolen Election of 1876.* New York: Simon & Schuster, 2003.

Murphy, Richard W. *The Nation Reunited: War's Aftermath.* Alexandria, VA: Time-Life Books, 1987.

Oubre, Claude F. *Forty Acres and a Mule: The Freedmen's Bureau and Black Land Ownership.* Baton Rouge: Louisiana State University Press, 1978.

Patrick, Rembert W. *Reconstruction of the Nation.* New York: Oxford University Press, 1967.

Perman, Michael. *The Road to Redemption: Southern Politics, 1869–1879.* Chapel Hill: University of North Carolina Press, 1984.

Rehnquist, William H. *Centennial Crisis: The Disputed Election of 1876.* New York: Alfred A. Knopf, 2004.

Simpson, Brooks D. *The Reconstruction Presidents.* Lawrence: University Press of Kansas, 1998.

Smith, John David. *Black Voices from Reconstruction, 1865–1877.* Gainesville: University of Florida Press, 1997.

Stampp, Kenneth M. *The Era of Reconstruction: 1865–1877.* New York: Vintage Books, 1965.

Stephens, Alexander Hamilton. *Recollections of Alexander H. Stephens: His Diary Kept When a Prisoner at Fort Warren, Boston Harbour, 1865.* New York: Doubleday, 1910. Reprint, Baton Rouge: Louisiana State University Press, 1998.

Trefousse, Hans Louis. *Impeachment of a President: Andrew Johnson, the Blacks, and Reconstruction.* Knoxville: University of Tennessee Press, 1975. Reprint, New York: Fordham University Press, 1999.

Wagner, Margaret E., Gary W. Gallagher, and Paul Finkelman, eds. *Civil War Desk Reference.* New York: Simon & Schuster, 2002.

Wharton, Vernon L. *The Negro in Mississippi, 1865–1900.* New York: Harper & Row, 1965.

Woodward, C. Vann. *Reunion and Reaction: The Compromise of 1877 and the End of Reconstruction.* Boston: Little, Brown, 1951. Reprint, New York: Oxford University Press, 1991.

Web Sites

Civil War Archive. http://www.civilwararchive.com/intro.htm (accessed on September 13, 2004).

The Civil War Homepage. http://www.civil-war.net/ (accessed on September 13, 2004).

Douglass, Frederick. "Reconstruction." *The Atlantic Online.* http://www.theatlantic.com/unbound/flashbks/black/douglas.htm (accessed on July 19, 2004).

"Famous American Trials: The Andrew Johnson Impeachment Trial." *University of Missouri–Kansas City.* http://www.law.umkc.edu/faculty/projects/ftrials/impeach/impeachmt.htm (accessed on July 26, 2004).

Hoemann, George A. *Civil War Homepage.* http://sunsite.utk.edu/civil-war/ (accessed on September 13, 2004).

Library of Congress. "African American Odyssey." *American Memory.* http://memory.loc.gov/ammem/aaohtml/aohome.html (accessed on September 13, 2004).

Louisiana State University. *The United States Civil War Center.* http://www.cwc.lsu.edu/ (accessed on August 31, 2004).

Osborn, Tracey. "Civil War Reconstruction, Racism, the KKK, & the Confederate Lost Cause." *Teacher Oz's Kingdom of History.* http://www.teacheroz.com/reconstruction.htm (accessed on September 13, 2004).

"Reconstruction." *African American History.* http://afroamhistory.about.com/od/reconstruction/ (accessed on August 31, 2004).

"Reference Resources: Civil War." *Kidinfo.* http://www.kidinfo.com/American_History/Civil_War.html (accessed on August 31, 2004).

"US Civil War." *Internet Modern History Sourcebook.* http://www.fordham.edu/halsall/mod/modsbook27.html (accessed on August 31, 2004)

Index

professional leagues, 218, 220, 223–24
Wright, Harry, 218, 219 (ill.), 219–25
Baseball (Eakins), 66
Baseball Hall of Fame. *See* National Baseball Hall of Fame
Bates, Edward, 48
"The Battle Hymn of the Republic" (Howe), 124, 127–28
Battle of Little Big Horn, 87, 120, 151
Battle of the Bloody Angle, 80
Belknap, William W., 87
Bell, John, 211 (ill.), 212
Bethlehem to Jerusalem, 74
Beyond the Mississippi (Richardson), 71
Bingham, John A., 142 (ill.)
Birchard, Sardis, 113, 114, 116
Black Codes, 76, 196
Black Friday, 82
Black Hawk War, 32
Blaine, James G., 116
Bland-Allison Act of 1878, 120
Bliss, Amos, 90
Bloomer, Amelia, 11
Bonds, 46–48
Bonnat, Léon, 64
Booth, John Wilkes, 174
"Boss" Tweed. *See* Tweed, William Marcy "Boss"
Boston Christian Register, 100
Boston Red Stockings, 223, 224
Bouchet, Edward, 24–25
Boutwell, George S., 142 (ill.)
Bozeman Trail, 148, 149
Bradley, Joseph P., 118
Brains. *See* Sweeny, Peter Barr
Bridgman, Laura, 125
Bristow, Benjamin H., 86
Brooklyn Atlantics, 224
Brooks, Preston S., 193 (ill.), 194
Brown, John, 35, 56
Brown, Joseph E., 37
Bruce, Blanche K., 17 (ill.), 17–22
Brulé Sioux, 147, 148
Bryant, William Cullen, 74
Buchanan, James, 170, 172, 197
Bull Bear, 147
Bureau of Indian Affairs, 87, 120–21
Butler, Andrew, 194

Butler, Benjamin F., 142 (ill.)
Butler, David, 81
Butterflies, 109

C

California land claims, 170
Cameron, Simon, 172, 172 (ill.)
Canal Ring, 204
Canals, Central America and, 121–22
Cardozo, Francis L., 23 (ill.), 23–29
Cardozo, W. Warrick, 25
Carmany, John H., 101
Carpetbaggers, 19, 41
Cartoons, editorial. *See* Editorial cartoons
Cartwright, Alexander, 220, 221 (ill.)
Cass, Lewis, 191
Casserly, Eugene, 158
Centennial Exposition, 64, 66, 73
Central America, 121–22
Century, 87
Century Building and Loan Association, 25
Channing, William Ellery, 190
Chase, Salmon P., 46, 47, 47 (ill.), 48, 137
Chemistry, industrial, 165
The Chemistry of Cooking and Cleaning (Richards), 165
Chemists, 161–67, 165 (ill.)
Cheney, Mary Youngs. *See* Greeley, Mary
Chess Players (Eakins), 66
Chevalier of the Order of St. Savior, 126
Cheyenne (Native Americans), 148, 149, 150, 151
Chicago World's Fair, 166
Chief Joseph, 87
Chief Smoke, 147
Children's literature, 4–5
China, treaties with, 120
Chinese immigration, 19, 120, 121 (ill.)
Chivington, John H., 149
Cincinnati Red Stockings, 218, 221, 222 (ill.), 223–24, 225
Citizenship, 57

F

G

Y